THE DANGEROUS TRADE

THE DANGEROUS TRADE

Spies, Spymasters and the Making of Europe

Edited by
Daniel Szechi

EDINBURGH
University Press

Edinburgh University Press is one of the leading university presses in the UK. We publish academic books and journals in our selected subject areas across the humanities and social sciences, combining cutting-edge scholarship with high editorial and production values to produce academic works of lasting importance. For more information visit our website: edinburghuniversitypress.com

First published in Great Britain in 2010 by
Dundee University Press

Edinburgh University Press Ltd
The Tun – Holyrood Road
12 (2f) Jackson's Entry
Edinburgh EH8 8PJ

Typeset by IDSUK (DataConnection) Ltd
and printed and bound in Great Britain

A CIP record for this book is available from the
British Library

ISBN 978 1 84586 060 8 (paperback)

In memory of Roger Absalom (1929–2009)

Contents

List of Illustrations

Notes on Contributors

Michael J. Levin received his PhD in Renaissance Studies from Yale University in 1997. He is currently Associate Professor of History and Director of Humanities at the University of Akron. He is the author of *Agents of Empire: Spanish Ambassadors in Sixteenth-Century Italy* (Cornell University Press, 2005).

Alan Marshall is a Fellow of the Royal Historical Society and Head of Humanities at Bath Spa University. He has written a number of books on the early modern period: *The Death of Nicholas Fairles: Law and Community in South Shields* (NEEHI, 2010); *Oliver Cromwell, Soldier: The Military Life of a Revolutionary at War* (Brassey's, 2004); *The Strange Death of Edmund Godfrey: Plots and Politics in Restoration London* (Sutton Publishing, 1999); *The Age of Faction: Court Politics, 1660–1702* (Manchester University Press, 1999) and *Intelligence and Espionage in the reign of Charles II, 1660–1685* (Cambridge University Press, 1994). In addition he has published a number of articles on seventeenth-century history. His current research in progress is on *'Killing Cromwell': The Death of the Leveller Party, 1649–1658* (History Press, 2011), which examines the nature of the transition of the Levellers from a moral force to a 'physical-force' group and focuses chiefly on the series of plots to assassinate the Lord Protector Oliver Cromwell. He is also working on a volume in the Palgrave History of Britain series: *Seventeenth-Century Britain, 1603–1707* (Palgrave, 2011).

Steve Murdoch, FSA Scot, FRHistS, is Professor of History at the University of St Andrews. His research interests include migration from the British Isles in the seventeenth century and all forms of interaction between early modern Scotland and the wider world. He has published extensively on the subject and his major publications include *Network North: Scottish Kin, Commercial and Covert Association in Northern Europe, 1603–1746* (Leiden, 2006) and *The Terror of the Seas? Scottish Maritime Warfare, 1513–1713* (Leiden, 2010). His major edited collections include *Scotland and the Thirty Years War, 1618–1648* (Leiden, 2001) and with Alexia Grosjean, *Scottish Communities Abroad in the*

Early Modern Period (Leiden, Brill, 2005). Also with Alexia Grosjean he has produced the widely acclaimed Scotland, Scandinavia and Northern European Biographical Database, online at www.st-andrews.ac.uk/history/ssne.

Paolo Preto was born in 1942, and received a degree in Italian literature at the University of Padua, where he has been Professor of Modern History since 1980. He is the author of several monographs, including: *Venezia e i turchi* (Sansoni, Firenze, 1975), *Peste e società a Venezia nel 1576* (Neri Pozza, Vicenza, 1979), *Epidemia, paura e politica nell'Italia moderna* (Laterza, Roma-Bari, 1987), *I Servizi segreti di Venezia* (Il Saggiatore, Milano, 1994), and *Persona per hora secreta. Accusa e delazione nella Repubblica di Venezia* (Il Saggiatore, Milano, 2003). He is also author of various articles on the history of the council of Trent, on the Jacobin era in Italy, and on intelligence services in early modern Europe. He has also written a number of bibliographical entries for the *Dizionario biografico degli Italiani*. He is currently working on a book on the subject of 'falso storico' (counterfeit sources) in the early modern era, a topic on which he has already published various articles.

Christopher Storrs is Reader in Modern History at the University of Dundee. He is the author of *War, Diplomacy and the Rise of Savoy 1690–1720* (Cambridge, 1999), *The Resilience of the Spanish Monarchy 1665–1700* (Oxford, 2006) and editor of *The Fiscal-Military State in Eighteenth-Century Europe. Essays in Honour of P. G. M. Dickson* (Farnham, 2009). He has published widely on seventeenth- and eighteenth-century European history, and is currently preparing a study of the resurgence of Spain as a power in the western Mediterranean and Italy in the generation after the War of the Spanish Succession.

Daniel Szechi is a graduate of the University of Sheffield and St Antony's College, Oxford, and after eighteen years as a Professor at Auburn University in Alabama, was appointed Professor of Early Modern History at the University of Manchester in 2006. He is a Fellow of the Royal Society of Edinburgh and the Royal Historical Society. His books include: *1715. The Great Jacobite Rebellion* (Yale University Press, 2006), *George Lockhart of Carnwath 1689–1727: a Study in Jacobitism* (Tuckwell Press, East Lothian, 2002); *The Jacobites. Britain and Europe, 1688–1788* (Manchester University Press, Manchester, 1994); with Professor G. Holmes, *The Age of Oligarchy: Pre-Industrial Britain 1722–1783* (Longman, 1993); and *Jacobitism and Tory Politics, 1710–14* (John Donald, Edinburgh, 1984). He has also published articles in *Past and Present, English Historical Review, Scottish Historical Review, Journal of British Studies, Historical Journal, Catholic Historical Review, Parliamentary History* and *Studies in Church History*, and a number of essays in collective works.

Acknowledgements

This book was inspired by Professor Chris Whatley, Vice-Principal of the University of Dundee. It was he who perceived there might be something here worth writing about, and asked me to consider the project. Like most of my generation, I had been raised on tales of desperate deeds of derring-do by heroic spies and special forces in World War II, to say nothing of the James Bond fantasy industry, yet it had never occurred to me to write about espionage or covert operations *per se*. Which is a bit strange, because I am best known for my work on Jacobitism. This was the underground movement dedicated to restoring the exiled main line of the Stuart dynasty, chased out by the revolutionaries of 1688, and it obviously operated for the most part in the twilight world of the dangerous trade. Before I finally decided to work on Jacobitism I had also contemplated working on a Jewish terrorist organisation, the *Lohamei Herut Israel* (Fighters for the Freedom of Israel; better known as the 'Stern Gang'), who fought the British in Palestine between 1940 and 1948, and in the mid-1980s I was very briefly considered as a potential recruit by the Secret Intelligence Service (MI6). Yet these moments had become curiosities of my youth, and my focus on Jacobitism was so tight that I had not realised how many of its activities were simply manifestations of a much larger phenomenon. Chris Whatley's suggestion thus came as a surprise. With typical perceptiveness he saw that my familiarity with the workings of the Jacobite underground was tolerably good preparation for thinking about the secret world of espionage and covert action as a whole, and urged me to take the project on. I am very glad he persuaded me to do so, and I owe him my happy thanks for getting me into the intriguing, frustrating, compellingly nasty world of the dangerous trade.

This book is, though, very far from being mine alone. By myself I could never have produced a work that spans a continent and three centuries. If, as I hope, this book is a worthy contribution to the burgeoning field of early modern intelligence studies it is above all owing to the fine contributions from my fellow authors: Michael Levin, Alan Marshall, Steve Murdoch, Paolo Preto and Christopher Storrs, and I thank them one and all. Alan Marshall, Steve

Murdoch and Christopher Storrs also kindly read and commented on the long introduction below. It greatly improved as a result, and any errors that remain are mine, not theirs.

I owe two further debts of gratitude that I must mention. The first is to my father, Roger Absalom. He was a historian of modern Italy who was best known for his work on the peasants of the north, and in particular their enthusiastic participation as helpers, guides and guardians of the thousands of Allied escapers trying to make their way back to the Allied lines in southern Italy after the collapse of Benito Mussolini's government in 1943. He was delighted that I was working in a kindred field to his own (by 2009 he was happily absorbed in researching SOE operations in Italy) and helped me enormously by translating Paolo Preto's essay below from its original Italian. His fee was going to be two good dinners in Edinburgh, a city neither of us could ever get enough of, but sadly I was never able to honour that debt: he died after a sudden illness on 9 October 2009. Hence my final debt of gratitude. Despite his own travails, my very kind colleague at Manchester, Paolo di Martino, selflessly helped me by translating sundry questions and communications into Italian. I thank him most sincerely.

Daniel Szechi

Abbreviations

AHR	*American Historical Review*
AST	*Archivio di Stato*
BCRA	Bureau Central de Renseignements et d'Action
CHR	*Catholic Historical Review*
CIA	Central Intelligence Agency
CSPDC	Mary Anne Everett Green, ed., *Calendar of State Papers, Domestic Series, 1649–1650 (–1659–1660)* (13 vols, reprint edn, 1965)
C.S.P. Venetian	Rawdon Brown, ed., *Calendar of State Papers and Manuscripts, Relating to English Affairs, Existing in the Archives and Collections of Venice, and in Other Libraries of Northern Italy* (38 vols, London, 1864–1947)
CSPI	R. P. Mahaffy, ed., *Calendar of the State Papers Relating to Ireland Preserved in the Public Record Office: 1625–1632 (–1670)* (8 vols, London, 1900–10)
EcHR	*Economic History Review*
EHR	*English Historical Review*
GCHQ	Government Communication Headquarters
HJ	*Historical Journal*
HMC	Historical Manuscripts Commission
HR	*Historical Research* (formerly: *Bulletin of the Institute of Historical Research*)
IJIC	*International Journal of Intelligence and CounterIntelligence*
INS	*Intelligence and National Security*
ISR	*Irish Studies Review*
JEcH	*Journal of Economic History*
JEMH	*Journal of Early Modern History*
JIH	*Journal of Interdisciplinary History*
MH	*Media History*

NSA	National Security Agency
OSS	Office of Strategic Services
RPCS	J. H. Burton and David Masson, eds, *The Register of the Privy Council of Scotland* (14 vols, Edinburgh, 1877–98)
ScJH	*Scandinavian Journal of History*
SIS	Secret Intelligence Service (MI6)
SOE	Special Operations Executive
SP	*State Papers*
SRA	Swedish Riksarkiv
SRP	N. A. Kullberg et al., eds, *Svenska Riksrådets Protokoll, 1621–1658* (vols 1–18, Stockholm, 1878–1959)
TSP	T. Birch, ed., *A Collection of the State Papers of John Thurloe* (7 vols, London, 1742)

Introduction

The 'Dangerous Trade' in Early Modern Europe

Daniel Szechi

There is a well-known adage that if prostitution is the world's oldest profession, espionage is the second oldest.[1] And, leaving aside procreation, spying certainly does revolve around two of the most basic social activities undertaken by *homo sapiens sapiens*: speaking to each other and remembering what was said. For in a sense, listening to, or prompting, conversations between your friends and neighbours, or watching and analysing their behaviour, then telling others about them to win favour or reward, is in many respects the essence of espionage. If you add the organisation of secretly planned attempts by groups of humans to steal other humans' goods, or intimidate, or murder them, you have the beginnings of covert operations in all their myriad forms and thus all the basics of the dangerous trade.

The affinity between human malice, greed, envy and violence and the twilight world of espionage and covert operations is self-evident from its basic characteristics outlined above, and would probably be enough on its own to inspire fear and loathing of its practitioners among the mass of humanity. But when you add the fact that a great deal of officially authorised covert activity is often directly criminal in terms of contemporary legal codes, the general detestation in which it has usually been held throughout the ages becomes easily comprehensible.[2] Who likes being informed on, blackmailed, intimidated or murdered? The masters of secret services have, moreover, often found the psychotic, the 'deviant' and the straitly criminal to be useful tools for achieving their ends.[3] Those who are already alienated from society are less likely to be squeamish about contravening its mores. Thus prostitutes, thugs and thieves (or those willing, for whatever reason, to engage in such activities) and those categorised as sexually, or socially, deviant by their societies, have always had a role to play.[4] The dangerous trade has correspondingly been tainted by association. What kind of official activity is it that uses, rewards and protects such people? How could the state's use of such methods and such people ever be legitimate?

The answer, of course, lies in the purpose behind the clandestine activity in question. Where the state, or its local equivalent, is believed to have used such intrinsically distasteful means to defend itself against its own people and their grievances, any state agency that operates in such a fashion, for example the Spartan *Crypteia* and Ivan the Terrible's *Oprichniki*, is liable to be viewed negatively at the time and by posterity.[5] Where the state or its equivalent is believed to be using nasty methods and unpleasant people to safeguard the interests of all, the state agencies undertaking the covert action are liable to meet with at least grudging approval. Thus spying, deceit, assassination, blackmail and murderous violence were part of the regular toolkit deployed by SOE, OSS, the BCRA and other secret agencies during World War II, but there was very little criticism at the time, and not much subsequently, because the general consensus was and is that it was in a good cause.[6] The principled argument for fighting fire with fire, evil with evil, is now generally characterised as Machiavellian, though the practice certainly existed before the Florentine diplomat Nicolo Machiavelli articulated it in response to the cutthroat world of early sixteenth-century Italian politics.[7] And it was and remains the underlying justification for espionage and covert action for good or ill, down to the present.

The scope for such 'principled' clandestine activities, though, depends on circumstances. In this book we are going to be dealing with espionage and covert action to defend or advance the interests of the state in early modern Europe.[8] There were, of course, other individuals and institutions who used one or both to defend, or promote, their interests. Throughout the early modern period the church in Spain, with the blessing of the state, used the Inquisition to ferret out the alleged enemies of the faith (and the reigning dynasty) through a nationwide network of investigators and informers, and after the restoration of the monarchy in England several zealously Anglican bishops developed private networks of informers to identify lax clergymen and religious Nonconformists.[9] In a more secular vein, in the early nineteenth century Lloyds of London used its agents overseas to collect foreign intelligence which it then passed on to the British state in return for commercially valuable information about the Royal Navy's military deployments.[10] But these operations were never in the same league as the espionage and covert action networks run by the early modern European states.

There were two branches to this clandestine extension of the state's reach. One was relatively new and semi-public, in that its chief operators were well known: the resident diplomats from foreign states who were an increasingly commonplace element in international relations. These men were the officially accredited representatives of their governments, and their persons and residences were increasingly viewed as sacrosanct with respect to local law and customs.[11] By the sixteenth century every significant state in Europe was deploying these 'great spies'. As formal agents of their respective states they were supposed to keep a careful eye on their host's politics and economy and report secretly, fully and regularly. Wherever possible they were encouraged discreetly to cultivate an espionage network that could supply good quality intelligence on the inner workings of the host country's government and an overlapping system of 'friends', who in modern parlance might be described as agents of influence, men and women who could be bribed, flattered or otherwise moved in favour of the ambassador's country's interests.[12] An ambassador was thus more than: 'an honest man sent to lie abroad for the good of his country', in the famous words of Sir Henry Wotton; he was expected to get good intelligence and find ways of influencing the host country's politics by fair means or foul.[13] It should not be assumed that all ambassadors therefore behaved like Guerau de Spes, the Spanish ambassador to the court of Elizabeth I, whose enthusiasm for English Catholic plots and intrigues (including encouraging a major rebellion against the queen) finally precipitated a virtual Cold War between England and Spain in the early 1570s.[14] Most were more discreet, as it was manifestly going to sour relations in the long term if they acted too obviously as spymasters and plotters when resident in friendly or neutral powers. In such circumstances, early modern ambassadors and other diplomats behaved themselves in public. But behind the scenes their role as spymasters, and even directors of covert operations, was fundamental to their role as representatives of their respective states.

The second branch was a very old one, and consisted of networks of agents of all kinds sometimes directed by princes, but more often controlled by powerful courtiers and ministers of state. These networks often (usually?) dealt only with internal security. In a few early modern states, such as Venice and Russia, they even developed into an enduring internal security organisation, but this was rare.[15] Most of these espionage and covert action networks were thus highly personal in terms of the relationship between spy and spymaster, and they were developed by individual ministers and great noblemen the better to serve their princes and themselves.[16] They were apparently ad hoc, in that particular ministers, such as Robert Harley in England and Armand de Plessis, Cardinal Richelieu, in France, hired spies and other agents to scout particular problems and work on resolving them in various (sometimes subtle, sometimes brutal) ways, all without official organisation, authorisation or legal sanction.[17] Moreover, because of the personal quality of the spies' and agents' relationship with their employer these networks were always fundamentally transient. When the 'great man', or very occasionally, 'great woman', fell or died their agents found themselves immediately unemployed unless they could work their passage into the service of his/her successor (which few succeeded in doing). A variant on this branch of clandestine activity was the regular establishment of espionage (and sometimes covert action) networks by senior military officers in time of war, or when war was looming.[18] These obviously focused on enemy military activity and expanded and contracted according to the state of international relations. Yet all this transience and volatility was more apparent than real. Though these proprietary clandestine networks expanded and contracted, and thus spies and other agents came into the dangerous trade and fell out of it all the time, there was always a network (or networks) out there. At any given moment someone in every early modern European government was always setting up or running espionage and covert operations.[19]

The spies and agents employed by ministers, generals and diplomats basically fall into two categories: the professionals and the amateurs. Professionals were those whose livelihoods depended on the dangerous trade. Not that this meant that their involvement secured them either a particularly good, or a regular, living. The payment they received was rarely generous and usually only fitfully paid.[20] The archives are correspondingly full of letters from impecunious agents lamenting their poverty, reminding their employers of the dangerous service they have undertaken for them and begging for money.[21] This even applied to those agents who were technically salaried servants of the state. Like many officials in early modern European government service, they were irregularly paid and often then only part of the arrears owing to them. Most professionals, however, did not even have that much security of employment; like Giacomo Casanova (see Paolo Preto's essay below) they were paid by results. The inevitable corollary was that some professionals consigned to the piecework system tried to inflate the value of the intelligence or services they provided, or chose to be as loyal and committed to their employers as their employers were to them, as was apparently the case with the Sicilian abbés and sometime servants of Philip V of Spain, Giambattista Platania and Giuseppe Caracciolo (see Christopher Storrs' essay below). The sixteenth to eighteenth centuries were thus the heyday of the mercenary spy and secret agent. Between the late 1580s and the early 1590s the Portuguese Manuel de Andrade, for example, worked successively for the exiled claimant to the Portuguese throne, Dom António, Philip II of Spain and Elizabeth I of England.[22] In the same vein, between the 1650s and the 1680s Ignatius White, a Catholic Irishman, at various times worked for the militantly anti-Catholic English republic, the only slightly less anti-Catholic Dutch republic and the devoutly Catholic governments of Spain, France, the Holy Roman Empire and James II's England, picking up a modest fortune and a title (marquis d'Albeville) on the way.[23] Yet we should not assume from this that the professionals generally did not do their best to serve their employers. The hallmark of professionalism is that you can effectively deliver a particular service, and the professional spies and secret agents of early modern Europe, such as the David Passi mentioned in Michael Levin's essay below, more often than not sought to do their job efficiently and well.[24] Passi, indeed, did his well enough to receive the personal thanks of Philip II, despite the fact that Passi was Jewish and Philip II (like most contemporary Spaniards) was reflexively anti-semitic. We should not be surprised that this was the case, for how else was a professional, mercenary agent going to be able to move successfully from employer to employer? Nor should we assume that just because a spy or agent was a paid professional that s/he did not care about the cause, or country, s/he was serving. Nathaniel Hooke, one of whose covert operations is analysed below, was born a Protestant Irishman and grew up to be a fierce opponent of Stuart absolutism in the British Isles, but in the course of events he ultimately became an outstandingly effective and loyal servant of the aggressively Catholic, absolutist Bourbon dynasty in France.

In the early modern era as much as in the modern world the professional spies and agents often worked alongside amateurs of various kinds. Indeed, it was usually the case that most spies and agents were probably amateurs, drawn to the business for a variety of reasons that will be examined below. This had a considerable impact on the general perception of the world of espionage and its associated activities. Because the amateurs, men like Edward Greg, a sometime agent of, and then a clerk in, Secretary of State Harley's office, tended to be sloppy in terms of their tradecraft and clumsy about concealing their activities, they were quite frequently detected and caught despite the very limited forensic capability and crude surveillance techniques available to state authorities. Greg, for example, openly filched the intercepted correspondence of French prisoners of war, hid copies of letters he had written to French ministers in the middle of quires of paper in his closet and used codes a child would have easily seen through.[25] The information they supplied was often of little consequence and when interrogated they also had a tendency to break down and tell all they knew, which was usually not much (as was the case with Greg). The net effect was to give the impression that the murky world of espionage and covert operations was full of silly enthusiasts and that the threat they posed to state security was minimal. Indeed, according to contemporaries like Jonathan Swift, claims that there was any threat at all were political humbug, designed to deceive a credulous public and allow greedy politicians to plunder the estates of wealthy rivals.[26]

There is a sense, moreover, that this scepticism was well founded. Contemporary statesmen certainly did get a great deal of mileage out of a good spy/traitor scandal, and the period is full of examples of statesmen manipulating public anxiety on the subject to consolidate their own political power or undermine that of others. Oliver Cromwell, for example, made good political use of plots against the Protectorate to consolidate public support for his government, Robert Walpole ingratiated himself with George I in large part by his vigorous investigation of the Atterbury plot and, perhaps most notoriously of all, during the French Revolution Maximilien Robespierre boosted his political career by periodic discoveries of nests of 'traitors' and 'spies'.[27] But just because politicians manipulate such discoveries to further their own interests does not mean that the clandestine activity they were exploiting had no basis in reality. To take the cases cited above: for eleven years the Royalist underground worked hard (albeit ineffectively) to overthrow the Protectorate by any means to hand, including attempting to assassinate Oliver Cromwell; the Jacobites Walpole industriously hunted down were deadly serious about their plan to set off a nation-wide rebellion in England with French help in 1722; and the 'counter-revolutionaries' Robespierre was pursuing included networks of French royalists supported and funded by the British government who were absolutely committed to overthrowing the French republic and massacring its adherents.[28] *En masse* the amateurs could also pose a serious threat to the existing authorities' hold on power, as may be seen from the success enjoyed by the very minority Dutch Protestant uprising in 1572, and individually they acted to extend the capabilities of the professional spies and secret agents.[29] A professional spy or agent was, too, intrinsically expensive, in that, at some point, his or her employers were likely to have to pay for his/her services. Amateurs, though they did need occasional payments to encourage them, were usually a great deal less expensive, and could often be persuaded to work for an espionage network or as part of a secret operation cheaply or even free of charge.[30] Given that the financial resources available to early modern Europe's spymasters were distinctly limited (Europe's rulers generally felt they got a better return by investing their money in soldiers, sailors and artillery), this was very helpful. In particular, it greatly extended the reach of the professionals. Without the networks of amateurs their professional agents, such as Sir James Spens, working on behalf of Sweden (see Steve Murdoch's essay below), built up in support of their covert operations it would, indeed, be fair to say that most of Europe's states would have been lucky to glean much information about their enemies by means of espionage and would have had only a minimal capacity for undertaking covert action.

Observing that the espionage and covert ops fraternity can be roughly broken down into professionals and amateurs naturally leads us to the question of where the spies and agents came from. As is the case in the modern world, there were many different trajectories leading them into the dangerous trade. Many of the professionals (or would-be professionals) came from the official diplomatic service of their respective states. Spens and Diego Guzmán de Silva (see below) were both career diplomats of this kind. For such experienced agents of the early modern state, setting up espionage networks and – less frequently – organising covert operations was part of their regular duties. Less happily, from his employer's point of view, the accomplished eighteenth-century French diplomat

François de Bussy used his experience to spy undetected for the British.[31] It should not be imagined, however, that they were trained in any of these activities. Entry into the diplomatic service of France, Sweden and Spain, to take Bussy, Spens and de Silva as pertinent cases, came about through the ordinary processes of patronage and connection by which all contemporary government appointments were made.[32] They then served what were effectively apprenticeships to established masters of the trade, before rising (due to a certain extent to merit, but usually also due to the continued working of connection and patronage) to the level of official Resident or Ambassador to the various states their masters wanted watched or cultivated, or, in Bussy's case, to senior clerk to the minister. In essence, then, they learned on the job.[33]

Much the same might be said of another discernible subgroup among the professionals: military officers, though there seems to have been a notable minority among them who did not learn their new trade so well. Unlike the diplomats the soldiers tended to turn their hand to spying or covert operations only when other, more orthodox, avenues to career advancement closed to them.[34] Sir Robert Walsh, in Alan Marshall's essay below, illustrates the category very well. Finding himself out of the business he had grown up in, soldiering, he thought he would turn to one of its ancillaries, spying. Though a military man might have been expected to have learned the virtues of secrecy, careful observation and fast, sharp decision-making, he appears not to have done so and ended up making a hopeless fist of it. In this he was not exceptional, and the unfortunate Major John André, Sir Henry Clinton's aide-de-camp and spymaster, who was captured and shot by the American Patriots in 1780 after a singularly inept performance in the field is a reminder that professionals who failed in the job could do a lot worse than suffer the contempt and oblivion that was to be Walsh's eventual lot.[35] Nathaniel Hooke, though a professional soldier by the time we encounter him, had a very different career track which may go some way toward explaining his unusual effectiveness both as an agent and an operator able to promote himself within the intelligence system. He began as an amateur participant in the clandestine preparations for Monmouth's rebellion of 1685, then switched to a semi-regular military career (with periodic forays into covert operations in the Jacobite underground) and only returned to the twilight world as his military career temporarily peaked. He was, too, apparently typical in terms of the consequences for his career of this renewed involvement with what turned out to be high-profile covert operations. Senior level involvement in major covert operations, which is to say, operations that really mattered to the princes these officers served, often had, it seems, distinctly beneficial effects for the careers of those involved, as compared with officers who delivered equally sterling service in straightforward military intelligence operations.

There are numerous examples of this sub-pattern in the careers of those involved in the dangerous trade. In January 1634 the Holy Roman Emperor, Ferdinand II, secretly ordered the murder of his own generalissimo, Albrecht von Wallenstein, duke of Friedland, whom he suspected of treason, by a company of picked men led by senior Irish and Scots officers in imperial service (Walter Butler, Walter Leslie and John Gordon). On the night of 25 February the assassins first surprised and slaughtered the officers commanding Wallenstein's bodyguard while they were at dinner and then stormed his lodgings and killed him on the spot.[36] All those involved in the operation – and particularly the senior officers, who all received noble estates – were well rewarded. 'Thomas O'Croli' (also known as Thomas MacDonnell), the assassin who shot the regicide John Lisle in the back on his way to church at Lausanne in 1664, very likely at the behest of Charles II's sister Minette, duchess of Orléans, was probably the Miles Crowley who is recorded as living in France in 1694 as a naturalised, ennobled French subject.[37] Nicolò Montalbano murdered the Electress Sophia Dorothea's lover, Count Philipp von Königsmarck, for Georg Ludwig, elector of Hanover (later George I of Great Britain) and he and his accomplices dumped the body in the Leine river in a sack full of stones. For thus preserving the integrity of the Electoral succession, Montalbano received the personal gift of a princely 150,000 *Taler*, and his accomplices all received well-paid, honourable appointments in the Electoral bureaucracy.[38] In the same vein, but without having had to murder anyone (that we know of), Hooke ended his days as a wealthy, ennobled Brigadier-General in the French army. By contrast, Arthur Wellesley, duke of Wellington's, two highly successful intelligence officers in the Peninsula War, Major Colquhoun Grant and Lieutenant John Grant, had a much less happy experience. Neither was able to parlay their services into substantive early advancement and both ended their careers embittered and with their services essentially unrecognised.[39]

The amateurs, too, usually fell into the spying and covert operations business for want of a better alternative.[40] The entry into the business of Melchor de Macanaz and Giacomo Casanova (as related in the essays below by Christopher Storrs and Paolo Preto) was principally motivated by desperation. Both had run out of other career options in that Macanaz had fallen from high office and could see no other way to rehabilitate himself and Casanova was nearly destitute. Their cases, though, do illustrate the divergent effects of their origins. Macanaz was able to trade on his old network in Spain, most of whom survived in office for many years after his fall, to secure himself a relatively honourable, semi-diplomatic, role and substantial monetary rewards (which, of course, were greatly moderated by their intermittent nature). He was also working towards a definable personal goal: the retrieval of his career as a senior servant of the Spanish empire, which he achieved, at least temporarily. In this respect Macanaz is a very good example of an uncommon, but recognised, way of retrieving one's political fortunes: winning back royal favour by working as an agent of the state. The same technique was used, with similarly limited success, by Henry St John, Viscount Bolingbroke, whose service to his (re)adopted monarch, George I, primarily consisted of ratting out his former comrades in the Jacobite underground, though he may have drawn the line at appearing as a witness against them.[41] More spectacularly, the Dutch renegade and – briefly, in 1725–6 – Spain's premier minister, Johan Willem, duke of Ripperda, tried to repair his fortunes by transferring his services (and all the information he had garnered in the course of his former service to Philip V) to another prince, and does not seem to have been particularly fussy who it was: he first tried George I and then, allegedly, Philip's enemy in North Africa, the Moroccan Sultan Ahmed ed-Dehebi.

Casanova's experience was very different. Despite a promising start working in association with the Venetian diplomatic service, he ended up on a piece rate in the grubby, anonymous world of the Venetian street informer. This was fairly typical of the more humble amateurs who drifted into the dangerous trade. George Eliot was a former servant of Lady Petre of Ingatestone who in 1581 exploited his acquaintanceship with the Catholic underground to discover when and where the future martyr St Edmund Campion was celebrating mass, then led a raid by the local authorities that eventually found Campion and his companions. He got little for it, however, beyond the infamy of having betrayed a man soon regarded as a saint by most of Catholic Europe.[42] In the same vein it is significant that the names of the local Loyalists who identified and delated the American Revolutionary Captain Nathan Hale, who was trying to spy on the British camp on Long Island in 1776, are lost to history.[43] Colonel Robert Rogers got all the credit for his capture. Whatever reward Rogers' unknown (but essential) assistants received was undoubtedly minor and certainly did not include any kind of recognition.

Lowly informing on friends and neighbours was, though, at the least unsavoury end of the spectrum of services such amateurs rendered to the spymasters of Europe. We know about Casanova's involvement only because he was famous for entirely different reasons and thus stands out among the records of the Council of Ten (*Consiglio Dei Diece*). Among the ranks of the broken men (and sometimes women) who provided the majority of 'services' other than spying incidental to the dangerous trade were also to be found many unidentifiable, virtually anonymous individuals willing to do pretty much anything to earn a reward, and these provided muscle for lower profile contemporary covert operations of all kinds, including kidnapping, violence and assassination. Thus in 1668 Louis XIV personally ordered his greatest general, Marshal of France Henri de la Tour D'Auvergne, Vicomte de Turenne, to arrange for the abduction of the Huguenot conspirator Claude Roux de Marcilly from imperial territory, and then had Marcilly executed once he was back in France.[44] The kidnapper, one Captain Mazel, was and remained obscure; whatever reward he received does not seem to have been large or made much difference to the course of his life. In a similar vein, in 1548 in Venice the otherwise obscure Captain Francesco Bibboni murdered Lorenzino de Medici on the orders of Duke Cosimo I de Medici of Florence, who had had Lorenzino condemned to death in Florence for the murder of his predecessor, Duke Alessandro de Medici.[45] Likewise in 1688 unknown agents in the employ of the future William III and II waylaid and murdered the Seigneur de Tellières, a French spy who they feared was close to discovering the secret of William's planned invasion of England.[46] Again, we do not know what reward they received for their services, but the mystery that hangs over their identities strongly suggests it was so small as to leave no record for posterity.

Hence, while Macanaz seems to have had no misgivings about what he was doing (which, after all, was only a little removed from a regular diplomat's activities and thus perfectly honourable in contemporary terms), it is not surprising that Casanova was clearly deeply embarrassed by his service to the Council of Ten and quietly avoided the subject in his memoirs. Neither man, however, is representative of a key further source of amateur recruits for the secret service of Europe's states: the ideologically committed.

Though early modern Europe did see the rise of political ideologies, such as Republicanism, that were not explicitly tied to religious belief, the vast majority of the population 1500–1800 took their politics from their religion.[47] There were, of course, many shades of belief and different strains of commitment within the two great religious camps of Protestant and Catholic, but on each side of the divide there was a minority whose commitment was sufficient potentially to carry them into activities, such as espionage and covert operations, that they believed would further God's cause. Where their religion was shared by the state and the majority of the population such zealots could and did serve their faiths by acting as unpaid, unsolicited informers on the sinful and dissident. Thus Domenico Scandella ('Menocchio') a miller of Friuli, was denounced to the Inquisition by his local priest in 1583, and by an acquaintance he was chatting to in the square at Udine and an innkeeper of Aviano in 1596.[48] Where the faithful of a particular religion were in the minority – Protestants in Catholic states; Catholics in Protestant states – they obviously had less opportunity to express their zeal after this fashion, and in such circumstances the zealot minority became a good recruiting ground for enemies of the prevailing order. Principal amongst these were foreign states aligned with the opposing religion. There still had to be a sufficient number of the minority religion for it to be worth the while of other states' secret services recruiting them. There was no point, for example, in cultivating Protestants in solidly Catholic Spain or Catholics in solidly Protestant Sweden: they were so few and so deep underground that they were difficult to locate and survived by lurking in isolated places off the beaten track. They were thus of little use as spies or covert operatives. But in states where there was a substantial number of the religious minority among whom recruits could be found, and where their moving through, and blending in, with the rest of society was an everyday occurrence, it was distinctly to the advantage of that state's enemies to establish friendly relations with said minority. In practice this meant that until 1685 (and to some extent afterwards) England and the Netherlands quietly maintained connections with France's Protestant Huguenot minority,[49] Sweden publicly presented itself as the protector of Protestantism throughout the German-speaking lands of the Catholic Holy Roman emperors[50] and Spain and France sympathetically patronised expatriate Irish, English and Scots Catholic communities who in turn maintained a strong connection with home.[51]

Such religious minorities, then, provided a steady stream of useful, cheap agents. For the most part entirely for their own reasons they supplied intelligence to professional spies and spymasters, particularly ambassadors, and could be recruited to act as covert operatives for other missions when the need arose.[52] Swedish Lutheran ministers, for example, apparently provided intelligence and other help for the Swedish forces attacking Elbing in 1655, leading to the fall of the city and Irish Protestant officers and civilians provided invaluable intelligence and support for Williamite military operations in Ireland in 1688–91.[53] On occasion, agents could also be recruited from dissident religious/political groups that would otherwise seem to be antithetical to the power they were working for on the age-old principle of my-enemy's-enemy-is-my-friend. Devoutly Catholic Spain thus entered into a secret alliance with the fiercely Protestant English Republican underground after the restoration of Charles II in 1660, and at the same time as Louis XIV was savagely persecuting the French Protestants his ambassador in London was on very friendly terms with the leaders of the strongly anti-Catholic Whig party in England, to the extent of regularly supplying them with French money to further their campaign to force Charles II to concede more and more anti-Catholic measures.[54] This served French interests by producing confrontation between Charles and his Parliaments, which in turn neutralised England on the international scene. In the round, however, it was minority co-religionists who were the most generally useful source of amateur agents. There was, though, always a risk that they might get the bit in their teeth on particular issues and go further than their allies wanted. Although Philip II had publicly put a price of 25,000 *écus* on the head of William the Silent, Prince of Orange and the military commander of the Dutch rebel forces, in 1580, Alessandro Farnese, duca di Parma and commander in chief of Spanish forces in the Netherlands, who was the man on the spot, does not seem to have been very enthusiastic about providing money, support or explicit authorisation for William's assassination. Indeed, he seems to have quietly sought to obstruct the Catholic fanatic Balthasar Gérard when he proposed to do the deed.[55] Gérard, however, refused to be discouraged, independently planned the assassination and then, ironically, finally financed it with money he had begged from the Prince of Orange himself, who believed Gérard to be a penniless Huguenot refugee. On 10 July 1584 he duly encountered William coming out of a dining room and speaking to petitioners in the *Prinsenhof* and shot him at point blank range, mortally wounding him.[56] As Parma may well have feared, the wave of outrage and revulsion which followed consolidated rather than diminished support for the rebels and, even worse, led directly to English military intervention on their behalf.[57] In the same vein, the 1605 Gunpowder Plot in England, which envisaged bringing in a Spanish army to re-Catholicise England at the point of a sword, was cooked up by fiercely Catholic English veterans of the Spanish Army of Flanders in time of peace and at a point when Anglo-Spanish relations were not only good but improving.[58] The abiding problem, then, with the religiously-inspired amateurs so commonly used by rival early modern European powers was that they could easily run wild.

Which brings us to the broader question of how intelligence gathering and internal security, and their attendant covert operations, were directed and controlled. Because the organisation and direction of clandestine networks were in part effectively sub-contracted by the state to individual ministers and generals there were always potential problems with rivalry, duplication and the quality of the intelligence procured.[59] In rare cases, such as Venice, of course, there was a single centrally directed, regularly organised and reasonably well funded state intelligence service, but even this was no guarantee of operational effectiveness from the point of view of the state. By the early sixteenth century the Council of Ten in Venice had effectively turned itself into an autonomous agency above and beyond the law and was more dedicated to serving its own interests than those of the Lion Republic, and it took a long political struggle, culminating in a major confrontation and crisis, to bring it back under the control of the Venetian Great Council in the 1580s.[60] Rivalry and duplication are, of course, problems with which modern intelligence services are all too familiar, and in a sense the rivalries and duplication of the early modern era were inspired by broadly similar circumstances. Then as now those individuals and officers (i.e. intelligence chiefs) who had developed intelligence networks used the information they gathered and the operations they could set in motion both to serve the state and to further their own careers. The difference in the early modern era was the absence of any institutional loyalty. Although careerism and ideology can and does degrade good intelligence work now as much as then, there is a crucial difference: the normative expectation now is that modern SIS, CIA, etc, officers' primary loyalty will be to the institution and the state it serves rather than their bosses.[61] In the early modern era, except in rare cases like Venice, the agents were not part of any institution. They were personally attached to particular individuals. On the eve of the French invasion attempt of 1708, for example, Captain John Ogilvie, one of Harley's agents, avowed to his recently politically disgraced master:

> If you had been in your place at this minute I should have either lost my life or you should have known all the particulars both of their ships and numbers of their troops; and I fancy I could have been very useful to you after they had landed, for I could have advertised you of every step they had taken. But since your honour is no more concerned I have done, and I promise you that it shall never be in the power of another minister to cause me ever venture my life or my honour for all the kings or princes on earth further than a soldier is obliged to do.[62]

This feature of early modern European intelligence and covert action networks made it even more vital for their controllers to make good political use of their intelligence assets, principally by outshining or discrediting their rivals with the intelligence they could bring in and the operations they could pull off.[63] This was because of the very different role society expected men like Sir Francis Walsingham, Richelieu and Oxenstierna to play with respect to their agents, as compared with the modern heads of intelligence services. Simply by taking men and women into their service these spymasters incurred a range of social obligations. This stemmed from the fact that statesmen in this period were always the heads of great clientage systems, which is to say broad networks of kinsmen, neighbours, friends and servants who looked to the man at the top for political leadership and patronage. In return, successful politicians sought to find grazing (i.e. government jobs, pensions and handouts) for their people.[64] This was not necessarily to the disadvantage of the early modern state. Powerful ministers rarely found it advantageous to appoint fools and wastrels to responsible offices and so the placement of tolerably competent, politically reliable, men selected from among their network of clients in medium and lower level public offices was a practical way to ensure the government's business got done. The upshot was that a major part of a statesman's 'job' focused on furthering his clientage network's interests.[65] Which in turn meant that if statesmen like Jean Baptiste Colbert de Croissy, marquis de Torcy, and Prince Eugene of Savoy did not win the approval of their masters – by pleasing them or carrying out their duties effectively – their people's prospects of honour and reward diminished, and by implication the 'great man's' own honour, status and authority declined.[66] As with so much else in early modern European politics, the smile of a prince could make a man's career, and a frown could end it.

This meant that the intelligence networks commanded by statesmen and generals were not simply add-ons. Good intelligence, then as now, was very valuable indeed, and could make or break a prince's policies and strategic decision-making.[67] So supplying good intelligence was an excellent way of winning the prince's favour. The problem facing contemporary spymasters was that their means of gathering and communicating information were very much more limited than those available now. And at this point it would be helpful to review some of the essential principles of intelligence gathering.

Modern intelligence organisations have spent a good deal of time and effort developing a coherent analysis of the organisational structures, field techniques and general approaches that make for good, effective intelligence operations and successful covert action. This has been part of the professionalisation and institutionalisation of the secret services now attached to every significant state. They now train their core staff in professional schools dedicated to that task, where formal principles of how to get, and use, intelligence, and how to plan, and execute, covert operations are taught by experts on the subject. Within the field of twenty-first century practical intelligence studies the crucial distinction is between signals intelligence ('sigint') and human intelligence ('humint'). Sigint, which is to say, the interception of communications of all kinds (e.g. letters, telephone calls, e-mails, etc), is now the dominant mode of intelligence gathering.[68] Humint, i.e. information provided by human observers and listeners, is much less important because it is so variable in quantity and quality, and so subject to human failings.[69] Covert action, though popularly believed to be primarily carried on by the likes of elite soldiers like the SAS and *Spetznatz* and fictional supermen like James Bond, also now often has a strongly sigint quality. More damage can usually be inflicted on modern states by a cyber-attack on their commercial and government e-infrastructure than by assassinating a hostile politician or blowing up Mr Big's secret industrial complex.[70]

The balance in the forms of intelligence gathering was, though, completely different in the early modern world. Sigint meant simply the interception and deciphering of the enemy's letters and other correspondence. This was regularly done by early modern states, and the relatively primitive quality of cryptography (the science of ciphering) meant that it was often highly effective.[71] But unlike the modern world, where organisations like the NSA in the United States and GCHQ in the United Kingdom literally pluck their intelligence from the air by monitoring, sampling and diverting the rivers of data flowing through the ether, sigint in the early modern era was far more dependent on good humint to detect secret channels of correspondence, and entirely dependent on human agents for the interception, deciphering and analysis of such material.[72] Thus in 1586 Walsingham's key counterstroke in penetrating the Babington Plot, a conspiracy by the eponymous Anthony Babington and a number of other well-connected young Catholic zealots to assassinate Elizabeth I and replace her on her throne with her cousin, the imprisoned Mary I of Scotland, was his insertion of Gilbert Gifford into the ranks of the plotters. Gifford assumed the role of courier, carrying letters between Mary and the conspirators brought out in empty beer barrels by a local brewer (who was also working for Walsingham); and every letter Gifford conveyed was opened, copied and deciphered by Walsingham's cryptographer, Thomas Phelippes. The outcome was an intelligence triumph: when the moment was right Walsingham caught not only the conspirators but also Mary. The operation yielded more than enough evidence to secure her trial and eventual execution – exactly the result Walsingham had long aimed to achieve.[73] In sum, in Europe between 1500 and 1800 the exact reverse of the modern situation applied: good humint was absolutely crucial to successful intelligence operations. This was also true of covert action. It did sometimes take forms akin to modern covert operations, notably with respect to targeted or black propaganda (such as the Dutch agent Pierre du Moulin deployed so effectively to sap English public support for the Third Anglo-Dutch War, 1672–4), but there was a tendency for more physical direct action, as we have already seen with respect to the assassination of William the Silent.[74] Thus assassinations and kidnapping, secretly negotiating with dissident groups to promote armed uprisings against enemy states (as in the case of Nathaniel Hooke, below), and so on, were far more prominent activities than in the modern world.[75]

Yet despite the disparity between modern and early modern intelligence operations and covert action, many of those who have worked in or on modern security organisations agree that the principles of intelligence operations, and by extension, covert action, now taught at the professional schools are timeless.[76] This is a proposition calculated to raise the hackles of most professional historians, but it is worth closer examination. In 1986 F. Reese Brown, Editor in Chief of the *International Journal of Intelligence and CounterIntelligence*, asserted:

> 'Intelligence' consists of actionable knowledge or decision-making information.
>
> 'Intelligence' increases the probability of making the best decision under the circumstances.
>
> 'Intelligence' reduces uncertainty by reducing the element of surprise.[77]

This is an analysis with which Elizabeth I and Frederick II would probably have agreed, and correspondingly suggests the operating principles of modern intelligence work may have something to offer in an analysis of early modern European espionage and covert operations. In addition, Winn L. Taplin (a former CIA officer) expanded on these principles in 1989 by further breaking down the process of intelligence gathering and adding covert action:

> Intelligence consists of the collection, analysis, evaluation, and dissemination of information for 'positive' intelligence and counterintelligence and the conduct of Special Activities (covert action).... Special Activities means activities and related functions conducted in support of national foreign policy objectives. They are planned and executed so that the role of the sponsoring government is not apparent or acknowledged publicly.[78]

These, too, have a generic relevance to the early modern era, and will therefore be used as a theoretical framework for the analysis that follows.

So what was early modern Europe's experience of the dangerous trade, as illustrated by the cases below? Taking Taplin's categories in order (but leaving aside the special case of covert action), the collection of intelligence was a constant in interstate relations. Ambassadors and other diplomats really were 'great spies', and thus men like Spens, Guzmán and Macanaz (below) spent most of their working lives listening to, and then recording, the news and gossip they encountered at social and other gatherings as well as identifying potential spies and informers in their host community, securing their services and feeding the information they gathered back to the states they served.[79] On the domestic side every state in Europe at least intermittently paid men like Walsh and Casanova to spy on home-grown dissidents, delinquents and renegades and the information they and agents like them procured was used to keep their governments as well informed as possible about their internal enemies.[80] Because those working under diplomatic cover were part of the burgeoning early modern bureaucracy of international relations their reports tended to be copied and re-copied for the consideration of ministers and princes at home and thus preserved in state archives. Our best sources thus tend to be related to international espionage and secret operations abroad. Which is potentially a problem, because domestic espionage tended to be far more ad hoc and was much more strongly associated with individual ministers and senior military officers. Hence, when those ministers and generals went out of office for whatever reason records of this kind of internal covert activity tended to go with them, making their survival down to the present day a great deal more precarious than its external, official counterpart. The upshot of this is that, because of the partial survival of the evidence, it would be easy to get the impression that the states of Europe (with exceptions like Venice and Cromwellian England) spent far less time spying on their own people than on their foreign enemies.[81] Theoretically this could still in fact be the case, but overall it seems unlikely, given the internal threats and challenges faced by most of the significant European powers. We can only, however, guess at the scale of intelligence collection of all kinds. That said, this writer's guess is that it was probably on a scale comparable in relative terms to modern intelligence-gathering operations.

Intelligence analysis and evaluation is quite rightly seen as absolutely crucial by modern intelligence organisations, and is something presently done by well-paid in-house experts in security organisations, clandestine think-tanks dedicated to that task alone and the like.[82] But as former British army intelligence officer Jock Haswell observed some time ago: '[T]he spy, no matter how good he is, will seldom make any headway against the prejudice of his masters.'[83] Which is to say that good intelligence only becomes effective if those in receipt of it understand and accept its implications. And in the early modern era (except, possibly, in Venice) because the interpretation of intelligence was the remit of particular ministers and princes, analyses tended to be highly individual, i.e. of very variable quality and highly subject to partial interpretation in the light of broader, local and personal political issues. In a sense this is still true, and even in the twenty-first century it can have dire consequences (as in the case of the 2003 invasion of Iraq), but in the early modern era such haphazard modes of interpretation substantially increased the likelihood of errors and misunderstandings leading to catastrophic outcomes. Thus despite all the intelligence he had received on the subject Jan de Witt, the senior minister and virtual director of the Dutch republic in the early 1670s, could not believe until early 1672 that France would so go against what he believed to be its own (secular) best interests in foreign affairs as to attack its former ally, the United Provinces, on ideological/confessional grounds.[84] But in fact deep-seated hostility towards the Calvinist republic was indeed Louis XIV's principal motivation in every move he made with respect to the United Provinces between 1667 and 1672.[85] As a result, when the French declared war in April 1672 the Dutch were taken by surprise in strategic terms, suffered disastrous defeats and only stopped the French army by the desperate expedient of breaching the dykes and allowing the sea to flood some of their most agriculturally productive regions. The price de Witt paid for this mistaken evaluation is a grim reminder of the potentially horrific personal consequences for early modern European statesmen of a military disaster (stemming directly from a failure of analysis) of this order. On 20 August 1672 a frenzied mob of hundreds of his own fellow-countrymen shot, stabbed and bludgeoned de Witt to death. His corpse was then hanged before being gruesomely dismembered and parts of it exultantly eaten by some of his attackers.[86] In 1688 King James II and VII similarly refused to believe, or failed to comprehend, the stream of intelligence he had received indicating that, not only was his nephew and son-in-law William, Prince of Orange, about to invade England with a Dutch army, he was going to be backed by a network of conspirators in the English army and the English provinces who were secretly pledged to rise against James and overthrow the main line of the Stuart dynasty.[87] As a result when the invasion came James's army was paralysed, his government collapsed and he fled the country a broken man. By comparison with de Witt he got off lightly. Taplin observed that: 'clandestine collection is the fundamental element of intelligence, but it is wasted effort if the information produced is not brought into play'.[88] The net impression these and other failures give is that early modern intelligence analysis was not only limited and partial, it very likely often did not make best use of the data supplied. Guzmán's inability to make sense of the intelligence he received, and thus comprehend what was going on in Venice on his watch (see below), is a stark case in point. The spymasters and governments of the period were, it seems, better at collecting intelligence than understanding and using it.[89]

As regards the dissemination of intelligence analyses, the early modern states were even worse at it than their modern counterparts. Whereas in the modern world dissemination tends to be blocked and diverted by bureaucratic boundaries, so that one organisation will jealously, or unthinkingly, hoard intelligence that may be of value to a rival agency, in the early modern period the information and its associated analysis was in effect the personal property of the minister who had built up the network that provided both.[90] In such a case it is not surprising that ministers did not share well with each other. Secret information was valuable and tended to move (when it moved at all) between the man who had sponsored its collection and the prince he was serving. The prince might then choose to disseminate it more broadly, but there was no system for coherently updating an entire government. Thus in December 1707 Harley, then British Secretary of State for the North, received very good intelligence from the John Ogilivie mentioned above that the French were about to launch an invasion of Scotland.[91] He was at the time, though, engaged in a bitter, losing political struggle with a coalition of ministerial rivals and, whether out of sheer cussedness or the fact that he was fighting for his political life, did not choose to impart this information to them. After he fell from office his enemies belatedly received further intelligence that finally alerted them to the threat, but Britain was consequently caught strategically unprepared and was very lucky to escape unscathed.[92]

All of which implicitly raises a final question. What was the impact of all this spying and other covert activity? How far did it influence the course of European affairs? Going by the cases below, the answer seems to be 'not much'. Intelligence gathering of the kind carried on by Spens, Guzmán and Macanaz was, in principle, useful to their masters, but much of the information they provided was not especially valuable and probably could have been picked up by debriefing merchants and travellers who had visited the country in question. Nor, because of contemporary communications problems, could the information be transmitted in a timely fashion. Early modern Europe moved at the speed of a walking horse, which meant that much of the intelligence statesmen and princes received was long out of date by the time they received it.[93] The professional operators, in other words, did not add much value to the information stream that was already there and readily available to anyone who wanted to tap in to it. In the case of Guzmán the money his master invested in Venetian espionage operations was almost certainly wasted, though this impression may be unfair. Guzmán was, after all, being silently opposed, and may ultimately have been thwarted, by one of the very few fully professional counterintelligence organisations operating in early modern Europe. The Council of Ten well knew how to neutralise foreign ambassadors. As for Macanaz the intelligence he supplied was intermittently useful (which may in part explain why he was also only intermittently paid), but he did not conduct himself with appropriate discretion and several times embarrassed his masters. They might have been better off to have been spared both the extra intelligence (Macanaz was, after all, ancillary to Spain's official diplomatic representatives in France, who were also busily gathering information) and the embarrassment. Spens provided more value for money, though even he was at his best not as a supplier of intelligence but as a director of covert action. Taken in the round this is not a fulsome record of success, and it suggests that such foreign intelligence gathering operations may have become ubiquitous more because of what they promised than what they delivered. Also, once the big players, France and Spain, began planting resident diplomats and their associated intelligence networks everywhere, investment in this mode of securing information became, in a way, expected of great powers, or even those simply aspiring to greatness.[94]

Given that neither Walsh nor Casanova provided particularly valuable services with respect to domestic security, it might seem that they, too, were a waste of time and money. Here, though, the disappointing performance of the agents in question may be more apparent than real. Domestic security operations are more about monitoring what is going on in society and among suspect groups than delivering crucial strategic intelligence that must be acted upon. Hence reports indicating that things are quiet, and that nobody is up to anything the government needs to worry about, are in fact quite valuable. The calmness with which the Council of Ten dealt with Casanova and his reports, and the insouciance with which they generally tolerated a great deal of mischief, fraud and minor crime, is indicative of a domestic surveillance system doing its job efficiently. They well knew Venice was in no danger from anything they were hearing from their network of informers. Even the incompetent Walsh was useful from a domestic security point of view. He singularly failed to provide John Thurloe and the Cromwellian regime with much in the way of usable, accurate intelligence, but his blundering around very usefully helped poison the waters among the Royalists. Prompting would-be conspirators and insurrectionaries to suspect each other of treachery by the exposure of double agents in their midst is a very effective way of paralysing their activities and encouraging the development of an atmosphere of paranoia among them.[95] And by the mid-1650s the Royalist underground was indeed effectively neutralised by internal disputes and claims and counter-claims of treachery between its various factions.[96] Thus, in a sense, Casanova and Walsh (and their ilk) were more effective servants of the early modern European state than many of their grander, more prestigious diplomatic and semi-diplomatic counterparts.

With respect to covert action, we have two cases below which well illustrate the promise and peril of such operations. The two operations Spens's network managed: the smearing, and thus discrediting, of Francis Gordon, the representative of the three kingdoms of the British Isles in the ongoing conflict between Sweden and Poland, and the disruption of Sir Robert Stewart's planned invasion of Sweden on behalf of Sigismund III, king of Poland, using forces recruited in Scotland, were both completely successful. The second of these, furthermore, thwarted a serious military threat and directly boosted Sweden's prospects of securing its wider strategic objectives. Oxenstierna's investment in Spens and his network was thus amply repaid. Spens, though, was fortunate to be working through a network of agents he had personally built up. Many of his agents were also veterans who had worked for Sweden for some time. The upshot was that they were tried and tested and worked well together. Hooke had a far more difficult operation to manage. He had to work with and through an independent underground organisation that was (rightly) suspicious of his master's motives and he never received the full backing of the French state. Hooke's operation was unpopular with two key actors: the French army and navy, and consequently at the mercy of the slightest shift in the strategic situation that might give them the excuse they wanted to abandon it. The operation's very nature: a surprise invasion of an enemy country, calculated to set off a major internal rebellion, conducted at the height of the annual bad weather season in that theatre of war and in the face of enemy naval superiority, also made it chancey and the outcome unpredictable. Given all of which, it is amazing it got so close to at least short term success (i.e. securing a landing and provoking a rebellion). In a grand strategic sense, moreover, from France's point of view Hooke's Scottish operation was at least a partial victory.

Interestingly, both these cases confirm Taplin's modern argument that for covert operations to succeed, 'the planners had better know the intimate subtleties of the population group they are trying to influence.'[97] Both men's lives up to that point had left them very well prepared to work in the milieu in which their operations were set and they were correspondingly highly effective. Spens and Hooke's stories suggest, furthermore, that when it was properly managed, covert action in the early modern world could achieve significant results in a way that espionage – even good espionage – rarely could. Of course such a judgement is to an extent unfair. Neither Spens nor Hooke could have carried on their operations without a continuous flow of good intelligence which enabled them to identify where and how to act and who to employ to serve their masters' ends. Nonetheless, the contrast between their eventual fates and those of Guzmán, Macanaz, Walsh and Casanova is very striking. Guzmán and Macanaz at least did not die in penury like Walsh and Casanova, but they did not do very well out of their careers in the dangerous trade. Guzmán did please his master well enough for Philip to ask that he receive a cardinal's hat, but this was for his services as a procurer of fine art, not as a procurer of good intelligence, and Macanaz spent most of his final years in prison. Meanwhile both Spens and Hooke were richly rewarded and ennobled; Hooke despite the fact that his most important operation failed. Perhaps the key to success in the dangerous trade in early modern Europe – at least from a personal point of view – was not so much the intrinsic value of your achievement to your employer as the impression it made on him or her. Even when they failed, dark and dramatic operations trumped the steady accumulation of good intelligence.

CHAPTER ONE

Diego Guzmán de Silva and Sixteenth-century Venice

A Case Study in Structural Intelligence Failure

Michael J. Levin

Being a spy can be dangerous for many different reasons. Obviously the job often involves physical danger, but there is also the peril of getting things wrong. A spy is only as good as the information he can obtain; when his sources conflict, or deceive him, the result is often political disaster for him and his masters. That is what happened to Diego Guzmán de Silva (d. 1578), an ambassador and intelligence gatherer for Spain in late sixteenth-century Venice. Guzmán was skilled and determined, and he served the greatest imperial power in early modern Europe, but at a critical moment he failed both as a diplomat and as an intelligence agent. While he did not fear for his life, he exemplifies another risk of the spy trade: being made to look like an idiot. Despite his best efforts, Guzmán could not determine what the Venetians intended to do, nor bend them to his will, and a crucial military alliance collapsed in consequence. Given that in other respects Guzmán enjoyed a highly successful diplomatic career, it is all the more notable that he failed in this case, his single most important assignment.

Guzmán started out with a number of advantages. To begin with, his king, Philip II of Spain (r.1556–1598), possessed one of the best spy networks in sixteenth-century Europe.[1] Throughout his reign, Philip was obsessed with collecting accurate political information, and received thousands of reports from around the globe.[2] Much of this intelligence came from his ambassadors. Then, as now, resident embassies were widely understood to have a parallel function as spy centres.[3] Ambassadors reported on events, evaluated their hosts' intentions and motivations, and often made use of paid informants and outright spies. The Spanish diplomatic corps, first created by Ferdinand the Catholic in the late fifteenth century, was particularly successful at this diplomatic game. Ferdinand established embassies in a great ring around France, Spain's greatest rival in Western Europe.[4] Ferdinand's successors, Charles V and Philip II, expanded this diplomatic system, and were particularly careful to maintain and further develop a network in Italy, a crucial strategic base for the Spanish Habsburg empire. By the late sixteenth century, Spanish resident embassies had been established in Rome, Genoa, and the Duchy of Savoy.[5] But in terms of intelligence gathering, perhaps the most important Spanish embassy in Italy was in the Republic of Venice.

Throughout the Middle Ages and the Renaissance, Venice stood at a crossroads between East and West. Venetian merchants spread through the Mediterranean and beyond, while commercial and political agents from Europe, the Levant and Asia Minor flocked to Venice.[6] As a result, news and information of all sorts flowed through the city.[7] Naturally this led to Venice becoming one of the great espionage centres of the world.[8] The Spanish Habsburgs (among others) particularly depended on Venice for information on the Ottoman Turks.[9] The Republic of Venice and the Ottoman Sultan exchanged formal embassies, and so communicated on official levels. The Venetian trading empire also extended into the Levant, and so was able to gather a great deal of information informally. The Spanish resident embassy in Venice tapped into these sources, and thus served as a clearinghouse for intelligence on the Turks (as well as Spain's other enemies). One recent study claims that espionage was the real reason for the existence of the embassy, and that the ambassador's diplomatic functions merely provided legal cover.[10] This perhaps overstates the case, for, as we will see, diplomacy was very much a part of Guzmán de Silva's job description. Clearly, however, Guzmán spent a lot of his time collecting intelligence. Indeed, in his initial instructions to his new ambassador, Philip stressed that he, 'must take particular care to know and understand whatever news there may be, through whatever channels, means or forms you can find.'[11] This command referred not only to information received from the Venetians, but also to intelligence *about* them.

The Spanish Habsburgs depended on Venice for much more than information. The Venetian navy was among the most powerful in the world, and the Spaniards needed its aid in their wars against the Turks. Furthermore, Venice itself was a major regional power in northeast Italy. Spanish kings hoped to enlist Venice on their side, against France, in their efforts to establish hegemony in Italy. Throughout the sixteenth century, the Venetians often did fight alongside Spain, but not in a dependable manner. They remained stubbornly independent, fighting Spain's enemies only when it suited them.[12] The Spanish resident ambassador in Venice, therefore, constantly struggled to maintain a working alliance with the Venetians, and just as constantly spied on them to figure out their intentions and strategies. The critical questions were, would the Venetians fight the Turks, and if so, could they be depended on to keep fighting? Almost as importantly, could Venice be trusted to support Spain in its perennial struggles with France for hegemony in northern Italy? These are precisely the issues that would plague Guzmán.[13]

Guzmán served as resident ambassador in Venice from 1571 until his death in 1578. On the surface, he seemed an unlikely candidate to be a spy. For one thing, he was a cleric, a friend of Bartolomé Carranza, the Archbishop of Toledo, and a canon of that city's main cathedral. He also had a relatively short diplomatic career. Before his appointment to Venice, he first served as ambassador to England from 1564 to 1568. His tenure there was successful, if only because he managed not to infuriate the English, as did most of the other Spanish ambassadors to Queen Elizabeth.[14] After returning to Spain, he received his posting to Venice in 1569, but King Philip II temporarily reassigned him to the resident embassy in Genoa when the ambassador there died.[15] So when Guzmán finally arrived in Venice in March 1571, he had less than eight years' experience as a diplomat, less than four years' experience in Italy, and no experience in Venice itself. He had to learn on the job, quickly.

To make matters worse, there was no one at the embassy who could train him or introduce him to people. Ordinarily, a new ambassador could depend on his predecessor to smooth his entrance, but the Spanish resident embassy in Venice had been unoccupied (save for secretaries and staff) since 1558. The last ambassador, Francisco de Vargas, left the city in a huff after the Venetians refused to grant him public ceremonial precedence over the French ambassador.[16] Perhaps to punish the Venetians for their offense against his ambassador's honour, Philip did not replace him for thirteen years. So Guzmán had no support system or functioning intelligence network within Venice to rely on at first. He must have felt enormous pressure to build a new network as rapidly as possible. Philip's instructions specified that in addition to his routine reports to the king and various councillors in Madrid he should regularly correspond and share intelligence with the resident ambassadors in Rome, Genoa, France, England, and the court of the Holy Roman Emperor, along with the governors of Milan and the Netherlands, the commander of the Spanish fleet in the Mediterranean, the viceroys of Naples and Sicily, and Cardinal Antoine Perrenot de Granvelle, the senior Spanish minister in Italy.[17] Guzmán would be one strand in the gigantic Spanish intelligence web, and he had to produce. Furthermore, the political situation in early 1571 called for speedy action.

Guzmán took up his post at a delicate moment. Spain, Venice, and the papacy were in the midst of contentious negotiations concerning a Holy League, or military alliance, against the Ottoman Turks. War had been looming for years, particularly after the Turks besieged Malta in 1565.[18] Pope Pius V (1566–1572) was especially eager for a new crusade against the infidels. Philip of Spain was slower to commit, for he was already fighting several wars and in particular a difficult, long-term one against his rebellious subjects in the Netherlands.[19] But the recent bloody War of the Alpujarras (1568–70), a war against Moorish rebels in Spain itself, made Philip more willing to consider a campaign against the Turks; it was better to take the fight to the enemy than to risk inviting a blow against Spain, where the Turks might find local fellow-Muslims to help them. That left the Venetians, who were the least desirous of open war against the Turks. Venetian and Ottoman business interests in the Mediterranean were strongly interconnected, which made war extremely costly, but in recent years the Ottoman Sultan, Selim II (1566–1574) had become much more aggressive. In 1570 a Turkish force invaded and captured Cyprus, a crucial Venetian colony, which convinced many in Venice of the necessity of war. Many, but not all: this is where Guzmán came in. He had to persuade, cajole, or bully the Venetians into committing themselves fully. But would he be up to the task?

Guzmán did not have the most forceful of personalities. Unlike some of his contemporaries in the Spanish diplomatic corps, he really was 'diplomatic' in the modern sense: outwardly calm and reasonable, not given to displays of temper or pride (as perhaps befitted a clergyman). He seems to have made a good first impression on the Venetians. A secretary in the Spanish embassy noted that when Guzmán formally presented himself to the Venetian government, he was 'very well received' and the Venetian senators, 'showed much contentment and satisfaction with his person.'[20] Guzmán's own initial report said much the same thing. Without going into details, he explained that he had said what 'seemed appropriate' to the Venetians, who responded, 'with many fine words and great eloquence.'[21] These traditional diplomatic rituals were all very polite and formal. But Guzmán's restraint masked a deep anxiety. The day after this ceremony, Guzmán wrote to Don Juan de Zúñiga, the Spanish resident ambassador in Rome, concerning the urgent necessity of developing new intelligence sources on Venetian-Turkish relations.[22] The Venetians seemed willing to discuss war with the Turks, but Guzmán clearly did not trust them. Neither did Zúñiga. Three weeks later Zúñiga responded with his own suspicions that the Venetians were negotiating a Holy League only because they hoped to leverage better terms for a peace treaty with the Turks.[23] And in fact, in January 1571, the Venetians had sent an envoy to Constantinople in a last-ditch effort to come to terms.[24]

Part of the ambassadors' nervousness and distrust derived from their inability to determine Venetian motivations. The inner workings of early modern Venetian government were famously opaque, and deliberately so. The Doge was the nominal head of state, but his role was partly ceremonial; actual power lay in the Senate and various councils, which were often divided into factions.[25] Outsiders thus had a very difficult time analysing how policy-making actually worked. Furthermore, the Venetians carefully controlled the flow of information out of their political institutions. One particular government body, called the Collegio, was responsible for making announcements.

At least in theory, foreigners could not get information from any other source inside the Venetian government, and in 1542 the government passed a law forbidding any contact between foreign ambassadors and Venetian nobles (the political class of sixteenth-century Venice), whether or not they held political office.[26] Guzmán complained about this more than once. 'Here they proceed so secretly,' he wrote in June 1571, 'and with such caution and reserve, that not only do [government officials] keep silent . . . but also so do the other nobles, and thus it is dangerous for me to state opinions for I cannot say anything for certain.'[27] Nevertheless Guzmán worked diligently to uncover what he could.

Within a few weeks of arriving in Venice, Guzmán had begun to gauge the level of support for a war against the Turks among the general populace. On March 29, he reported that the city was deeply divided. Some wanted to launch an immediate offensive, others preferred to defend what they had. Interestingly, Guzmán detected tension along class lines. Old established noble families tended to be more belligerent, while newer houses favoured peace, because they feared for their business ventures in the eastern Mediterranean. But Guzmán warned that his assessments were based on sketchy information. He complained to King Philip that he had no intelligence sources in the city, perhaps because the Spanish embassy had been unoccupied for so long. Whatever intelligence networks Spain used to have in place had clearly deteriorated and Guzmán indicated he was unsure how to proceed.[28] Three weeks later, as far as he could tell, nothing had changed. He complained bitterly about the indecisiveness of the Venetians, because, 'the Turk does not sleep, and could do much damage.'[29]

Meanwhile in Rome, the site for the negotiations over the Holy League, Zúñiga was equally frustrated. The three teams of representatives (Spanish, Venetian, and papal) argued over everything, from who would command the combined fleet to who would pay for supplies.[30] Perhaps the worst disagreement, however, concerned strategy. The Venetians wanted to send the fleet to the eastern Mediterranean, to protect their outposts and colonies, while Philip called for an invasion of North Africa, to head off an attack on Spain. Pope Pius favoured the Venetian position, as he ultimately hoped for a renewed Crusade in the Holy Land, but above all he urged a strike *somewhere* before the campaigning season ended. Yet as late as 7 May 1571, Zúñiga despaired of ever reaching an agreement.[31] His suspicions regarding the Venetian willingness to fight were in fact well founded: even as they negotiated the Holy League, the Republic had sent an envoy to Constantinople to discuss terms.[32]

Back in Venice, Guzmán did his best to prod Doge Alvise Mocenigo I (1570–1577) and the Senate into war. He made speeches before the entire assembled government, and met privately with the Doge and his councillors. He warned them of, 'the necessity of haste, and the great harm which could result from being irresolute, [such as] strengthening the enemy's spirits while weakening those of your friends.'[33] Over the next few weeks Guzmán's reports wavered between cautious optimism and total dejection. On 10 May 1571, he sent a particularly downcast letter to Philip about a recent meeting with the Senate. He had tried to reassure the Venetians that he had no purpose other than to please them, but they were unmoved. The Senators criticized both him and his king, and blamed the Spaniards for the delays in the Holy League negotiations.[34] There seemed little chance of realising an alliance.

Much to Guzmán's relief, however, on 21 May the delegates in Rome actually concluded a formal treaty. The breakthrough had less to do with the Spanish ambassadors' efforts than with the breakdown of Venice's negotiations with the Turks.[35] Indeed, we see here a pattern that would hold true for the next three years: Guzmán's diplomacy apparently had little effect on Venetian actions, while Venetian actions caught Guzmán by surprise. But in some ways he must have won the Venetians' respect. The Doge publicly announced the conclusion of the treaty, and ordered citywide celebrations. Guzmán would play an important role in these rituals. As he wrote to Philip:

> Their Lordships determined yesterday to announce [the conclusion] of the League with great solemnity and demonstrations of contentment . . . two days earlier His Holiness's Nuncio [that is, resident ambassador] came to talk to me, saying that he understood from [the Venetians] that because this proclamation was to be done with great authority, all of the princes' ambassadors who are here would take part, and they had determined to send to me to ask if I would do them the honor of celebrating the mass that day, being certain that my assistance would be very appropriate.[36]

This represented a tremendous diplomatic coup for Guzmán. In Venice, ceremonial political rituals were important displays of power and prestige.[37] That Guzmán, a mere canon, should be chosen to perform this rite, rather than any of a number of Venetian prelates, was a singular sign of official approval. The Spanish ambassador returned the favor by hosting eight days' worth of festivals and feasts in his official residence.[38] These happy events, however, would be eclipsed by the celebrations three months later.

On 7 October 1571, the Holy League fleet crushed the Ottoman Turks at the famous battle of Lepanto. News of the great victory reached Venice eleven days later, sparking jubilation on a scale rarely seen before, and lasting for weeks.[39] Again, Guzmán played a very public role. On 22 October he reported that during a routine appearance before the Senate, the Doge spontaneously asked him to give him and the entire Senate communion, as well as to celebrate a mass in memory of those killed in the battle. Guzmán complied, and later informed Philip that: 'I accepted it all with the appropriate goodwill and grace, so in everything they would know the honor which Your Majesty wishes to do them.'[40] This typically laconic statement tells us much about Guzmán's diplomatic technique, as well as his worldview. No doubt it pleased the devout cleric to perform this service, but he also perceived it as a political gesture. As the representative of the King of Spain, Guzmán's participation in these rituals expressed Philip's benevolence; it also underlined the religious significance of a Spanish-led military triumph over the Muslims. Philip II promoted himself as the secular champion of the Church, and in this moment of victory over the infidel, his ambassador performed a Catholic rite that symbolised God's special relationship with Spain.[41] But Venice of course had also fought and suffered, and so Guzmán 'honored' them. At the same time, by 'gracefully' accepting their compliments, he made it clear who was in charge.

A few days later, Guzmán struck an even more dramatic public position during a grand celebratory procession down the canals of Venice. At one point the ambassador symbolically addressed the Doge and the crowds in a short Latin oration: 'Serenissime Principe, concordia parve res crescunt, discordia maxime dilabantur; et dux noster Jesus Christo dixit, Hoc est preceptum meum, ut diligatis invicem, sicut dilexi vos.' ('Most Serene Prince, small things grow great on concord, great things are destroyed by discord; and our lord Jesus Christ said, this is my commandment, that you love one another, as I have loved you.').[42] By combining a passage from the gospels (John 15:12) with a quote from Sallust (often used by Renaissance diplomats) Guzmán was ostentatiously displaying both his religious and Renaissance humanist learning.[43] As a clergyman/ambassador, he was perfectly representing His Most Catholic Majesty Philip II, the defender of the Faith and the most powerful prince in Western Europe. The subtext of his words was clear: Venice had made the right choice to ally with Spain, and God had rewarded them. After the procession, Guzmán returned to his residence accompanied by the Doge and other government officials, where they feasted together. 'They say it has been the day of greatest joy and devotion together that has ever been seen in this city,' he proudly reported.[44]

Was all of this public posturing effective? At least to begin with, Guzmán believed so. In the afterglow of Lepanto, the Venetians seemed ecstatic about the Spanish alliance. As Guzmán wrote to Philip:

> [The Venetians] demonstrate nothing but great contentment and joy for this most happy success. Such are the praises for Your Majesty and their debt to you that no words can express them. They never stop thanking God for the favor He has done them by uniting them perpetually with

> Your Majesty. I have seen their gratitude in their tears of joy, and the delight with which they declare their allegiance. . . . In the streets and houses they say nothing else out loud except 'Long live King Philip the Catholic!' and many add, 'our lord.'[45]

It is likely that the ambassador's own emotions coloured this account. We have no corroborating evidence that Venetians shouted these actual words; it would have been unprecedented if anyone in Venice had in fact referred to the king of Spain as their lord. Most descriptions of the celebrations emphasise the heroic role of Philip's half-brother Don John of Austria, the supreme commander of the League fleet.[46] (Supposedly when Pope Pius V heard the news about Lepanto, he quoted Scripture: 'There was a man sent from God, whose name was John.').[47] In any event, Guzmán's belief that God had 'perpetually united' Spain and Venice would prove overly optimistic.

Given the festive mood in Venice, Guzmán could be forgiven for being overconfident. A few days after the celebrations ended, he spotted a newcomer to Venice: François de Noailles, Bishop of Dax, a man the Spaniards knew to be an intelligence agent for France. Ordinarily Dax's appearance in Venice would have alarmed Guzmán, for many suspected the Frenchman of trying to sabotage the Venetian commitment to the Holy League (which indeed he was).[48] Guzmán, however, casually dismissed Dax's presence as harmless, now that the Venetians felt such gratitude to Spain. At the same time, Guzmán sounded an oddly cautious note. After mentioning Dax's arrival in Venice, he stated: 'What I can say about this city is this: that one can be sure of them, *unless they deceive me*.'[49] It is difficult to interpret this message. Did Guzmán have some premonition of disaster? He seems to have been undermining his own intelligence report. What is clear, is that even in this moment of triumph, Guzmán did not entirely trust the Venetians. Over the next months, his sense of unease would only increase.

The goodwill amongst the partners in the Holy League did not last very long. In Rome, a mere three weeks after Lepanto, the Venetian ambassadors complained loudly about not receiving grain shipments the Spaniards had promised, as well as perceived slights by Spanish officers in the fleet against their Venetian counterparts.[50] But once again the worst arguments reflected the League members' different military priorities. The Venetians and Pope Pius wanted to press their advantage in the eastern Mediterranean, while Philip and his advisers again urged an attack on North Africa. Fernando Alvarez de Toledo, the third Duke of Alba, one of Spain's leading military strategists, pointed out that, since the Turkish fleet had been neutralised, the next logical step was to destroy their land bases, starting with those close to Spain and Italy.[51] Philip concurred, although he allowed that a North African campaign could be postponed if both the Pope and the Venetians demanded it – but even then, he insisted that Don John should have the last word on the matter.[52] In any case, nothing would happen immediately. Don John, under orders from Philip, withdrew the Spanish ships from the fleet, and spent the winter in Sicily.

This move made sense from the Spanish point of view. From Sicily, Don John would be in a position to strike at North Africa. He would also be able to defend Italy against a French invasion, a threat that seemed increasingly likely in the spring of 1572.[53] Spain's tactical withdrawal from the eastern Mediterranean, however, disappointed the Venetians, who felt abandoned. Guzmán sensed their anger. In January, for example, Guzmán reported a conversation with an unhappy Doge Mocenigo. The ambassador relayed a request from Don John that the Venetians should increase their efforts to spy on the Turks. The Doge said he would dispatch more agents into the field, and suggested that the Spaniards should do the same, perhaps with the aid of Jews, or of Christians pretending to be Jews.[54] Given Spanish sensitivity about Jewish ancestry (and European stereotyped beliefs about Spaniards), this was a not-so-subtle insult.[55] Meanwhile, Guzmán spent months trying to argue that by destroying the Turkish fleet, Spain had already proven that it would fulfil its obligations, but this weak excuse did him no good.[56] By March, the anti-war faction in Venice had clearly grown in strength, along with anti-Spanish sentiment. Guzmán, who had now been in Venice for a year, had evidently established some intelligence sources inside the Venetian government, and he did not like what he learned. On 19 March Guzmán reported that the Council of Ten, a government body that debated, 'the most secret and important matters of state,' had met for three straight days. An anonymous informant told Guzmán that a senior noble named Nicolò da Ponte (who would become Doge in 1578) had spoken in the meeting against staying in the League. Worse, he had castigated Philip and all Spaniards as insolent and imperialistic ever since Lepanto. While some Council members argued for the League, others had agreed with Da Ponte. Such evidence of resentment against Spain must have worried Guzmán, who blamed French agents for spreading disaffection throughout the city.[57]

The rising anger against Spain no doubt made it even harder for Guzmán to find sources willing to talk to him. Conversely, those who did contact him could not necessarily be trusted. One odd letter he sent Philip on 8 April illustrates his situation. Guzmán began by explaining that Venice was full of 'inventors' who made wild claims. Some offered war machines, or new ship designs, or 'other various things,' but all of them had to be dealt with carefully. One should not believe them, the ambassador warned, unless they truly seemed to be offering something, 'feasible and useful for Your Majesty's service.'[58] Guzmán then went on to describe an encounter with one such individual. This person approached

Guzmán through a third party, and refused to disclose his name until the ambassador agreed to a face to face meeting. Through other sources Guzmán determined that the mystery man was wealthy, and probably either a Venetian native or a resident in the *terrafirma*. In any case, Guzmán agreed to meet with him. As it turned out, the man (who remains unnamed in the letter) wanted to sell a get-rich-quick scheme to the Spaniards. He claimed that if Philip paid him 5,000 gold *escudos* up front, plus an annual salary of 1,000 *escudos*, he would reveal a surefire method of increasing Spain's tax revenues by 50,000 to 70,000 *escudos* a year. Unfortunately we do not know if Philip ever responded to this offer, but it is interesting to note the atmosphere of secrecy surrounding the incident. Obviously the 'inventor' was skirting the law against speaking with ambassadors, and was probably also trying to impress Guzmán with the importance of his wares. He may also have wanted to avoid being seen with the Spanish ambassador in particular. It is also interesting that Guzmán reported this episode at all. Whether or not he took the man seriously, he was earnest in his quest to find Venetians willing to aid Spain.[59] Fewer and fewer seemed likely to do so.

In April 1572, the Holy League suffered several critical blows. One was the death of Pope Pius V. Pius had been the driving force behind the League, and his demise increased everyone's doubts about the alliance's survival. In Rome, Zúñiga lamented the great loss, 'both for Christendom in general and for the particular affairs of Your Majesty [King Philip].'[60] In Venice, Guzmán did his best to keep the League afloat. Before the Senate, he announced, 'that I greatly sorrowed for the loss of [Pope Pius], especially at this time. But while God has seen fit to gather up [his soul], I was certain that the general business of the League . . . would continue without fail.'[61] This show of confidence, however, lacked conviction, for Guzmán knew that his own king could no longer be counted on either. First of all, after the death of Pope Pius, Philip became even more determined to send Don John to North Africa.[62] But then an entirely different factor entered the equation: the Netherlands erupted in a second and even more massive revolt against Spanish rule.[63] Philip's attention would be riveted on the Dutch Revolt for the rest of his life. Guzmán personally believed that the war against the Turks should remain Spain's highest priority, but he would find it increasingly difficult to pretend that Philip agreed.[64] With Philip so obviously distracted, the Venetians now had another reason to doubt Spanish support, and another excuse for abandoning the League. Guzmán's fears about losing the Venetians redoubled, and deservedly so. On 6 June the Council of Ten began to send feelers out to Constantinople, concerning a possible peace treaty.[65] From this point the alliance between Spain and Venice was doomed.

Guzmán did not know about Venice's renewed discussions with the Turks, but his intelligence reports reflected his suspicions, as well as his own misgivings. On

2 July 1572, he sent Philip a curious account of what he had heard in the streets and on the canals of Venice. 'Many speeches are being made here,' he wrote, 'because Your Majesty decided not to order our fleet to proceed, and everyone is making judgments without knowing the facts. But that is an ancient malady of Italy which cannot be cured.'[66] This sneering remark about Italians was fairly typical for Spanish ambassadors in Italy.[67] But then Guzmán made some unusual statements concerning what 'people' in Venice were saying about Spain in general, and Philip in particular. He cited a rumor that perhaps Spain was not as powerful as everyone believed, and that Philip's refusal to continue the campaign in the Mediterranean proved his impotence. Worse, Philip, whose promises, 'have been inviolable until now,' had shown himself to be untrustworthy. Then Guzmán's language shifted away from a description of what Venetians had said, and into a more personal mode. The Venetians had already been suspicious of Spain, Guzmán warned, but now they would never believe Spanish promises. Furthermore, 'the princes of Italy will be more hesitant [to ally with Spain], as it seems to them that when Your Majesty deliberates about policy, you care more about your particular concerns than about the common good.' At this point we have to wonder what Guzmán was really saying, and whose opinions he was truly expressing. He never identified the 'people' making these speeches, or the audience, or the circumstances. In fact this entire report has an odd, artificial tone. Which Venetians believed that Philip never broke his promises? What Italian Renaissance prince would be shocked that the King of Spain acted in his own self-interest? It seems possible we are hearing Guzmán's own disillusionment with his monarch. Perhaps he was chastising Philip indirectly, by putting these sentiments into the mouths of Venetians?

In any case, Guzmán was not the only Spanish official in Italy unhappy with Philip's policies. Zúñiga, his brother Don Luis de Requeséns (formerly an ambassador in Rome, and currently the Governor of Milan), Cardinal Granvelle, and Don John himself, all complained that the king's unwillingness to send the fleet into the Mediterranean would drive the Venetians straight into the arms of the Turks.[68] This united front, plus additional pressure from the new pope, Gregory XIII (1572–1585), forced Philip to relent.[69] On 4 July he informed his delegates in Rome that in order to satisfy the pope, and keep the Venetians in the League, he would command Don John to proceed to the Levant with a large part of the Spanish fleet.[70] Unfortunately, however, the gears of Spanish bureaucracy ground very slowly. Don John did not receive his orders to proceed until 12 July.[71] The Venetian and papal ships had already set sail by then, and they engaged the Turks in an inconclusive battle off of the island of Malvasia. The Spanish fleet did not rejoin the rest of the League forces until early September. Quarrels between Venetian and Spanish officers again broke out.[72] A month later, after much indecision about what to do next, Don John declared the campaign season over for the year; the League's efforts to capitalise on the victory of Lepanto had been a pathetic failure. Guzmán reported much grumbling among the Venetians about Don John's poor performance, and indulged in some griping of his own. 'These people who are in their houses and at their leisure fight very well by sea or land,' he remarked sarcastically.[73]

For Guzmán, the winter of 1572–73 was truly a time of discontent. He experienced agonizing uncertainty about whether the Venetians would sign a separate peace with the Turks; his opinion sometimes changed from week to week. Philip, in a classic example of too-little, too-late, promised to shoulder a greater proportion of League costs in an effort to keep the Venetians happy.[74] But the Venetian response was ambiguous at best. In early January, Guzmán reported that the Senate had demonstrated 'contentment' with the king's offer, but he warned that such concessions did not guarantee support for the League. In fact, he admitted painful ignorance about the true state of Venetian-Turkish relations. 'It hurts me not to be able to clarify nor give any specifics about [Venice's] intentions in this business, as I have said before,' he wrote. 'I believe they could very well make peace with the Turks, as some lean that way, while others the contrary.' He then relayed assurances from the Doge that Venice would remain in the League, which, oddly, Guzmán claimed to believe. But he concluded the letter on a grim note: 'It is appropriate that Your Majesty should make provisions so that whatever happens . . . you will be prepared.'[75] In other words, Guzmán had no idea what was going to happen and hoped for the best, but he feared the worst. This is a remarkable acknowledgement of failure as an intelligence officer, and a foretaste of his failure as a diplomat.

Still Guzmán did not admit total defeat. He continued to harangue the Doge and the Senate, albeit with perceptible desperation. In one open letter to the Venetian government, for example, he thundered that it would be blind, stupid, and wicked of the Republic to abandon its allies. Then in an abrupt change of tone, he begged them in the name of God, King Philip, and, 'the particular love I bear for this Most Serene Dominion', to act in the common interest.[76] Clearly, Guzmán was unsure whether blustering or pleading would be more effective, or indeed whether anything could be done. By this time so many rumors about peace negotiations were flying around the city that Guzmán considered confronting the Venetian government openly. But a Venetian noble (Guzmán did not identify him) talked him out of an open confrontation, arguing that a display of mistrust would offend too many people, which presumably would strengthen the anti-war faction.[77] One wonders whether this anonymous Venetian was manipulating the ambassador, but there is no way to know. A week later the Doge himself assured both Guzmán and the papal nuncio that

Venice would remain in the League, a story that other sources seemed to confirm.[78] Were they lying, or was there still hope for the alliance? Guzmán did not know, and he vented his frustration: 'On the twenty-fifth [of February] when I spoke to the Senate on Your Majesty's behalf it seemed to me that they were happy and content; today I could judge the opposite . . . Please God the devil does not deceive them. I am acting with the necessary care, but also with the distress of not knowing the truth about what is happening.'[79] Again, Guzmán revealed his inability to determine what the Venetians would do. Evidently he still hoped that the Venetians would resist the Evil One's temptations to make peace with the infidels, but he also feared that it would take an act of God to prevent it.[80]

Unfortunately for Guzmán, his prayers would not be answered. After some hard negotiations, the Venetians signed a peace treaty with the Turks on 7 March 1573.[81] Guzmán, however, would not know this for nearly another month. Until their ambassadors returned from Constantinople with the actual treaty, the Venetians pretended that nothing had changed. The mixed signals they sent out must have driven Guzmán to distraction. As late as 17 March for example, he stated that the Venetians had declared themselves to be, 'totally determined to remain in the League.'[82] Later Guzmán would learn this was a bald-faced lie, but at the time he seemed to accept it. He did not say why anyone should believe the Venetians, given all of the contrary evidence, but perhaps he still hoped for a miracle. Then, on 3 April reality finally made an appearance, in the shape of two messengers from the Levant. Guzmán's description of events gives us a fascinating insight into the atmosphere of secrecy surrounding the Venetians' dealings with the Turks. The dispatch itself was written in code, indicating the importance and sensitivity of its contents. As the Spanish ambassador wrote:

> This morning I was advised that yesterday at nightfall there arrived two men in a ship from Ruvino, who did not want to present themselves before the ministers of the city, as is the custom for all foreigners, as they wished to go directly to the Doge . . . Having been given permission, they were taken from the ship in a covered gondola so they would not be seen. They went by a somewhat isolated canal to St. Mark's, and afterwards they returned there, and according to what I was told they had been with the Doge. The more important of the two men came dressed in crimson damask, and the other in black, both in Levantine style.[83]

Guzmán did not say who tipped him off to these developments, although he clearly had some kind of surveillance system in place, watching for new arrivals to the city. Whoever Guzmán's source was, he had carefully tracked the movements of these strangers, and observed their clothing. Guzmán had probably been dreading the arrival of Turkish ambassadors, or Venetian messengers from Turkey, for months, and would have been on the lookout for them. In any case he proceeded to investigate, by quizzing the other resident ambassadors in Venice:

> The papal nuncio was in the College this morning. I went to his house to ask if he knew anything about these events. He told me [the Venetians] had told him nothing. . . . But the emperor's ambassador had sent to him to say that the son of the *bailo* [the Venetian ambassador in Constantinople] had arrived, and had brought with him a signed peace treaty with the Turks. I went to look for the [imperial] ambassador and met him on the street that leads to the nuncio's house and from there to my residence. I asked him what he knew, and he told me that a highly placed source had told him the *bailo*'s son had come with a signed peace treaty. I asked him if he knew anything more specific, but he said no. I asked him to try to discover more, and I would do the same.[84]

We see here the diplomatic community in Venice at work, as the various ambassadors combined their intelligence resources. It is interesting that Guzmán asked for help so directly. He apparently still did not have many highly placed informants inside the Venetian government, if he had to rely so heavily on other people's sources. It is also remarkable that Guzmán did not seem embarrassed to ask for assistance, or to risk appearing desperate. But the truth was evident and undeniable: Venice had in fact abandoned the League, and Guzmán had failed in his primary diplomatic mission.

The following day the wrathful Guzmán, accompanied by the papal nuncio, met with the Doge and his councillors. The Doge made a long speech justifying their decision to make peace, and asked that King Philip, whose, 'desire for the common good and [Venice's] in particular', was well known, should accept this development with the, 'benevolence, prudence, modesty, and good will that he has always shown in our affairs.'[85] It is difficult to determine if the Doge spoke sarcastically, but the Spanish ambassador certainly took it that way. He reminded the Venetians of everything Philip had done to aid them, and then acidly remarked that, '[i]f this peace was indeed made in the service of God and the common good, and for the conservation and growth of this Republic, then I definitely believed that Your Majesty would receive the news with the good will and love which [the Doge] alluded to.' But of course Guzmán made it clear that that the Venetians had done anything but advance the interests of

Christendom, or Venice itself; indeed, he sneered, the Venetians had better look to the defenses of the lands bordering those of their 'new friend.'

Guzmán's anger at the Venetians was genuine, but he was also upset with himself. Despite all of the ominous signs, and his evident suspicions, the actual announcement of a peace treaty seems to have caught him by surprise. In the same letter that described his stormy meeting with the Doge, Guzmán included a coded note, which expressed his dejection and embarrassment. 'These past days I have been deceived in this business by the notices I received from good people,' he admitted. 'I could not on my part have made greater efforts [than those] I have described to Your Majesty in my previous letters. I have told you about what I did here, which was much less than I wished. . . . I confess some fault in this [failure] rather than in my will and desire to serve Your Majesty.'[86] Guzmán knew that he had been hoodwinked; his intelligence sources had either erred or lied to him, and his lack of accurate information had contributed to a major diplomatic disaster. Zúñiga sent a similar letter from Rome, claiming that he had done everything he could to keep the League intact.[87] Interestingly, Zúñiga assured Philip that Venice's defection was in no way the king's fault; it is unclear if he was trying to console the king, or himself, or even if he meant it as an implied criticism of the king.

Word of Venice's defection slowly rippled through Western Europe. As faulty as Guzmán's intelligence may have been, he still discovered the truth relatively early. Pope Gregory XIII did not know for sure until the Venetian ambassador in Rome, Paolo Tiepolo, officially broke the news on 6 April 1573.[88] Gregory exploded, hurling curses and threats of excommunication at the ambassador and all of Venice.[89] King Philip, by contrast, maintained his famously icy composure (at least in public). On 17 April the Venetian ambassadors in Madrid, Leonardo Donà and Lorenzo Priuli, admitted to Philip what their government had done, and sent the following report:

> The king listened to us very attentively . . . His face gave no hint of what he was thinking, except that at the moment when he heard that the conditions of the peace treaty had been accepted his mouth moved ever so slightly in the very fleetest of ironic smiles, almost as if His Majesty wanted to say, without interrupting us, 'In short, you've done it, just as everyone told me you would!'.[90]

According to Donà, Philip then claimed that the news came to him as a complete surprise, although it obviously did not. Philip, as much as his ambassadors, had hoped that Venice would remain in the League, and felt betrayed. Whatever his public pose, Philip shared Guzmán's hard feelings. In a private note to one of his councillors, probably written that same day, the king reported the Venetian defection, and then spat: 'I hope to God [the Venetians] get the worst out of that deal!'[91]

In the aftermath, Guzmán endeavored to learn exactly what had gone wrong. On 8 April he reported that, as best as he could determine, the Council of Ten, and specifically Nicolò da Ponte, had initiated the peace negotiations.[92] This confirmed his intelligence reports about Da Ponte from the previous year, although of course it did Guzmán no good to discover that for once he had had accurate intelligence. In public the Venetian government blamed Spain for forcing it into signing a separate peace. The Doge and Senate pointed to Don John's tardiness in joining the League fleet, and the subsequent failure of the 1572 campaign, as evidence of Spain's culpability. Or at least, as Guzmán pointed out, that was the 'story' (in Spanish, *ficción*) that the Venetian government proclaimed. Guzmán claimed that many Venetian citizens grieved over the defection, and refused to meet the ambassador's eye, 'like embarrassed and ashamed people.'[93] No doubt many Venetians did indeed feel shame, although Guzmán may also have been projecting his own emotions.[94]

Whatever Guzmán's feelings, however, he still had a job to do. For the rest of his tenure in Venice, he would argue for renewed hostilities against the Turks. It may be a tribute to his faith, or perhaps his stubbornness, that he never gave up hope. In January 1574, for example, he sent Philip a long coded letter, in which he reported that many Venetians were 'dissatisfied' with how long it was taking to hammer out the details of their peace treaty with the Turks.[95] Once again Guzmán perceived a split in the Venetian populace: some wanted to accept whatever conditions the Turks demanded, while others argued the opposite, saying that Venice, 'ought to look to the honor of the Republic.' Sensing an opportunity, Guzmán explained, '[i]t seemed to me [best] to make some effort to encourage our friends and to compel everyone with general words. I went to the College yesterday and spoke to them in secret, saying in substance what I have been telling them from the beginning.' The ambassador delivered a typical diatribe, hitting all of the same notes he had been singing for years. For the good of Venice, its allies, and all of Christendom, they must rejoin the fight against the infidel; besides, had not the Turks repeatedly proven their untrustworthiness? The Doge answered with bland words, pointing out that he had heard all of this before. He assured Guzmán that neither he nor any in Venice would ever forget the gratitude they owed to Spain, but he was clearly not moved to change his mind. Guzmán then switched tactics, trying to persuade the Venetians that whatever Spain's faults in the past, it was now ready and able to fight at any moment. King Philip was in perfect health, and while the Dutch Revolt was still a problem, things were looking up there too. Don Luis de

Requeséns, the new Governor-General of the Netherlands, was, 'very hopeful that affairs in Flanders had taken a turn for the better.'[96] But the ambassador's arguments fell on deaf ears. Although many Venetians may in fact have been unhappy about the terms, the peace treaty held. In March 1574 Guzmán's sources informed him that a messenger had arrived in Venice with a confirmed and signed document.[97]

It is worth noting that Guzmán's responsibilities as an intelligence officer did not cease after the Venetians abandoned the League. For one thing, he continued to collect information on the Turks, with or without the Venetians' help. The Turkish threat had not disappeared, even if Venice would no longer fight, and Philip no longer paid as much attention. Long after the demise of the League, Guzmán worked as diligently as ever in his role as intelligence agent, both to assess the danger of another Turkish assault, and to ascertain the true state of Turkish-Venetian relations. Ironically, in some ways Guzmán would be more successful building an intelligence network in these later years, when it no longer mattered as much.

Guzmán never stopped seeking better sources of information on Levantine affairs, or ceased complaining about the inadequacies of his agents. In July 1573, for example, he told Philip that he did not bother passing on some of the intelligence he collected, because of the unreliability of his sources. 'Eastern spies' could not be trusted, the ambassador warned, and Venetians living in the East were no better, because of their 'permanently ambiguous attitude.'[98] Guzmán's exasperation with his lack of good informants perhaps explains his willingness to work with questionable people. That same month he made an odd request of the king. He explained (in code) that a certain gentleman named Don Cesar de la Mara had contacted him, offering important information about the Turks. De la Mara, it seems, was a Neapolitan currently living in Ragusa (modern-day Dubrovnik), bordering on Ottoman territory. De la Mara, however, was also an outlaw: he was in Ragusa because he had murdered his own mother and then fled Naples. In return for his information, he demanded a royal pardon. After describing this situation, Guzmán recommended that, given the difficulty of finding good intelligence sources, the king should make the deal.[99] Obviously, the needs of state trumped whatever scruples Guzmán might have had as a cleric. We do not know how Philip responded in this particular case, but we do know that the king approved other sources he or his ambassador might have found objectionable. Some of Guzmán's best intelligence agents, for example, were Jews.

The Ottoman Turks were relatively tolerant of Jews living in their lands, and Jewish merchants traded and traveled freely throughout the eastern Mediterranean.[100] As a result, these Jews saw and heard quite a lot, and many came through Venice with valuable information. The Venetians took advantage of this situation, and used a number of Jewish informants. For example, the Venetians received much intelligence from a man named Solomon Ashkenazi, a Jewish doctor and diplomat in the personal service of one of the Ottoman Sultan's chief ministers. Ashkenazi also played an active role in the Turkish-Venetian peace negotiations.[101] Guzmán evidently learned from this example, and employed several Jewish spies, once again demonstrating that whatever his personal feelings as a Spanish priest, he would not let a good source of information go to waste. Sometimes these men remained anonymous in Guzmán's reports, such as a Jewish member of a Turkish ambassador's entourage, who discussed the current state of Turkish-Venetian relations with Guzmán in June 1574. Guzmán mentioned that this man was a native of Milan, and thus one of Philip's subjects (which perhaps explains his willingness to spy for Spain), but we do not learn anything else about him.[102] Other times, however, Guzmán described these sources in great detail. In August 1573, for example, a man named David Passi offered his services to Guzmán. Passi was a diplomat and a career spy, who worked for both Christian and Muslim masters.[103] Guzmán apparently examined Passi's background closely, and sent Philip a thoroughly researched report:

> A Jew named David has arrived here from Ragusa, who was in that republic during the recent conflict with the Turks. According to my sources, he is the nephew of the Jewish doctor who negotiated peace [between Venice and the Turks]. He speaks Spanish, and claims to be a native Spaniard, and to have debts there, and as a Spaniard he desires to enter Your Majesty's service. He has been serving the Venetians, but claims to be dissatisfied with them because they have not paid him; but you cannot trust Jews. . . . He tells me he knows for certain that the Venetians always intended to seek peace [with the Turks], and that no one would know better than he, because he handled many of the negotiations.[104]

It is interesting that despite his obvious bigotry against Jews, Guzmán was impressed by Passi's depth of knowledge, and evident value as a highly placed intelligence agent. Passi's observation about the Venetians always wanting peace no doubt confirmed the suspicions Guzmán had had all along, and perhaps also indicated that he was telling the truth. In any case Guzmán overcame his distaste for working with Jews, and accepted Passi's offer. Over the next few years Guzmán's correspondence contained numerous references to Passi and the intelligence he gathered on the Turks. Some of the information Passi provided was alarming. In January 1575, Passi told Guzmán that the Bishop of

Dax was again making trouble for Spain, this time by trying to arrange an anti-Spanish alliance between France, Venice, and the Turks.[105] Nothing ever came of the French agent's machinations, but Guzmán was no doubt very upset at the time by the bare possibility of such a plot. Whatever intelligence Passi could obtain, however, Guzmán clearly appreciated his efforts, as did Philip. At one point Guzmán relayed to Passi the king's personal thanks for his good work.[106] Not even King Philip, famous for his profound Catholic faith, allowed religious prejudice to get in the way of utilising a good spy.

Despite the improvements in Guzmán's intelligence network, however, he still had very little good news to convey. In June 1574, for example, Guzmán sent Philip a report about a meeting between the assembled Venetian government and their ambassador to the Sultan, Marcantonio Barbaro, along with Solomon Ashkenazi. Guzmán was not present at this meeting, but the level of detail he was able to provide indicates a very good informant inside the Senate. But having good information would have been cold comfort, given the meeting's subject: friendly relations between Venice and the Turks. As Guzmán wrote:

> On the eleventh of this month I wrote to Your Majesty that the *bailo* Barbaro and the Jewish doctor had arrived here, and the reason for it was not known. Yesterday Barbaro went to the *Collegio*, accompanied by the procurators of Saint Mark's, as is the custom . . . the Jewish doctor went with them and was treated as an ambassador . . . The words [Barbaro] spoke were in substance as follows: 'The Most Serene Prince [the Doge] and the Senate sent me to His Most Serene Great Lord the Emperor of the Muslims [the Sultan], in order to confirm the blessed and holy peace, and to certify that [Venice] will always be most prompt to observe and guard its obligations. . . . On the part of the Most Illustrious and Most Excellent [Sultan] I have an order to kiss your hands, and to advise and certify you that as far as may be possible, he will be a good friend and will live up to his obligations, and for the sake of greater clarity and certainty, he has given me this credential letter, which concerns no other particular business except this message alone.[107]

So Guzmán was able to produce a first-rate intelligence report, describing what was said in a closed meeting of the Venetian government, but once again it only confirmed what everyone already knew. The Venetians would remain at peace with the Turks, and could even exchange diplomatic pleasantries with the Sultan. Guzmán must have been bitter to have his failure underlined so clearly.

But Guzmán did not have time to brood. While the war against the Turks had consumed him for years, he also had other political powers to worry about. France, in particular, had to be watched. Like all Spanish ambassadors in Italy, Guzmán worried about French actions that might jeopardise Spain's domination of the peninsula.[108] The Spanish Habsburgs were always haunted by the possibility of an Italian power inviting a French invasion in the hopes of improving its own lot. Guzmán thus monitored Venice's relations with France closely, looking for signs that the Republic was becoming too friendly with Spain's main European rival. In July 1574, it suddenly became his primary focus, because of a state visit to Venice by the new king of France. When King Charles IX died in May 1574, his brother Henry III (1574–1589) was in Poland (which he had ruled as king for less than a year). Henry decided to take a leisurely tour of Italy on his journey back home, enjoying fetes and festivals along the way. Venice in particular honoured him with a week of elaborate celebrations.[109] Guzmán, however, did not enjoy the party. While he participated in the ceremonies, he could not help but be suspicious and resentful of this show of amity between Venice and France.

Even before Henry arrived, Guzmán's intelligence reports indicated the building excitement and anticipation in Venice. Three weeks before the event, he remarked on the grand apartments the Venetians had prepared for the king's use, and the ten gondolas, covered with scarlet satin, which would convey Henry and his entourage through the city.[110] Once Henry made his entry, Guzmán's reports become even more detailed; Venetian civic rituals were highly symbolic, and Guzmán noted every nuance. For example, he reported that Doge Mocenigo met Henry at the outskirts of the city, and accompanied him personally to the Ducal Palace – the highest compliment possible for a visiting dignitary.[111] As the representative of the king of Spain, Guzmán himself was part of the welcoming party, along with the other foreign ambassadors in Venice. As he wrote to Philip, 'I said to [Henry] in a few words what seemed fitting for the occasion. The king responded graciously in Italian, that being what I spoke to him, knowing he understands no languages other than that and French.'[112] Guzmán here displayed his qualities as a Renaissance courtier: gracious, affable, and a touch condescending. He also noted that when Henry spoke with him, the king removed his hat, a clear mark of respect for the king of Spain's ambassador.

But these pleasant overtures masked political tension. Many nobles from all over Northern Italy, including Emanuel Philibert, duke of Savoy, and Alfonso II d'Este, duke of Ferrara, came to Venice to honour Henry, making Guzmán increasingly nervous. From the beginning of his reign, Philip II had been cultivating ties with the Italian aristocracy in order to solidify Spanish hegemony in the peninsula.[113] Now many of these nominal allies of Spain (including the duke of Savoy, Philip's own cousin) were ingratiating themselves with the king of France. In addition, as the historian Edward Muir suggests, the Venetians purposely designed their decorations and ceremonies around the theme of, 'courting French favour at the expense of the Spanish.'[114] Guzmán noticed, and appears to have been irritable and defensive the whole week. At one point, for example, Guzmán met with the duke of Savoy. The duke apologized for being late to their meeting, as he had been detained in another meeting with the duke of Ferrara, and (more ominously) Louis de Gonzague, the French duke of Nevers. Guzmán pointed out that Savoy could have included him in that earlier meeting. Guzmán rebuked the duke, saying, 'he wished to return later, so as to leave him and not disturb him in such good company.'[115] Guzmán reported that Savoy was amused by the remark, but it is not clear if the Spaniard meant to be funny; the ambassador did not appreciate being snubbed in favour of a Frenchman.

This incident fits the general pattern of a difficult week for Guzmán. The Spanish ambassador perceived King Henry's visit as a stunning success for French diplomacy. For him, even apparently comic moments during the week's activities had ominous implications. For example, the Venetians produced a spectacular mock battle for the king's amusement, in which two 'armies' fought for possession of the Rialto Bridge.[116] Guzmán explained to Philip that this game had been popular in Venice in the past, but had been banned for some years, because the casualty rate had been too high. In Henry's honour, however, the Venetians revived the old tradition. According to Guzmán, the king greatly enjoyed the spectacle, 'because many people were knocked into the water.'[117] The Spanish ambassador believed that the Venetians had been alarmingly successful at charming the French king, but interestingly, Guzmán's account disagreed with that of the Venetians. According to Venetian sources, the Doge and Senate were embarrassed because the 'fake' combat resulted in nine deaths. Worse, Henry was actually bored, and supposedly said that if the battle was in play, then it was too much, but if it was real, it was too little.[118] Guzmán, it seems, overestimated how greatly the Venetians had impressed Henry, an intelligence failure of a different kind.

Once again, Guzmán seemed unable to decipher Venetian foreign policy – in this case, the true state of Venetian-French relations. He focused on outward, and disquieting, signs of what seemed to be a growing rapprochement. The Venetian government, for example, added Henry's name to the Book of Gold, the list of Venetian families recognized as nobility (a much-treasured and jealously guarded privilege).[119] Guzmán also noted that Henry met privately with the Doge and Senate several times, but he apparently did not receive any intelligence on what was said. As the historian John Julius Norwich writes, Doge Mocenigo in fact complained to Henry about the, 'further increase in the already overbearing power of Spain', since Lepanto. The Doge further confided his hopes that France would help curb King Philip's ambitions. But Henry remained noncommittal.[120] In the end, none of Guzmán's worst fears were realised: Henry's visit did not result in an alliance between Venice and France against Spain, nor did the French invade northern Italy at the Venetians' behest. Guzmán, however, never knew for sure that this would be the case. About a year after Henry's visit, he reported that the Venetian government had erected a monument to commemorate Henry's visit. While some Venetians expressed doubts about the king of France's goodwill toward the Republic, the ambassador wrote, the monument illustrated the fondness many felt for Henry.[121] Again, Guzmán did not really know the strength of Venice's relationship with the king of France. He had no accurate, inside intelligence on the topic, and so had to guess, based on outward signs. Of course, this kind of guesswork (or 'analysis') was, and still is, integral to the very nature of spycraft, but some have better intelligence networks than others.

Failure is at the heart of this story: failure to persuade, and more importantly failure to comprehend. To be fair, Guzmán does not deserve all of the blame. First of all, he should not be faulted for his inability to compel the Venetians to act against their own best interests. Second, and more critically, he did not have a reliable intelligence network in place when he arrived. When Philip II chose not to replace Francisco de Vargas in 1558, he may have satisfied a question of honour, but it hurt Spanish interests in the long term. When Guzmán finally arrived in 1571, he had to build a new network from scratch; this certainly contributed to his difficulty piercing the veils surrounding Venetian politics.

It is also important to note that Guzmán accomplished a great deal during his time in Venice. As the resident ambassador, he had many tasks in addition to diplomacy and espionage; one of these duties, in which he excelled, was as a purchasing agent. Renaissance Venice was of course a centre of arts, learning, and culture, and as ambassador, Guzmán became a conduit for Venetian goods and services back to Spain.[122] King Philip in particular utilised Guzmán to obtain paintings, books, and religious artefacts, most of which ended up at El Escorial, Philip's great palace/mausoleum. During his time in Venice, Guzmán arranged for dozens of shipments of such commodities back to Madrid. Philip was so pleased with Guzmán's performance, both in this regard and in general, that in 1577 he petitioned Pope Gregory to make Guzmán a Cardinal.[123] Guzmán died before the honour could be granted, but the fact that Philip nominated him is evidence of the king's high opinion of his ambassador. Clearly Philip did not consider Guzmán to be a total failure, or think of his tenure in Venice as a complete disaster.

But Guzmán did have some definite faults as an intelligence officer. For one thing, he lacked subtlety, and was thus overmatched by the more devious Venetians. Even worse, he apparently lacked the ability to see things through Venetian eyes. Guzmán never understood that for the Venetians, the war against the Turks was not a moral cause, as he saw it, but a political and economic necessity. As soon as circumstances changed, the Venetians returned to what for them was the status quo. For Venice, peace with the Turks was the norm. As one recent study explains, 'Venice's rulers clearly understood that their city's economic and political viability was most closely linked to their ability to maintain good relations with the dominant Mediterranean power of the day,' the Ottoman Empire.[124] Guzmán could not accept this fact, and thus was doomed to fail as an intelligence agent. The best sources in the world cannot overcome a basic blindness in the people trying to interpret the information. So for two years, from 1571 to 1573, Guzmán floundered, never certain what the Venetians would do next.

After 1573, he would discover another danger of the spy trade: becoming irrelevant. The Venetians would not fight, so Guzmán's primary diplomatic purpose became moot. But Guzmán was also out of step with his own government. Philip would never again focus his attention on the Turks as much as Guzmán wanted him to. In reality, by the late 1570s both the Habsburg and Ottoman empires were too distracted by internal problems to carry on the struggle in the Mediterranean; between 1577 and 1584 Spain and the Sultan quietly negotiated a series of their own peace treaties.[125] But Guzmán would never know this (he died in 1578). In the end, international politics befuddled Guzmán as much as the Venetians ever did.

Acknowledgements

I would like to thank Mr John G. Ackerman and Ms Stephanie L. Munson at the Cornell University Press, for permission to use previously published material. I would also like to thank Ms Marta Fodor at Art Resource, Inc. for permission to use the images they provided. Finally, thanks to Professor Michael Graham and Professor Geoffrey Parker for their comments and suggestions.

CHAPTER TWO

Oxenstierna's Spies

Sir James Spens and the Organisation of Covert Operations in Early Seventeenth-century Sweden

Steve Murdoch

In recent years there has been an upsurge of interest in the diplomatic networking, clandestine information exchange and downright spying conducted on behalf of Sweden in the first half of the seventeenth century. Current research tends to focus on the activities of a particular individual using extant correspondence to evaluate the value of the information transmitted back to or on behalf of Sweden. Undoubtedly an influential source for surveys of this sort was provided by Leo Tandrup's excellent edition of the letters written to Sweden by the Swedish Sound Toll Commissioner (1621–1626), Anders Svensson.[1] These letters contain a mix of factual business reports and valuable information pertaining to a variety of subjects from troop and ship movements to the latest gossip emanating from one of Sweden's hostile neighbours, Denmark. A different geographical location was considered by Heiko Droste in his overview of the networks employed by the Swedish Resident in Hamburg, Johan Adler. Droste, among others, in his contribution to an edited collection in 1999, reminded us of the importance of correspondence networks and the development of social capital relating to Swedish agents.[2] In 2003 two further articles appeared in the *Scandinavian Journal of History* which dealt with the transmission of political information to Sweden and the agents who conducted this 'Business of News' through the work of double agents.[3] The authors of these articles, Marika Keblusek and Badeloch Noldus, were two of the three person editorial team who, in 2006, produced *Your Humble Servant*, dedicated to the role of 'agents' in Early Modern Europe, which contained work on Swedish agents along with articles by scholars whose interests lay in other locations.[4] The same year a discussion of a Swedish espionage network orchestrated by the Scot, General Sir James Spens of Wormiston, appeared in print, while the complete correspondence of Spens and another Swedish diplomat, Jan Rutgers, with Axel Oxenstierna (the Swedish Chancellor) appeared only months later.[5] This was complimented by a fine edition of the correspondence between Hermannus Samsonius, Sweden's Superintendent of Churches in Livonia, and Axel Oxenstierna, also in 2006.[6]

Among all this literature, and other similar writings, there are a variety of types of information exchange discussed, modes of dissemination considered and political agents unveiled. It is important to make a distinction between the contrasting types of information providers, few of whom could be meaningfully termed spies and many of whom were not the typical double agents conjured up by their description as such. Both Keblusek and Noldus use the term to mean an agent or representative who held two positions (such as a cultural broker who was also employed as a diplomatic representative), thus a 'dual agent' rather than a 'double agent'.[7] To many scholars the latter term carries the connotation of a spy who works for two, usually conflicting, employers. That said, one of those dual agents to whom Noldus referred, Peter Issacsz, certainly earned a third income above that which he received as a Danish Court painter and Dutch Commissioner for the Sound in Denmark. In 1620 he was persuaded by the Swedish commissioner to the Segeberg conference, Jan Rutgers, to become a 'Swedish correspondent' for an annual salary of 400 *rixdaler* (*rdl*) per year.[8] Because his principal employers were the Dutch and Danish governments, he may even properly deserve the epithet of 'treble agent', but it is still debatable whether this made him a spy (as stated) rather than simply an important informant in an old-style correspondence network. Noldus has amply demonstrated that Issacsz often got his information to Sweden covertly using 'art as cover', but lamented that much of his information might be described as hearsay at best.[9] Another correspondent specifically recruited for Oxenstierna, Francis Gordon, was purposely paid money to make him believe he was a trusted informant while his recruiter told Oxenstierna to disregard any information he actually gave to the Chancellor.[10] Spies, in contrast to these informants, had to deliver accurate information because this information was usually gleaned in order to directly influence occurrences rather than simply report upon them. For example, it was allegedly the work of, 'Swedish Lutheran spies among the city's clergy', in Elbing which facilitated the Swedish taking of the city in 1655, apparently against the wishes of the majority of the population.[11]

This essay reviews another of Sweden's spy networks and examines the differences between its *modus operandi* and the transmission of sensitive information as provided by 'news agents' such as Johan Salvius, Peter Issacsz and similarly paid informants. Oxenstierna's spies, unlike the 'news agents', seldom wrote to the Chancellor, either directly or indirectly. Indeed it was, 'by diplomatic convention', non-accredited agents who paid (and communicated with) spies.[12] Thus information on the activities of spies usually emerges through oblique references from other correspondents, such as the tantalising reference from Hermannus Samsonius that a pastor who, 'held certain secrets related to

Poland', lived under his roof and would, in due course, be introduced to Oxenstierna.[13] But what those secrets were, we are not told. The letter containing this snippet is part of the correspondence to and from Oxenstierna held in the vaults of the Swedish National Archives (*Riksarkivet*), a source which amounts to some 500 volumes in two main collections.[14] Much of it has been published or is now available online, and the collection contains extensive information relating to diplomats, agents, dealers, spies and double agents, though it is not catalogued as such.[15] By contrasting the high-profile individuals mentioned above in combination with limited references to lesser known figures, a clearer picture emerges of the place of the true spy among the other information providers Oxenstierna employed.

Diplomats, Information Gatherers and 'News Agents'

There is a fine line between the activities of accredited diplomats and those engaged in covert information gathering who were, 'operating in the twilight zone of legality',[16] compared to individuals who engaged in espionage. One should consider when discussing the dual agents noted above what degree of access they would actually have had to highly sensitive information. Certainly full ambassadors from opposing sides can be shown to have exchanged highly sensitive information on occasion. An early Swedish-Danish example of this arose from the employment of foreigners as diplomats, as exemplified by the Knäred negotiations of 1612–13. Curiously perhaps, both Sweden and Denmark employed Scots in their diplomatic corps as a result of James VI & I of Great Britain's clever policy of sending young gentlemen abroad to become embedded in the courts and societies of overseas powers to learn their languages and customs and later be activated as his own diplomats or agents.[17] Thus in Denmark–Norway, King James employed two Scots as full British ambassadors, both of whom also became fully accredited Danish ambassadors to Britain. These were Andrew Sinclair til Sinklarsholm (who became a member of the Danish State Council or *Rigsraad*) and Sir Robert Anstruther, who became Britain's most senior ambassador in Europe between 1612 and 1638.[18] Across the Scandinavian border in Sweden, the same role of 'dual ambassador' was undertaken by the soldier–diplomat, Sir James Spens of Wormiston.[19] These appointments would have significant consequences for the exchange of restricted information between the Scandinavian (and British) Courts – and ultimately for the Swedish espionage network of Sir James Spens.

In April 1612, while working to secure a peace treaty between warring Sweden and Denmark, the step-brothers Anstruther and Spens were both supplied with diplomatic instructions from the Stuart Court in London.[20] The two men exchanged information that can only be regarded as 'highly sensitive' in the form of royal correspondence between King James and the two respective Scandinavian kings. One letter was so fresh that Anstruther declared to his brother that he had not even had time to copy it in Latin, but wrote it out in Scots, telling his kinsman that the 'ornate et verbatim in Latine' would follow in the next dispatch.[21] The following day, Anstruther wrote again noting receipt of a copy of a letter of Gustav II Adolf to Christian IV, showing that the traffic in royal correspondence was a two-way affair.[22] By accepting James's embedded diplomats, the Scandinavians had unwittingly allowed 'Trojan horses' into the heart of their diplomatic community as both these men demonstrably placed their kin and dynastic allegiance to each other and the House of Stuart above their Scandinavian appointments.[23] For example, in October 1612, Spens signed an oath of loyalty to Gustav II Adolf, albeit insisting on a clause reaffirming that his ultimate allegiance remained with James VI & I.[24] The appointment proved highly advantageous for Sweden, but Poland–Lithuania eventually fell foul of this embedded Stuart agent within the Swedish diplomatic corps (of which more below). Importantly, however, it must not be forgotten that foreign diplomats were expected to try their hand at espionage. Axel Oxenstierna, writing to Duke Karl Gustav (the future Karl X of Sweden), paid little heed to such activity when he noted that an envoy of the Polish Court had arrived in Stockholm in 1652. Ostensibly the reason for the Frenchman Henri de Canazille's mission was to ask Queen Christina to be godparent to the king of Poland's son (who tragically died before the offer could formally be made). However, as Oxenstierna casually noted, 'apart from spying', the real motive for his mission was not known.[25] And if it was expected that diplomats would at least attempt some form of espionage, then the same was true of many other agents, including some of those correspondents already discussed.

In discussing Michel le Blon's role as, 'news agent in general', at the Hague on behalf of Sweden, Keblusek argued that, 'his intelligence work from Amsterdam may not have been perceived by the Dutch authorities as necessarily damaging, since they sided with Sweden politically'.[26] The implication here is that le Blon's activities were known to the Dutch, which – if correct – reflected a remarkably tolerant attitude; few governments wish their secrets to be shared with either friend or foe. Simultaneously, there was actually little the Dutch could do to prevent the distribution of information already in the public domain, or observed by a foreign diplomat or sympathiser, or passed on to them by an embedded spy. A major point made by Droste and Keblusek refers to the importance of establishing and controlling correspondence networks by Swedish agents in order to distribute this information.[27] Droste has detailed the pains that Salvius went to in Hamburg to install his chosen postmaster (his nephew Hendrik Schute) in 1639, even in the face of opposition from Axel Oxenstierna who wished Frans Mathias Schiller in the position.[28] Not trusting the post, or even the elaborate ciphers many letters were written in, led many covert information providers to employ trustworthy individuals to memorise information rather than send a letter. That this happened is frequently recorded, and naturally the information delivered is usually lost to us. Sir Robert Anstruther certainly favoured this method of information transmission noting to his brother that, 'without forder troublen your L[ordship] I taik my live, referring much more unto the bearer than to this peaper [. . .] I trust much in Mr Fenton's memorie'.[29] James Spens in turn employed James Ramsay as a courier between himself and Axel Oxenstierna specifically because he was a kinsman and well versed in Spens' affairs for over 20 years. He told the Chancellor, 'you can trust him as you would me in person', and to explain all matters accurately and faithfully, especially those that Spens would not want to be caught putting on paper.[30] Perhaps this traffic in information was, for the most part, legitimate, but on some occasions it was blatantly obvious that the information exchange involved espionage.

In one Anstruther letter from 1624 we learn that Sir Robert had passed information to James Spens relating to the withdrawal of the Danish envoy, Peter Galt, from Stockholm. Crucially, Anstruther affirmed that this was 'secret information'.[31] Not only that, but this sophisticated diplomat, embedded at Christian IV's Court, actually contracted himself as a correspondent of the Swedish Chancellor after having met him during the Knäred treaty negotiations.[32] James Spens undoubtedly served often as the go-between for his brother and the Swedish Court as hinted at in Anstruther's correspondence.[33] Anstruther thereafter referred to Oxenstierna as an intimate friend, and they met numerous times throughout the duration of Anstruther's political career, though written communication was minimal. Oxenstierna always maintained a front, proclaiming Anstruther's loyalty to Denmark–Norway (calling him a 'good Dane'), though Anstruther's own actions suggest his respect for Christian IV diminished over time, particularly after the Treaty of Lübeck in 1629.[34] More importantly, Anstruther became a significant cog in the Swedish espionage agency, linked to it through his blood ties to Spens. Thus Spens fulfils one of the essential roles identified by Keblusek as fundamental to the orchestrators of an espionage network: to identify individuals in distinguished offices abroad who might supply sensitive information to the Swedish government.[35] However, problems remained in ascertaining how valuable such a person was, how reliable any information provided might be and indeed in determining if the targeted information provider was a double-agent in the spying sense. As will be seen below, this was something that concerned the spymasters themselves, including James Spens. For example, Robert Anstruther's few extant letters to Spens tend to give his brother 'information in advance' rather than truly revelatory intelligence. Spens did put together a network of spies and agents which was demonstrably successful in its operations, but the key target of their work was not actually Anstruther's Denmark, but rather the sprawling Polish–Lithuanian Commonwealth.

In 1598, Sigismund III Vasa was ousted from his Swedish throne and forced into 'exile' in Poland (if that is the correct word for a king in his own kingdom) after his defeat at the battle of Stångebro.[36] From his new base, Sigismund launched the Polish–Swedish War (1600–29) and established a Swedish Catholic 'Émigré Chancellery' in Poland headed up by Gabriel Göransson Posse.[37] One of his missions was the establishment of an espionage network to operate against the Protestant Swedish regime and for this he used a variety of anti-Swedish sympathisers including the Danish agent Frederick Ludvigsson (eventually exposed as a Polish spy and executed after diplomatic pressure from Sweden).[38] Other foreigners included Scots like Sir Andrew Keith who ran a network of some ten, 'well educated and intelligent individuals', in his anti-Swedish operations.[39] One of his spies, James Ross, is said to have begun working as a Keith agent around 1600, a position (if true) he managed to conceal very well.[40] Eventually suspected, Ross was interrogated by the Swedish *Riksråd* on 10 December 1628 and accused of espionage on behalf of Sigismund and Poland.[41] Whether Ross was convicted is not recorded in his trial notes, but his case is instructive with regard to the question of who made a good spy and why. Ross was no high profile diplomat, merchant consul, art dealer or public figure. He was a not particularly important merchant and maintained a low profile; he has left little trace in the public archives. Like many of the best spies he is barely visible historically – an unobtrusive agent who was in it for the long-term, waiting to either be activated by a handler or to stumble onto a big piece of information which would benefit his employer. Though working for the other side, men like Ross, not Salvius, Issacsz, Le Blon or Spens, were the real spies rather than simply information gatherers, news agents or diplomats. But spies need handlers, and in the Swedish case, Spens represents one of the best such operators.

Spies and Spoilers

As noted above, Sir James Spens bound himself from 1612 onwards to work tirelessly against Sweden's enemies, particularly Poland–Lithuania. Whenever Spens travelled to the Stuart Court he usually carried a specific request from

Gustav II Adolf for some form of military or diplomatic assistance against the Poles, even if Sweden and Poland were actually in a state of truce. At the end of 1614, for instance, Spens urged James VI to allow the recruitment of 800 Scots for Samuel Cockburn's (Cobron) regiment.[42] King James allowed this levy, specifically agreed to their use against Muscovites or Poles, and added that he would make sure Christian IV would not interfere with their transit to Sweden.[43] Ironically, as these troops prepared to go to war with Poland–Lithuania, James also found himself intervening in the most discreet terms with Sigismund III on behalf of a Scottish Catholic in Polish service, Captain Thomas Buik, who had a quarrel with both the civic leaders of Riga and Sigismund III himself.[44] The letters, which are written in very polite and friendly terms, tell us, if nothing else, that a series of courteous royal letters does not necessarily indicate a positive relationship – especially when one party has just authorised a military force for use against the recipient of such kind correspondence. More importantly, the letter shows that Buik was in contact with James Spens in Sweden, one of many 'Scottish-Poles' who became important to Spens's anti-Polish network. Another Scot of interest to Spens was Patrick Gordon, the British Merchant Consul to Danzig in particular and Poland–Lithuania in general. On one occasion during the reign of Karl IX of Sweden, Spens had tried to engage Gordon to supply him with information from the Polish Court, though the latter refused. However, when Gordon briefly left his Polish duties in 1615, it was on a mission to London on behalf of Count Krysztof Radziwill, the Calvinist Lithuanian nobleman.[45] Spens pointed out to Oxenstierna that Gordon might be worth targeting again since he was no longer under any binding obligation to Sigismund Vasa.[46] Spens had good grounds to think he might persuade him.

Patrick Gordon had been in Sweden in the 1590s where he served as tutor to Count (and later *Riksråd*) Gustav Eriksson Stenbock and his brother.[47] He had moved to Poland in the retinue of Sigismund, but left his Court and moved to Danzig, and there attempted to realise some unresolved financial claims in Sweden. Gordon certainly wrote directly to Axel Oxenstierna from London only months after Spens mentioned him as a possible agent, reminding the chancellor of his lengthy stay in Sweden, and that he still had some debts which he hoped to recoup.[48] He indicated his intention to visit Sweden to pursue these claims, or to send a factor in his place to do so. Gordon even suggested that future communication could be set up through Johan Forthelius once the Swede moved to Danzig from London, broadly hinting that through that man Oxenstierna might learn much about the state of Britain. This hardly amounts to definitive proof that he was prepared to engage in espionage, as Forthelius was a secretary of the Swedish Chancellery whom

Gordon had met in London and who Oxenstierna was well aware of anyway.[49] Furthermore, Gordon concluded his letter by emphatically stating that he had nothing to offer at that particular juncture.[50] However, there is a particularly interesting letter from Gordon in August 1617 to his, 'loving friend and brother', Archibald Rankin.[51] Rankin was both a Gentleman of the Bedchamber to Charles, Prince of Wales (the future Charles I), and the prince's representative in Sweden. He was also a close confederate of James Spens.[52] The contents of the Gordon-Rankin letter prove that Patrick Gordon was both passing on diplomatic information to Rankin about the French (for Swedish consumption) and seeking safe conduct from Axel Oxenstierna to travel to Sweden.[53] This he was granted by 1618, confirming a positive reception for his earlier letter to Oxenstierna in 1615. On this journey, Gordon revealed, he was to travel to Sweden in the company of a Swedish gentleman, though he does not name him. It is clear from another letter sent from Spens to Oxenstierna that, thereafter, Gordon did not mind sharing at least some information with Spens. Sir James reported that Gordon had shown him a copy of a letter detailing the schedule for the next meeting of the Polish *Sjem* and Polish fears relating to their nervousness about a Turkish/Tartar attack instigated, according to the Poles, on advice from Russia.[54] He also disclosed the imminent arrival of Johannes Weijer (John Weir) en route from Poland, allowing Spens time to investigate the circumstances surrounding his mission.[55] Weijer was described by Gordon as an envoy of 'Count Putskenski' (Maximillian Przerebski, Polish envoy in Vienna) but other sources describe him as an agent of Spain. This does not in itself mean that Gordon had been engaged as a correspondent by Spens, but he was clearly unconcerned about sharing information potentially useful to the Swedes through Spens or via Gordon's 'friend and brother' Rankin.

Spens also gleaned information about Polish plans to attack Sweden through the Scottish ambassador in the service of Denmark–Norway, Sir Andrew Sinclair. In 1617, Sinclair tipped Spens off that Christian IV had been asked to allow a Spanish fleet of Dunkirk vessels carrying 6,000 soldiers to sail through the Sound to bolster the forces of Sigismund III.[56] Archibald Rankin in London also knew what Polish plans were afoot and he kept Axel Oxenstierna informed through his various contacts with Dr James Robertson, Sir James Spens and other Swedish-based Scots, or Swedes with Scottish family like Johan Skytte (who was married to the Scot Maria Neave).[57] Rankin made it his business to keep a close eye on Swedes in the retinue of the Polish envoy in London, 'Herr Tinnagell', while Jan Rutgers in Copenhagen reported on Johannes Weijer's activities and his (unverified) claims to Christian IV that Sigismund was about to dethrone Gustav II Adolf.[58] In May 1618, Rankin divulged that he had gleaned information from an English skipper who claimed he had been approached to transport Sigismund III. The inference is that his destination was to be London, but that Polish-Vasa business was now to be pursued by 'the fool Tinnagell'.[59] It is in this letter of May 1618 that Rankin warns of a new Order of Chivalry called *Cavalieri de Jhesu* who intended to subdue Sweden with the 'Sword of Paul'. Rankin continued that, 'those old dogs, the Jesuits, have come up with these young dogs, for they cannot achieve anything with the Keys of Peter'.[60] Such information warned the Swedes in advance of an apparent plan to infiltrate (and invade) Sweden with the ultimate goal of enforcing a Counter-Reformation under the exiled Sigismund's direction.

Rankin continued his mission as an informant from his secure position in the royal household of the Prince of Wales. From there he maintained verbal and written correspondence with Sweden, particularly in relation to Polish activities.[61] Furthermore, King James had written directly to Gustav II Adolf urging him to form an alliance with his cousin Sigismund against the non-Christian Turkish threat. Thus the November 1620 request for troops from Jerzy Ossolinki seemed to James to make a great deal of sense.[62] Yet despite Stuart diplomatic efforts, Swedish–Polish hostilities had already commenced in July 1621 when Gustav II Adolf landed an army of 17,850 men at Pernau.[63] James sent his kinsman, Sir Robert Stewart, to Poland to discuss the situation but Sir Robert chose to use his visit to promote himself with Sigismund III.[64] Sir Robert contracted himself on 20 April 1623 to raise 10,000 men for Sigismund's service in what was alleged to be a force designed to attack Sweden. He was to command these soldiers in an invasion of Älvsborg (Gothenburg) while Sigismund and the Spanish under Johan Weijer would attack Sweden's eastern coast at Kalmar, from Danzig. Simultaneously, disaffected fifth-columnist Swedish nobles and Catholics would rise within Sweden itself.[65] News of Stewart's activity quickly filtered back to Sweden from agents in Poland, Britain and Denmark, particularly through the dispatches of the Swedish Toll Commissioner, Anders Svensson.[66]

By June 1623, it was believed that Stewart had been granted permission to recruit an army in Britain and Ireland, although he had still not managed to gain an audience with Christian IV to obtain their free passage through the Sound.[67] Axel Oxenstierna immediately instructed the Swedish representative negotiating a truce with the Poles to ensure that a condition of that truce would be that any troops raised by Stewart could not be used against Sweden.[68] To guarantee that would be the case, Gustav II Adolf drew up a set up instructions for Sir James Spens which were explicit in their content. He was to proceed with haste to the Court of Great Britain and do his utmost to prevent

Robert Stewart and his accomplices from raising soldiers for the king of Poland's service. He was also to add, however, that, should King James allow both sides to recruit, then the Swedish king would be satisfied of James's neutrality in the conflict.[69] The same instructions also urged that James Spens junior be allowed to raise a regiment of Scots to be transported to Gothenburg the following spring.[70] By October 1623, however, an Irishman known simply as 'Michael', en-route to the Polish king, brought news to Svensson that King James had said that Stewart could hire as many men and ships as he needed to transport them, and that they were already preparing a rendezvous in the north of Scotland.[71] While Anders Svensson pondered the best ways of dealing with Stewart's proposed invasion of Älvsborg, the situation continued to deteriorate from a Swedish perspective. Two Scottish sea captains, formerly in Christian of Brunswick's service, had visited Sigismund III and offered to join his service. He in turn sent them on to join Robert Stewart to give him a fledgling fleet with which to conduct his invasion force to Sweden.[72] Gustav II Adolf protested to the Scottish Privy Council and King James about such support for the Poles, both help which was raised privately and any that might stem from the British governments in Edinburgh and London.[73] The Swedish king also ordered Spens to undertake direct negotiations with King James to reverse any such support for Sigismund that might already have been granted.[74] It was during this period that the Danish agent, Frederick Ludvigsson, was exposed as a Polish spy, leading to an embassy being dispatched from Stockholm to Copenhagen to prosecute him. He was eventually tried, convicted and executed for espionage in a remarkable and unusual show of Danish–Swedish solidarity (Ludvigsson being an expendable pawn at a time when Denmark hoped for Swedish help against the Holy Roman Empire). But in a desperate bid to save himself he tried to accuse the stalwart Swedish agent Anders Svensson of passing sensitive information to him – something Ambassador Gabriel Oxenstierna strongly denounced as a lie to his brother Axel.[75]

Beyond the high-level diplomatic manoeuvrings, Spens undertook contingency plans, which included orchestrating covert operations against the Polish representatives in London aided by the long-term Swedish agent, Archibald Rankin. Through his network of associates in London, Spens managed to intercept a copy of a letter from James VI & I to Sigismund III, revealing the current thinking of the Stuart king to Axel Oxenstierna, though whether with James's approval is not revealed.[76] Rankin had also sent copies of the speeches of English parliamentarians and King James on the subject on to Sweden.[77] In one of two letters he sent on 10 March 1624, Spens made several notable requests. One of these was that in the event his step-brother, Sir Robert Anstruther, was sent to Sweden as an ambassador, Oxenstierna would only show Anstruther transcripts of letters sent to Oxenstierna by Spens. This was in case Spens' handwriting gave away his authorship of sensitive information, hinting that Spens did not yet fully trust Anstruther not to blow the whistle on his step-brother's espionage activities.[78] As a further subterfuge, Oxenstierna was to postmark the copies of sensitive letters as if they had been sent from Holland (and thus make them attributable to the Swedish resident there, Jan Rutgers). Spens claimed that he had seen to it that the English Secretary of State, Sir Edward Conway, composed a letter to Stewart in such terms that it contained no hint of an obligation from James to Sigismund for military support.[79] Naturally Robert Stewart was none too happy about this development, but continued with his plans anyway.

More interesting from the espionage perspective are the methods by which the information had been collected. Spens had been given his copy of the royal correspondence by the Aberdonian, Thomas Reid, poet and Latin Secretary to James VI & I.[80] Reid had obtained a copy of the letter from Robert Middleton, another Scot, who was a former secretary to the Vice-Chancellor of Poland and Robert Stewart's trusted secretary in London. This was at least the second time Reid had passed on sensitive correspondence to Spens, having previously done so in 1622.[81] Whether Middleton was complicit or Reid was simply an effective agent is not made clear in the Spens correspondence. However, Reid probably gained the trust of the 'Polish–Scots', being an experienced Baltic and Northern European traveller himself, and sometime lecturer in Rostock and Leipzig between 1608–13. Unaware of Reid's activity and Middleton's possible (though unproven) duplicity, Stewart was also unaware that another Swedish agent had also infiltrated his circle. The Scotsman, John Fairbairne, had been sent to London from Danzig by the Swedish government with instructions to infiltrate Robert Stewart's pro-Polish circle.[82] With Spens acting as his handler in Britain, Fairbairne quickly gained Stewart's confidence and learned the most intimate details of his plans. This was despite the fact that Stewart knew Fairbairne had previously worked for the Swedes. In fact, this seems to have been seen as a benefit, as Stewart believed that Fairbairne's knowledge of the country could be advantageous to the Poles, presumably in the same way he intended to deploy his own knowledge of the country. Unsuspecting of his countryman's motives, Stewart offered Fairbairne the position of Quartermaster General of his army, set to consist of 8,000 men recruited in Britain, backed by a fleet of 20 ships. From his vantage point as a senior staff officer in the proposed Stewart expedition, Fairbairne was able to send the most detailed information back to Sweden. Gustav II Adolf learned from him that, after the invasion of Älvsborg, Stewart intended to quadruple the size of his army and, with the help of disaffected members of the Swedish nobility and some (undisclosed) Papal backing, seize the whole of Sweden and place it under Sigismund III's control within three months.[83] This new initiative would undoubtedly have included both financial assistance from the Papacy and the involvement of the *Cavalieri de Jhesu* Rankin had warned about just a few years previously.[84]

In order to cover his tracks, Fairbairne established several routes by which his information could reach Sweden. On 10 October 1623, he had entered a contract with Jerome Hostier of Amsterdam to receive his post for a period of six months. He also requested that Anders Svensson in Denmark guarantee that his future correspondence would be routed through Lehonard von Sorgen, a Swedish correspondent in Hamburg mentioned a number of times by Jan Rutgers.[85] Unfortunately for Fairbairne, within a few months he was exposed as a spy when he was caught in the act of sending letters directly to the Swedish envoy to Danzig, Christoff Ludvig Rasche.[86] This blow led to financial troubles for him in London, which in turn caused Spens to request money from Gustav II Adolf to bail him out. As Spens noted, he had, in any case, completed his agreed period of service to the Swedish crown.[87] During that time, Fairbairne had been responsible for luring three important Scottish nobles and one Englishman away from Robert Stewart and into Swedish service, thus negatively influencing the outcome of the Polish recruiting drive.[88] One of these Scots was Andrew Schaw (Shaw) who went on to act as a trusted courier and agent between Axel Oxenstierna and James Spens, his loyalty guaranteed, Spens noted, by his Protestantism.[89] Another was Andrew Stewart, former diplomat of Karl IX, who refused the Polish commission in favour of returning to the Swedish fold.

During the meetings between King James and Spens in London, Sir James had been able to persuade the British king to withdraw his unconditional consent for the Polish levy, insisting that the troops should not be used against a Christian enemy i.e. Sweden. The ambassador duly informed Gustav II Adolf that he doubted Sweden had anything to fear from Poland and highlighted how his intercessions with James VI & I had overturned Stewart's plans.[90] By July 1624, Spens was able to assure Gustav II Adolf that there was no reason for the Swedish king to be concerned about Sir Robert Stewart's levy. King James had built in such conditions that any troops he raised would be forbidden from landing in any of Sweden's territories or from fighting his forces elsewhere, just as Oxenstierna had previously wanted.[91] Fairbairne confirmed that the troops raised in Britain were now only for use by Sigismund against the Turks and Tartars.[92] King James even wrote to Spens to say that he doubted that the Stewart levy would ever materialise due to all the restrictions and logistical problems placed in the way.[93] With both the diplomatic and clandestine campaigns of Sir James Spens having taken their toll, Robert Stewart's efforts to raise his troops fizzled out, although mention of the levy continued intermittently throughout late 1624, with Sir Robert Anstruther being noted as a source of information on its progress.[94] As Svensson noted, Robert Stewart had proved not to be the man Sigismund III had hoped – he was unable to raise either money or men.[95] Spens's spoiling mission had been a complete success. Not only did Stewart not get his army from Britain, but Spens had received permission for his son and namesake to raise a regiment for Swedish service. The Danish historian, Leo Tandrup, has attributed Stewart's ruin directly to the diplomatic intervention of James Spens with James VI & I.[96] However, the network of informants and spies built up by James Spens undoubtedly deserve as much credit as his astute diplomacy.

It did not take long for Spens and his Scottish party of pro-Swedish partisans to get back into action against Poland – or at least, the Scottish pro-Polish network operating there. He did so from London, where he was reported to be held in great esteem by the new king of Great Britain, Charles I.[97] In 1625, Patrick Gordon indulged in a bit of nepotism and ensured that his nephew Francis Gordon, a former secretary to Sir Robert Anstruther, took over as the Stuart Consul and Factor in Poland with an annual salary of £200 sterling.[98] In this Francis Gordon had the support of Christian IV of Denmark–Norway who also paid him 400 *rdl.* to act as Danish factor in the same location.[99] James Spens believed that, working under the cloak of being a public representative of both monarchs, Francis Gordon had actually been retained to conduct secret negotiations between Charles I and Sigismund III.[100] Having newly wrecked Robert Stewart's Polish levy, Spens now set about impeding the appointment of Francis Gordon as official Stuart agent to Poland. He confirmed to Oxenstierna that he had recruited, 'a prudent and learned gentleman' at the Polish Court who would supply Spens with information relating to Gordon's mission, especially if there was any link to an anti-Swedish Jesuit conspiracy.[101] Given the amount of Scottish–Jesuit activity in Poland previously reported by Patrick Gordon himself – let alone indigenous and other foreign Jesuit missions there – these fears were not without foundation.[102] Little wonder then that Gustav II Adolf seized the Jesuit seminary at Braunsberg in 1626. According to Oskar Garstein: 'The ecclesiastical authorities with the help of the temporal arm in the Scandinavian North regarded Braunsberg as a source of many of their troubles, and they set out to liquidate it at the earliest opportunity once its significance had become firmly established.'[103] To further alleviate Swedish fears, Spens received orders from Sweden that he should try to have Gordon's mission cancelled to prevent any secret negotiations from taking place.[104] For the same wages as Gordon would be paid by the Danes (400 *rdl.*), Spens' man in Poland would be paid by the Swedes to ruin his mission.[105] The man selected for this was none other than another Scotsman, Hugh Mowatt, a former British envoy to the Polish Court of Sigismund III in 1624.[106] This appointment saw Mowatt contract himself to the Swedish government (for the usual correspondent's fee) to serve as their agent in Poland–Lithuania with the explicit brief of destroying Gordon's mission and reputation.[107] New ciphers were drawn up for Spens, Oxenstierna and Mowatt, who prepared his departure for Poland–Lithuania at the end of July 1626 with payment being made secretly through the 'merchant' in Hamburg, Anders Svensson – the veteran Swedish agent previously located in Denmark.[108]

While Mowatt prepared the groundwork for his new Polish assignment, Spens began his assault on Gordon from his base in London. Without even a full knowledge of Gordon's brief, Spens believed that he might be trying to negotiate a new levy of troops to be raised in Britain and sent to Poland. At an audience with Charles I, he pointed out the danger of such a move and urged any such aid to Poland to be blocked. As a bargaining chip, Spens tantalised Charles I with the prospect of Swedish intervention in Germany on behalf of the king's brother-in-law and sister, Frederick V of the Palatinate and Elizabeth of Bohemia.[109] As a final encouragement, Gustav II Adolf made it clear to Spens that during Swedish military operations in Poland and Prussia there would be no loss of trade to any 'friends of Sweden'.[110] Of course the threat behind that thin veil was that any support for Sigismund III by the House of Stuart would be detrimental to British trade and result in punitive action against British merchants by the Swedes in the Baltic. These actions were actually unnecessary in the short term, however, since Spens had already effectively won the argument in London. He had successfully persuaded Charles I that Francis Gordon could not be trusted and informed Oxenstierna that the Mowatt mission being prepared against Gordon had received the approval of the British king.[111] Clearly Charles I had started to doubt his own diplomatic appointment to Poland–Lithuania.

As Francis Gordon set out for Poland, he was instructed by Charles I to stop first at The Hague and then visit the Vasa court in Sweden. The hapless envoy carried with him a letter of introduction to Gustav II Adolf prepared by Spens as part of a devious plan to entrap him – only one of several snares which had been set to catch him. Ludwig Camerarius, the Swedish commissioner in The Hague had been briefed about the Gordon mission and received instructions (probably from Spens) to try to engage Gordon as a Swedish 'correspondent'.[112] The next phase of the plan hinged on Gordon travelling to the Swedish Court where Spens had already encouraged Gustav II Adolf to overtly treat Gordon with 'great kindness and admiration' thus stalling his arrival in Poland and allowing Mowatt more time to proceed with his character assassination in Danzig, Warsaw and Cracow. By winning Gordon over with hospitality, Gustav II Adolf could then test what Spens described as his 'dubious and mercenary' nature by promising him a reward in return for some favour, such as serving as an embedded Swedish correspondent in Poland–Lithuania. This, Spens believed, would be the moment at which Gordon would reveal his lack of integrity by signing himself up as a Swedish agent. Indeed, Spens added that if he contracted himself, the Swedes should not trust any information they got from him as it was bound to be dubious, adding that he would leave the reception of any information supplied by Gordon entirely up to the king's discretion.[113]

The entrapment plan was really quite brilliant, if something of a 'Catch 22' for Gordon. Francis Gordon arrived in Sweden having been told to go there by the monarch he served and presumably trusted. Even if Gordon declined the Swedish offer, Hugh Mowatt could still point out to Sigismund III that Gustav II Adolf had entertained Gordon beyond the normal degree required for a merchant consul and thus raise doubts about his character and intention in his mind. To add grist to the mill, Francis Gordon did become a correspondent of the Swedish government. Between 1627 and 1636 Gordon wrote a number of dispatches to Axel Oxenstierna thus seeming to damn him as the double agent Spens believed him to be.[114] What must be considered, though, is that Gordon's correspondence with Charles I and Sigismund III Vasa has not yet come to light. We simply do not know how he viewed his Swedish mission or how he described it to the two monarchs he was officially supposed to be representing. It is very possible he understood his situation well and passed only non-sensitive and erroneous information to the Swedes. Oxenstierna doubted some of the information he received from Gordon, adding in one letter to Herman Wrangel that, whatever the truth of the information he had received, the Swedes should take precautions anyway.[115] However, the majority of surviving letters from Gordon to Oxenstierna refer to Gordon's official role in the Swedish–Polish negotiations of 1629 working with Sir Thomas Roe, in which capacity he had orders from London (and Warsaw) to communicate with the Swedish Chancellor.[116] Sometimes, however, the dispatches contain just a little more than one would expect from someone in Gordon's position. He was a Stuart representative and may have been required to pass information to the Swedes by Charles I. That does not explain the fact that he recommended officers from Polish service like his cousin [Lieutenant] Alexander Falconer, or countryman [Lieutenant] James Keith, both of whom did go into Swedish service thereafter.[117] Not only that, but he also sent sensitive information relating to Roe, Sigismund III and Christian IV to Oxenstierna and tellingly added that once Oxenstierna was through with the dispatches he needed them back![118] Only Gordon knew if he crossed the line of his Stuart brief and became a fully fledged double agent. Rightly or wrongly, Francis Gordon's loyalty was always subject to doubt thereafter and he never rose above the level of merchant consul. Although tasked with several light diplomatic duties by Roe, Gordon eventually suffered the indignity of having to return to London in 1637 to face charges of treason.[119] Clearly some of the mud thrown by the Spens network had stuck. Although Gordon was cleared, it was only at the expense of yet another blow to his reputation, and long after he could have been effective in preventing Spens and his cohorts carrying out their sabotaging missions against the Poles.

With the prospect of Charles I providing military support for the Poles now over, Spens set about his task of getting positive support from the British kingdoms for Sweden. As war with Danzig loomed, Spens offered the usual Swedish inducements to Charles I. Unhindered trade with Elbing, and free British trade as far as Poland by way of the river Nogat (which the Swedes claimed they could make navigable to the Vistula), were proffered.[120] Charles I liked the plan and, through Spens, congratulated Gustav II Adolf on his military successes. He informed Spens that he would not only allow recruiting by two Scottish colonels in Swedish service, but also the British merchants at Elbing would lend 15,000 *rdl.* to support the project.[121] To make matters worse for the Poles, Charles I ordered Spens back to Sweden where he was also to serve as ambassador and negotiate a peace between Sweden, Danzig, Brandenburg and Poland–Lithuania, undoubtedly the most hostile appointment to Sigismund III Vasa that Charles could make.[122] Of course the main aim of this mission was to ensure continued free trade for British merchants in the Baltic. His counterpart on the Polish side was none other than the ever-unfortunate Francis Gordon, now dealing face to face with a man who had effectively destroyed his reputation.[123] Furthermore, Archibald Rankin again proved active in his subtle collection of data, sending in reports to James Spens, Johan Skytte and Axel Oxenstierna throughout this period.[124]

During this embassy, Spens once more became involved in covert work for the Swedes. In August 1627, Colonel Patrick Ruthven, a fellow Scot in Swedish service, approached him with an offer from the Swedish king. Ruthven intimated that Gustav II Adolf wished Spens to secretly abandon his role as British ambassador in order that he might orchestrate the covert recruitment of Scottish troops for Sweden. Spens replied to this request by saying that he would be delighted to do so.[125] Given the ongoing war with Poland–Lithuania, it must have been clear where the Swedes wanted these troops to go. In order to avoid the suspicion of any members of the British community, Spens requested that Axel Oxenstierna should delay the departure of British ships from Elbing so that his men missed the last boat before the following spring. In that way Spens could have time to organise his agents for their return trip to Britain and make it seem that they were simply travelling home on the first ships they found in harbour.[126] After Spens' agents were on board, the British ships were free to leave. It is not known for certain who these representatives were, but it can be readily guessed. In November 1627, Lieutenant James Kinnaird and the regimental secretary John Sommerville received a pass from Axel Oxenstierna to travel to Scotland and recruit troops for a Captain James Bannatyne.[127] It is easy to surmise that these were Spens's agents since Bannatyne's company formed part of James Ramsay's Scottish regiment based around Elbing, and Ramsay himself was Sir James Spens' son-in-law.[128] The use of trusted officers drawn from a regiment commanded by a kinsman seems to follow the patterns of kith and kin network building favoured by Spens.

The Swedish campaign against Danzig and Poland–Lithuania continued into 1628. Despite pleas from an unnamed Scotsman in Danzig, probably Francis Gordon, for Gustav II Adolf to come to a peaceful arrangement with the city, Spens had clearly adopted a hard line pro-Swedish approach. He had not been fulfilling his instructions to settle a peace with either Poland–Lithuania or Danzig and, indeed, he gloated over Polish defeats to Sir John Coke in London.[129] Spens' career as the Stuart arbitrator in the Swedish–Polish dispute effectively came to an end in 1628 after Gustav II Adolf finally destroyed any illusion of impartiality when he created him Baron Spens of Orreholm while serving at the Swedish Court in Elbing. Spens remained the permanent ambassador between the Swedish Vasa and Stuart monarchs for the duration of his life but, despite his arrival in London, replacements were found to negotiate the peace. The Danzigers chose as their envoy to Charles I the unsuspecting Francis Gordon, whom they instructed to win over Charles, the main mediator in the dispute, not realising that their legate's reputation in London had been seriously compromised.[130] Sir Thomas Roe eventually negotiated the peace after some crucial help from Sir James Ramsay, who had to repair the damage Roe had done by ignoring his brief and visiting Sigismund before Gustav II Adolf.[131] Thereafter Francis Gordon must be credited with continuing Roe's work after the ambassador left Danzig, particularly in trying to settle disputes concerning British merchants.[132] These endeavours ended in failure, again due to the fact that Gordon's position had been compromised by his countrymen in the city who were working for, or sympathetic to, the Swedes. Archibald Rankin, Oxenstierna's agent, arrived in the city in 1629 and continued to keep the Swedes informed of the various projects of the Danzig magistrates for the next year.[133] As a distant relative of Francis Gordon he would have aroused little suspicion with him, and may not have done anything to harm him directly. Yet Rankin certainly kept up his correspondence with the Swedish Chancellor, and also verbally via the Scottish officers Patrick Ruthven and John Hepburn (Hebron) who additionally arranged Rankin's 'New Years Gift' of 200 *rdl.* from Sweden.[134] Rankin could report that the Poles and Danzigers had had enough of the conflict with Sweden and were enjoying the armistice which they hoped would lead to 'eternal peace'.

The James Spens espionage network had played a significant, albeit largely unrecognised, role in thwarting Sigismund III Vasa's ambition to reclaim the Swedish throne. Sir James Spens returned to the Swedish Court in Germany where he remained for the last two years of his life, dying just before the king he had served so long and faithfully. The other correspondents, agents and spies carried on about their business, reaping the benefits of their loyalty to Sweden, gaining promotion, respect and pensions. Francis Gordon remained in Danzig until the 1640s and he probably never knew that failure of his career had been contrived and conducted by four fellow Scotsmen: James Spens, Archibald Rankin, Hugh Mowatt and Charles I.

Conclusion

Sir James Spens fulfilled many roles for Sweden: diplomat, general and correspondent – but he was not himself a spy. His dual loyalty to Britain and Sweden was too well known by all sides for that to be possible. That said, he was both a skilled intelligencer and a very successful spymaster; his network included a spectrum of individuals from well-known ambassadors to unnamed informers, although their motive for participation in his network is not always clear. But whatever their reasons, the Spens espionage network exemplifies the differences that could exist between 'news agents' as information providers (Isaacsz, le Blon) and spies, as people who subtly influenced – or tried to influence – events by their actions (Fairbairne, Reid). For a man who worked for the Swedes, Spens could count on a startling degree of support in London for his activities. At the highest level he was able to ensure that both King James and Charles I were participants in his operations – a reward for his loyal service to the House of Stuart. Whether or not they knew that Sweden had embedded agents (like Archibald Rankin) in the royal household is not clear.

Top-level governmental support for James Spens in Sweden was obviously helped by the favourable inclination of Gustav II Adolf and Axel Oxenstierna towards the Scot. After all, his network was working directly for their interest.

Therefore the fact that Anders Svensson in Elsinore and Hamburg, Ludwig Camerarius in The Hague, Jerome Hoister in Amsterdam, Lehonard von Sogren in Hamburg or Christoff Ludovig Rasche and Johan Forthelius in Danzig provided logistical backing for the Spens network is unsurprising. Furthermore, Spens could also rely on family connections to gain information pertaining to the Danish Court from his step-brother, Sir Robert Anstruther. The two men demonstrably exchanged information before it was due to be released, but the extent of Anstruther's involvement in the Spens network as a 'spy' awaits further study. There are few direct letters from Sir Robert to Sweden beyond those he would be expected to send as a British ambassador and the weight of information communicated verbally is unknown. Thus the extent of his involvement as a Swedish spy, correspondent or sympathiser remains uncertain. Much more searching questions relate to some of the Scots who were resident in, or maintained strong connections to the Polish–Lithuanian Commonwealth.

From the evidence, it is clear that Patrick Gordon trod a narrow line in his loyalties, not prepared to be bought by the Swedes, but ready to deliver specific information on his own terms to certain individuals he knew were senior Swedish agents. Whether he acted through familial loyalty or auld acquaintance with Archibald Rankin, friendship with James Spens or simply to improve his own situation regarding his ongoing claims in Sweden, only Patrick Gordon ever knew.[135] As a respected member of the Polish–Scottish diaspora, Secretary Robert Middleton may simply have been a careless man, or may have allowed Thomas Reid access to royal correspondence through friendship, not suspecting that Reid would then turn the information over to Spens. No conclusions can be drawn from their involvement other than that Middleton provided important information indirectly, whilst Reid certainly knew full well Spens' relationship with Sweden. Like Gordon, Reid's motive remains his own but his actions place him firmly in the category of spy: a man unsuspected by his actual employer, yet demonstrably working covertly for the other side. Importantly, Thomas Reid was no correspondent of anyone in the Swedish government and to all intents and purposes, had no connections with Stockholm whatsoever. For others in the ring there is equally little ambiguity about their activities.

Right from the start, Archibald Rankin appeared unwavering in his role as a Swedish agent. His motives can be partly attributed to financial reward for sure, as he often mentions his payment as a correspondent in letters to Oxenstierna. Yet he never seems to have offered his services to the other side, which he was certainly in a position to do after moving to Danzig as part of a British diplomatic mission there. Numerous sources point to a very positive relationship with Sir James Spens over a number of years. The two other main agents employed by Spens were John Fairbairne and Hugh Mowatt, both of whom lived for many years in Danzig. It has been suggested that Mowatt resented the fact that Francis Gordon gained the position as British representative in 1625 rather than he.[136] Revenge is therefore a possible motive for his enthusiastic participation in the mission against Gordon. That may, or may not, have been a factor, as must simple financial inducement. It must also be considered that Mowatt was a long-time servant of the House of Stuart and so his actions might reflect straightforward dynastic loyalty to his sovereign. Quite what drove John Fairbairne can only be surmised. However, the very fact that he got caught in the process of passing information to Rasche suggests that he had an enduring understanding with that man in Danzig before he left the city for London. He also must have had an established relationship with James Spens. Why else would he have been selected as an infiltrator unless he had already been identified as a trustworthy participant in the espionage network? Fairbairne was clearly prepared to take great risks on behalf of the Spens network and Spens in turn fought to ensure he was rewarded once his cover as a spy was blown.

The failed pro-Polish network of Robert Stewart gives rise to some searching questions regarding his endeavours. Why would two successive Scottish monarchs who believed in the 'Divine Right of Kings' take the side of a 'usurper' such as Gustav II Adolf over that of the legitimate king Sigismund III of Poland–Lithuania (and Sweden)? The answer must surely lie in the growing confessional conflicts sweeping through Europe at the time. King James, while still playing the diplomatic card, was acutely aware of where the strength of European Protestantism might come to lie, and it was certainly not in Poland–Lithuania. Sigismund's southern flank had to be defended against the Islamic threat, but the Protestant cause in Western Europe needed strong military assistance from Denmark–Norway and Sweden. Stewart's familial link with King James was not as close as that of James (brother-in-law) or Charles I (nephew) to Christian IV. Nor did James wish to see Sweden collapse militarily or return to the Catholic fold under Sigismund III, particularly as Sweden was clearly the main Protestant power capable of standing up to the Habsburgs in northern Europe. Thus the events discussed above relate to a far wider European agenda – the war for confessional supremacy in Europe. With her demonstrable Jesuit intrigue and the ever present threat of Sigismund's support for the Habsburgs in Germany, Poland–Lithuania could easily be seen as a potential enemy of the House of Stuart. As such, first James VI & I's and later Charles I's co-operation with the anti-Polish Spens network is less than surprising. British Royal support for James Spens left both Robert Stewart and the many other 'Polish-Scots' in an awkward situation. Those prepared to get on with their mercantile business got full backing, while those who wished to alter the political balance in the Baltic were cut adrift and left to the onslaught of the covert networks of Spens and other Swedish agents. The ferocity with which the pro-Swedish agents pursued Robert Stewart and Francis Gordon therefore becomes easier to understand.

As demonstrated above, the espionage network of Sir James Spens was built upon a variety of elements, including kinship, friendships, trust and dynastic loyalty. It may also have been bolstered by financial incentives and extortion, though we may never know the full spectrum of motives that moved members of the network. What we can say for sure is that Spens' success as a spymaster places him in the top rank of such men in Swedish service during the seventeenth century. By drawing together the tantalising remnants of information pertaining to his agents we can see their importance in the business of information exchange in early modern Sweden. In so doing we can broaden out the excellent work already done to date on Swedish correspondents and news agents and at last get a glimpse of some of the men we can truly call 'Oxenstierna's spies'.

CHAPTER THREE

'Woeful Knight'

Sir Robert Walsh and the Fragmented World of the Double Agent

Alan Marshall

The game is so large that one sees but a little at a time

Rudyard Kipling, *Kim*

In many senses telling Sir Robert Walsh's history as a spy chronologically doesn't do justice to its nature. His can be seen as a life in fragments – we possess incidents in a series of manuscripts and self-publicising texts that emerge generally not as a whole, but as broken images. What these images do provide, however, are some insights into those other fragmentary and hidden areas of early modern life: intelligence and espionage. This essay seeks to explore Sir Robert Walsh at a particular period: when he was caught up in the coils of early modern espionage and in particular his actions in the 1650s when he tried, unsuccessfully, to engineer a career as a double agent in the Royalist exile community and within the Cromwellian intelligence system run by John Thurloe. By examining these events it is hoped that the reader will perceive in Walsh's example some of the pertinent characteristics of how that area of early modern government actually worked under John Thurloe and what sort of men it attracted, even as they thought to betray it as double agents.

Unusually enough, Robert Walsh's views of his own affairs are also available. He vigorously expressed these through both his private and public faces. In this process we can see Walsh continually negotiating between the two worlds, as he tried, in vain, to rescue his own fragmented narrative, his honour, his meaning of himself and his career. This fortunately allows us an insight into this particular spy's personality. There is no doubt that Walsh was a mercenary man and all too obviously trying to make his way in the real world and, if there is little romanticism in his account of his espionage activities in the 1650s, which ultimately proved rather more abortive than even he, or his various masters, would have wished, then that is because, *pace* James Bond, there is in fact little romanticism in this world at all.

Indeed, by most criteria Walsh's life was a failure. In the 1650s we find him as an exiled Royalist soldier of fortune, with a reputation for double-dealing, knavery and violence. As with many another Royalist, exile had brought Walsh nothing but trouble, poverty, bitterness and misfortune. If he found himself in trouble in France in the mid-1650s, he also found himself a prisoner in the Bastille. How had he reached this pass?

Background

Robert Walsh was born in Ireland, the son of Sir James Walsh, of Little Island and Ballygoner in Waterford, and Mary Sherlock. Robert Walsh was of 'Old English' descent, dating his family's rise from Edward I's reign.[1] By 1639 Robert Walsh was serving as a soldier in the Bishop's Wars under Thomas Howard, earl of Arundel, and may also have been one of the Irish troops brought over to the north of England for that purpose, where he served in a 'Troop of Guards' and at, 'his own cost furnish[ed] into the said Troop six horses and horsemen, and himself Volunteer'.[2] By 1642 Walsh was imprisoned for debt, a regular theme in his life, in the King's Bench Prison. He soon sought immunity as a 'sworn servant' of Henrietta Maria.[3] Walsh was to state that in the build-up to the civil war he was asked to serve in Parliament's forces, but instead chose to offer his sword to the king; he swiftly left London and rode to York. He was then placed in the horse regiment of Lord Henry Wilmot and, as captain, commanded Wilmot's own troop: '100 Valiant Brave men, most Gentlemen of Estate & Quality'. They included men such as Sir John Dongan, Sir Brien O'Neale and Sir Henry Talbot, and 'most of them [were] Irish'.[4]

In the first clash of arms at Edgehill in 1642 Walsh led the troop in battle. Edgehill was an event that Walsh frequently returned to in his writings, where it has a totemic quality as an expression of loyalty from a man who was often questioned in this respect. His actions – he managed to keep his troop in order and brought them back into the fray, taking a couple of cannon and recovering the lost standards of the king's regiment by the way – also led to him being knighted on the field. Moreover, he was rewarded with a medal: 'ever since carried at his Breast'.[5] This fact was never covered with false modesty and indeed he pushed it forward at the least opportunity. It was a way of Walsh's wearing his loyalty openly and in public and of disguising his more secretive dealings.

After Edgehill we lose sight of Walsh, but when he next appears it is in the southwest of England where Prince Rupert, with whom he had now become associated, was serving. Walsh was now a Lieutenant-Colonel of Sir George Vaughan's regiment of horse and in 1643 he was part of the besieged garrison of Devizes under Prince Maurice and was, according to Walsh at least, one of those who broke out to Oxford to report to the king and bring back assistance to the town; he subsequently served at Roundway Down.[6]

In 1643–44 Walsh was given a commission to raise troops in Ireland and this resulted in him raising one hundred cavalry whom he took to serve in England.[7] Various services followed, but when his patron Wilmot fell into disgrace and was imprisoned in Exeter gaol, Walsh threatened to resign. He claimed that only the kind words of the king gave him encouragement to continue to serve the cause. The collapse of the Royalist western army in 1645–46 left Walsh without a role. He soon returned to Ireland and, following talks there with the French envoy, agreed to raise Irish infantry for the French army. Walsh claimed that under this contract he was to have received thirty crowns for each man on landing in France and pension of 2,000 crowns *per annum* as well as other perks. He duly raised his men and also provided shipping. When some 950 soldiers were finally shipped out of Galway, Parliament's navy intercepted one of the vessels, the other got into Havre de Grace with some 600 men on board. As a colonel Walsh now served the French army, but he stated that he received little reward for all his pains.

One incident did make Walsh's name at this time, although not how he would have wished. In 1648 animosity spilled over in the exiles' councils in the Low Countries between Prince Rupert and John Colepeper, Lord Colepeper. The latter was an argumentative man and a suggestion by Rupert that Walsh was reliable enough to be given the task of an agent for the sale of prize goods led to an open quarrel between the pair, for Walsh had something of a reputation. Colepeper called Walsh a 'cheat'. Rupert, naturally enough, took this very ill and said when Walsh heard of it he would call Colepeper out. The latter refused to fight with Rupert, but nor, at first, would he ask for the Prince's pardon. While the pair eventually apologised to one another, it was a different matter with Walsh. On 23 October 1648 he accosted Colepeper in the streets of The Hague. While Colepeper said he would give Walsh satisfaction he was not wearing a sword so instead Walsh struck him a violent blow in the face and knocked him down, Walsh then stormed off. Such fighting in royal precincts – Colepeper had been on his way to the Prince of Wales' council – was not to be tolerated and Charles sent to the magistrates of The Hague to have Walsh arrested, and then promptly banished him from his court. Walsh, in a move that was to become part of a pattern in his life, issued a 'scandalous pamphlet' justifying his position and then, just as promptly, left for Ireland. Walsh had an undercurrent of violence about his character and more than once he was willing to defend his honour, as he saw it, by whatever means came to hand, but he was also proving a difficult man to deal with.[8]

Soon his continued dissatisfaction led him back to France and to join the Fronde. He served with the Frondeurs' army and fought at the battles at Faubourg Saint-Antoine and St Denis in May–July 1652 under Louis de

Bourbon, prince de Condé.[9] In the course of this service, Walsh was captured and imprisoned in the Bastille for three years; he was not exchanged.

Cromwellian espionage

Leaving Walsh languishing in the Bastille, it is time to examine the world in which he was about to become involved. The one outstanding name in seventeenth-century espionage has always been that of John Thurloe, the secretary of state who served Oliver Cromwell's protectorate and whose reputation as a father of English intelligence work has been an orthodoxy for some time.[10] It is indeed high time that the prevailing belief in the so-called all-seeing, somewhat Machiavellian 'little secretary', who kept his master and the republic safe with his multitude of plans, secret agents, spies and informers and, allegedly, helped to carry all the secrets of Europe in Cromwell's girdle, was re-examined. In a regime often plagued by internal conflict it is very clear that his power had limits and was not as all-encompassing as some have made out.[11]

In point of fact, it was not until July 1653 that John Thurloe fully moved into the world of intelligence by taking over the role formerly established in this area of government by his predecessor Thomas Scot, whom Thurloe personally disliked and whom he described as a 'noisy windbag'.[12] Effectively, Thurloe became Secretary of State, a role that he was to hold until 1659, and he was very much Oliver Cromwell's man. It was said that Oliver rarely trusted another as he trusted John Thurloe. Bulstrode Whitelocke noted on 2 May 1657 that:

> Several times he [Oliver] would send for the L[ord] Broghill, Pierrpont[,] Wh[itelocke,] S[i]r Charles Oulsely, & Thurlo & be shutt up w[i]th them 3 or 4 hours together in private discourse & none were admitted to come in to him, he would sometimes be very cheerfull with them, & laying aside his greatnes he would be exceeding familiar w[i]th them, & by way of diversion would make verses w[i]th them, & ever[y]one myt try his fancy, he commonly called for tobacco pipes & candle . . . then he would fall again to his serious & great business, & advise with them in these affayrs . . .[13]

If Thurloe became powerful, and a key part of the Protector's inner circle, he doesn't seem to have exploited his position, or at least he was not too open in his corruption.[14] That he was in general an unobtrusive, self-effacing man, very much the 'civil servant', whose main aim was to try to bring together the strings of administration, act as an intermediary to the Protector and screen supplicants from his master is clear; all of which in the end proved to be essential requirements to sustain his position.[15]

The Swedish ambassador noted of Thurloe that, 'it is principally he who transacts all business with the protector; and he is besides a pretty intelligent man', indeed, as the ambassador noted on another occasion: Thurloe was Cromwell's 'intimus', or 'right-hand man'. Or, as Cromwell himself noted, 'a man as well acquainted with all my affairs as I am myself'. Theirs was still, though, a relationship of master and servant and, while Thurloe was often a convenient intermediary with most of those who wanted to talk to the Protector, he also became an occasional excuse as to why something did not happen.[16]

Nonetheless, Thurloe was now the 'executive agent' of the government, especially in its foreign affairs.[17] By July 1655 he had also taken control of the government's printed newsbooks, the post office (as postmaster general), and most of the state correspondence of the regime.[18] While he did not control every avenue of intelligence, he does seem to have sought, as far as he was able, to centralise its flow and in doing so he was ably assisted by men whom he had largely chosen himself.[19] Thurloe was also deeply concerned in the censorship of the press and pamphlet world of the day, from employing the ubiquitous Marchamont Nedham, to engineering newsbooks and manipulating public responses to political events.[20] Additionally, and most notably in this instance, John Thurloe created a retinue of spies and informers for more secret work and used them to gather covert intelligence.

It would be a mistake, however, to suppose that John Thurloe always had a monopoly within this intelligence world, nor to presume that he got everything right, or had everything his own way. This was certainly not the case. Others on the Council of State were always dabbling in this particular pond. Others in the government could also sometimes thwart him or put him in his place.[21] The Cromwellian Council of State was in any case made up of some very strong-minded men, all aware of how much good intelligence could mean both to the state and their own future careers. The strongest-minded man of all, of course, was the Lord Protector himself.

It was, furthermore, always going to be a struggle for Thurloe to pull all of the intelligence threads into his own hands, for he was not only frequently ill in these years, but foreign commentators were quick to note that, '[the] secretary . . . [was often] overwhelmed by the mass of business and the burden of so many difficult affairs, the perfect digest of which demands an immense amount of time. For this reason their decisions move slowly'.[22] Having said this, it might also be suggested that the slowness of the Protectoral regime in coming to any decision may well have been a result of politic deliberation. One ambassador implied that the reason for having only a single secretary, a trend not followed under Charles I nor later still under the Restoration where two secretaries was the norm, was that one of the:

worst defects of the late Parliament . . [was that] what was not divulged by the members [of Parliament] was published abroad by the Secretaries, this method of everything passing through the hands of only one [secretary] has been adopted – a method, convenient in what concerns this purpose, but troublesome in that it makes negotiations very lengthy, and execution very slow.[23]

As a plus point, however, the Genoese ambassador noted that, '[t]here is certainly no government on earth which divulges its affairs less than England'.[24]

Thus, while Thurloe eventually came to control most of the Protectorate's espionage system, he did not have it entirely his own way. We know, for example, that John Lambert, a powerful man in the regime and not someone who was to be lightly crossed, ran agents for his own purposes.[25] As a military commissioner for the Ridings of Yorkshire and York, Lambert had agents around in 1655 and one of these was a 'young Tinker', who was a, 'subtlie & crafty younge man, at times full of simplicity, but one of notable dexterity in all sorts of games, as Dice or knavery'. The former talent, as well as an interest in hunting, seems to have given this man access to 'Gentlemen's houses' in the area, so as to gain information on their activities, which in turn was then passed on to Lambert's local agent and then on to Lambert himself.[26] Lambert was also rumoured to have placed William Swift in Ambassador William Lockhart's embassy to France to keep him informed of Lockhart's activities.[27]

Two other Cromwellians immediately involved in this world were George Monck and Roger Boyle, Lord Broghill. Both, for a time, were running an intelligence system from Scotland and depending on the information gathered by it to forestall any Royalist plots there. They were using their own informers, who gave them information for money, or to keep in with the regime within Scotland itself, and taking up professional spies of Scottish origins who could be sent abroad to the exiled court, or elsewhere, to gain information. A whole range of other techniques can also be seen in their work: the interception and seizing of letters; the rounding up of the 'usual suspects'; surveillance, imprisonment and heavy fines; as well as turning individuals around to work for the state.[28] Broghill noted to Thurloe that one of his agents had told him that one particular Royalist, who was due in Scotland, was already under scrutiny and that, 'what ever he does here we shall know it'.[29] He made it clear that the man was to be allowed in the country and then:

as soone as he lands . . . [we] cause him to be rob'd, and thereby get all his letters, which he looseinge upon a robbery, he will never doubt, can com

> to our knowledge, for the men, which give us the letters, to doe soe, must prove themselves to be theeves.[30]

In other respects Broghill doubted that he could recruit many agents in Scotland, 'as my inquireing after an honest able Scotchman to imploy as an agent, I have put in a way; but I much feare a person soe quallifyed will hardly be found in all this nation'.[31] Despite this, Broghill engaged the otherwise obscure Captain Maitland to spy on Archibald Campbell, Lord Lorne. This man was actually an intelligencer of Lorne's own choice, whom Broghill now recruited to play the double agent. An unforeseen consequence of this was that Maitland, 'as soone as he came into Argile . . . died suddenly; which truly is a very unhappy accident, for by that what I had from him already, I was cleerly convinced, that Lorne was playing the rog[u]e'.[32] Accident or not, some of Broghill's other agents were more successful or luckier. An agent sent to Flanders ended up in Amsterdam, where he informed Broghill about the correspondence going into London from the exiled Scots there. With names and codes at his disposal Broghill was then able to search the posts and ships plying between Holland and Scotland and warn Thurloe to keep an eye on the London letter office. Yet another agent, despite Broghill's apparent hatred of Catholics, seems to have been a Jesuit. He was sent off to Madrid in 1656 to relay intelligence from Spain.[33] George Monck, in his role as commander of the English army in Scotland, was to continue this type of work all through his tenure, recognising its importance. Nor did Broghill's work in this area stop when he left Scotland, for, as we shall see, he was to be closely associated with Robert Walsh.

John Thurloe's own seeming purpose in this world was much like Broghill's: to gain advantage in terms of knowledge and then to use this knowledge in both council and in his personal relationship with the Protector, as well as to protect the state. Thurloe seems to have been just as keen, furthermore, to spread as much dissention and uncertainty amongst any of the state's enemies, particularly those around the exiled Charles II, as possible and to undermine any of the inevitable plots and conspiracies that emerged. His tools for doing this were much the same general intelligence ones used by others both at home and abroad in the seventeenth century. Thurloe naturally sought to gather information via foreign relations, ambassadors and their minions. Specific secret intelligence gathering was undertaken by agents who were either volunteers or were press-ganged into the task. In each case, the worth of the agent needed to be assessed at the centre. There were always going to be some successes, some no-hopers, some 'ne'er-do-wells', some idealists (not many of these), some subject to the *ennui* of the exiles' life and some seeking to work their passage back to England, and Thurloe naturally exploited them all.

So, what were the techniques and tactics used by Thurloe and others in the world of intelligence? Who were their enemies, how did they work to preserve the government of Oliver Cromwell and, perhaps most significantly, how effective were they?

We must really begin with a political master who knew the value of good intelligence, for in the end Oliver Cromwell's former military career had gained him some very sound knowledge of this area of government and he proved to be the real master in this field. As a general on campaign Cromwell had garnered intelligence from a number of sources: his scoutmaster, spies, his own observations and the interrogation of members of the local populations his armies passed through. He was doubtless well aware from all of this that intelligence, especially good intelligence, had to be paid for.[34] Nor, when he was Lord Protector, was he above interrogating suspects himself, and he proved more than shrewd in using the evidence of plots uncovered for political and other purposes. Here, for example, is John Thurloe assessing the result of the crushing of John Penruddock's rising of 1655:

> [The] . . . advantages the Protector has got by this business: First, he has gained belief among all men that he made not a noise about plots and designs to get money out of the people's purses, but that the danger he had so often spoken of to the nation was real. Secondly, the army and the honest people of the nation are hereby become united. Thirdly our neighbours abroad, whom the king solicits for aid, do see that that family have no real interest in this commonwealth, but that the body of the honest and substantial people are against them . . . fourth: that the people will now the more willingly pay their taxes . . . fifth . . . the benefit of confiscations which will be through this business.[35]

Matched with John Thurloe, who continually built upon his own myth as the successes came in – more than half the battle it seems – Cromwell was both lucky and shrewd and if he had incautious opponents to deal with it was all to the good.

Generally, the Cromwellian regime's aim on this underground level was to seek to secure itself by the undermining and destruction of any plots against it. Some of these, once discovered, were to be allowed to mature sufficiently enough so that they could be broken at the opportune time and the plotters rounded up with the evidence upon them. Much political noise could then be made of the event in the press and in parliament. Others slipped by unnoticed, but all in the end were effectively dealt with. This regime would not fall through plotting. Naturally when dealing with might-have-beens, it is often very difficult to assess just how real some of these plots were in the 1650s and how many were all too obviously over-publicised by a regime anxious to establish itself as the supporter of stability against the 'wicked' Royalists/Levellers/Fifth Monarchists or what you will; their way, implied the government's reports, was anarchy, and look how well we keep it from you, was to be the official line. For, in the post-civil war nation, the fear of anarchy was ever-present amongst the more moderate members of society. Hence plot breaking was, generally speaking, used to quell this anxiety or at least to force it into useful channels.

In terms of actual conspiracies of the day the government had many opportunities and advantages in undermining and then destroying plots. For any conspiracy, communication was the main problem. If this was verbal, then meetings would have to be arranged and these of course would have to take place in either private or public places, during which suspects could be observed or watched. If the plot was one initiated and carried on by correspondence then this could be intercepted. The use of covert routes to relay correspondence was one solution, but couriers could be intercepted, ports were certainly watched and the 'usual suspects' were frequently hauled in for questioning. Moreover, at certain times any meetings would be dangerous, for the regime was not loath to flooding the streets of London with heavier patrols of troops than usual when it thought something was going on. In December 1655 the Genoese ambassador noted: 'The patrols or companies of horse quartered in the chief thoroughfares of the city are instructed to charge severely and arrest the promoters of any – no matter how insignificant – rumour of revolt among the people.'[36]

Of course, a disguised correspondence was one solution; through the use of cipher, mainly by letter substitution or merchant speech, some secrecy could be kept. But ciphers could be broken or easily read if the keys were found. Amateurish attempts to disguise secrets through the use of invisible inks, lemon juice for example, were easily discovered as such techniques were limited and usually well known.

In any case the actual decision-making processes of conspiracy were always problematic. It was often difficult to say who was to lead and where they were to be based: if in Europe then there was the problem of time and action. Far too often orders arrived either too late or bore no relation to the actual circumstances in the country. If the leader was based in England then the problem of infiltration was rife.[37] Additionally, any combination of groups seeking the same outcome, but with different ends, was fraught with difficulty. The usual environment for conspiracy, too, invariably proved problematic. Taverns and public houses, the classic environ of the plot, led to drinking (usually to excess, perhaps because of nerves), violence (against one another), short tempers and loud words, braggadocio and rowdiness, any one of which could and naturally did lead to arrests, interrogation and revelations. Suspicious actions in public were also likely to be picked up and commented on by the locals as the latter all too often minded each others' business and seventeenth-century plotters seemed to have had a fondness for doing suspicious things almost too obviously. Notice would then reach the authorities. All in all plotting was not an easy task. On the other hand for the regime there were also difficulties to deal with.

Trustworthy helpers to uncover plots were naturally difficult to come by. Agents or informers, as we shall see in the case of Walsh, were driven by many different motives. How far their reports could be relied upon depended on a reading of their character and ideals, such as they were. Even more significant was the ability to sift through the evidence and find the gold within. This was the true skill needed by any intelligence chief. So often it was the talent for sifting evidence at the centre rather than the mere collection of evidence that marked the genius from the commonplace. Of course leadership was a badly needed quality. Who was to make the final decisions and how long could the regime afford to leave the situation before arrests had to be made? These were more than significant factors. Certainly the final revelation of the plot to the public was an art in itself. To proclaim to the public that a plot had been uncovered, or broken, and the men involved taken, could lead to public disbelief if tried too often. If the regime was then seen to exploit the plot too openly, they were more often than not accused of invention, or of using *agent provocateurs*. Yet despite this the regime had to be on its guard all the time; the conspirators only had to succeed once; the pressure was therefore on the government to get their actions right every time.

Its security was naturally of significance to the Cromwellian regime and its members. And it is clear that at times of heightened tension in the 1650s there was an increased emphasis on physical security. At audiences with the Protector, for example, the Venetian ambassador noted that 'everyone who entered was narrowly scanned . . . the ambassador's attendants were not all admitted to the Protector's cabinet. To reach this it was necessary to pass four closed doors'.[38] In addition, the Lord Protector was always escorted by his lifeguard when he went on his weekend expeditions to Hampton Court – and occasionally his route was changed, to go by river instead of road. The garrison at the Tower was also frequently strengthened and put on alert, while numerous military patrols went out at night in London's streets, and sometimes these were doubled; passersby were stopped and searched, passes were examined and lodgings were periodically searched. Landlords had to provide lists of their lodgers to officials. Sentries also guarded the palace of Whitehall, and at times artillery was even placed on its approaches.[39]

If needed, raids on suspects were made, usually at night or in the early morning and usually when concrete information was available. Troops would batter down doors and then arrest suspects. A parallel to this technique, which gives some insight into the methods used by Thurloe, is the capture in 1655 of Percy Owen, a highwayman. Similar techniques were used for plotters. An agent had been set upon Owen's trail and provided Thurloe with information and a full description of the man:

> not full thirty . . . hayre browne, & long curl'd locks[,] an oval face[,] handsome, & black eyes, a cutt downe his under lipp almost to his chin on the left side of his mouth. His habit either black . . . or Grey-cloath suite with and old close stuffe coate almost to his knees.[40]

In addition, the agent also related the places Owen lurked; where he stabled his horse and how he spent his time. Further instructions, to cover the agent's identity, were given that those who were sent to arrest Owen should know little about him, but should be told, 'he is suspected for a priest'. An implicit threat of violence was then to be used on Owen in his interrogation: 'if he proves obstinate'. Finally, the government had an informer in their pocket, Charles Pitts, 'the only person hee stands in feare of (in paymt of peaching)', to bring in, if Owen did not tell all.[41]

On a personal level it was rumoured that Cromwell also took care of his own safety. In July 1654 it was said: 'He will allow no one to approach him, and to secure himself the better he has recourse to every artifice, using his own cunning and address; the force of arms and money.'[42] There is little doubt that he went personally armed. In the course of his famous accident of 1654 when the Lord Protector lost control of the six new horses and coach sent to him as a present by the duke of Oldenburg, he flung himself from the seat of the carriage he was driving and a pistol, secreted in his pocket, went off. Bruised, but otherwise unhurt, he may have seen this as yet another one of God's providences. Yet despite this it shows that he had a gun and it was loaded. Was this merely an old soldier's foible or something more sinister? It is clear that Cromwell, for all his trust in the Lord's providences, was also willing to take practical care of himself and his mission. 'On this account his body guards are most assiduous and watchful and he always carries firearms with him.'[43]

Spies

Information was gathered by both public and private means. In this respect Thurloe was a stern taskmaster and frequently demanded as much information from his correspondents, both at home and abroad, as he could get. At home he had, it was said, 'spies abroad almost in every County, and Citty, or town of note, who made it their great business to observe all such persons, and what houses they frequented'.[44] Links with those in authority in the localities were created and Thurloe pressed them into supplying information to him.

Intelligence abroad could normally be openly gathered by residents or ambassadors, or by the more secret and dubious means of employing agents to bring it in, or by merely paying for information from informers who proffered it to the regime. Such information tended to be military, political and diplomatic in nature and would assist the regime to make decisions in government.

Thurloe's use of spies was an obvious adjunct to this regular form; it was common enough practice, although there were never as many spies as some contemporaries thought. They were variously employed and came into Thurloe's orbit by a variety of means. As we shall see, Walsh's problems also allow us to see how one particular example of the double agent in this era emerged and some of the techniques that were used by such men when faced with two masters. We do know that 'safe houses' were frequently used to let such men report back to the secretary, for it was said that Thurloe's own lodging, 'was constantly watcht almost by all parties to see who came out, or went in, and consequently to finde out which of their brethren probably betrayed them'.[45] Indeed, Samuel Morland was given the task by Thurloe of finding and hiring discreet rooms in private places in the city, using a false name, 'on purpose to meet such persons in a disguise and receive their intelligence'.[46] Where they could not come in person the agent would correspond. Agents were given cover names and addresses from a list (also supplied to Isaac Dorislaus in the Post Office). The agent would then use this cover name and address to write back; the letter being intercepted in the post office, it would then be taken to the secretary.[47] In addition, agents were also covertly hired in ambassadors' retinues, 'who might be entertained as their domestique servants and therefore discover all manner of secrets'.[48]

Indeed Jerome Beverning, the Dutch ambassador, wrote to one correspondent: 'I dare not write much news. All our actions are spied. We have spies set to watch us in our houses. We cannot be certain of anything we do, that it shall not either be known or miscarry'.[49] Yet another Dutchman noted that, '[t]hey had spies amongst our domestics, and false informers, who did inform us of what they thought fitting for us to know'.[50] The Genoese ambassador also wrote that:

> Every foreigner who lands in places here has his papers and letters he has with him minutely examined, and transmitted to London, nor are they

> restored before being submitted to the rigorous examination and diligent requisition of the Secretary of State. No one can leave London for any foreign country without permission, signed by the protector, which obliges foreigners to an inopportune length of time and phlegmatic patience.[51]

Money was, of course, an essential factor in intelligence work. Here Thurloe's situation has often been exaggerated. We may leave aside Samuel Pepys' later sweeping assertion that the Cromwellian government had some £70,000 to spend on intelligence and thus Cromwell gained the secrets of all the princes of Europe at his girdle; in fact the money available to Thurloe was rarely above some £1,200–£2,000 a year. Naturally, he spent more and by 1659 he found himself in debt, being owed some £1,665 3s 2d for his expenses.[52] Money, however, was the one lever whereby individuals at home or abroad, especially near the exiled king, could be persuaded to turn, or be bought outright.

Predictably enough the Cromwellian intelligence system recruited some of its agents from the professionals of the contemporary espionage world. Amongst the professionals we can also find the bravos, murderers and hired killers who could be employed if the government wanted more violent tasks undertaken. The professional spy was naturally slippery in his loyalties. He would tend to serve an assortment of masters, sometimes all at once. Many were of foreign extraction and drawn from a swarm of professional rogues, adventurers, or dubious ex-diplomats who haunted the staterooms and corridors of the palaces of Europe. Their actual value was often questionable and their loyalty was usually to themselves.

The type of information the regime wished its agents to gather may be placed under five broad headings. First, there was intelligence concerning the whereabouts and activities of rebels and Royalist exiles. Second, there was obviously a need for intelligence on any possible conspiracies which might be emerging from that quarter. Third, the spies sent into Europe were, of course, required to obtain general military and naval intelligence useful to the government. A fourth area of concern normally lay in basic political intelligence, relating to the host country's politics, the activities of its government, or the state of public opinion. Lastly, there was also a need for some basic economic intelligence. The instructions given out would obviously vary with the task in hand. We do know that sub-contracting such work was a common practice. This provided a means of security for the agent, for the authorities would tend to pick up the lesser fry first, as well as a way of keeping information flowing. The other side of this picture was the domestic scene. Here the spy might be asked to attend religious meetings, lurk in London's taverns and inns, go into prison (or be there already as Sir Robert Walsh often was) in order to listen to the conversations of prisoners and report them, or 'escape' and rejoin his former comrades solely in order to betray them.

If the spy's life was dangerous, it was also morally dubious and often humiliating. In general, however, the profession did not involve physical brutality. Indeed it seems to have been far better for such men to cultivate the art of listening, to have a fawning manner and to put victims at their ease. The accepted rules in such work seem to have been threefold: try to gain the victim's confidence; never drop your guard; and achieve your masters' purpose. The financial and personal rewards for a spy in the regime's service were not that high and much depended upon the quality of the information, the use of the agent, his position and the regularity of his intelligence, yet for some, such activities represented a chance for redemption.[53] Of course, in the end one could still be betrayed, especially if engaged in a double cross.

A mission for Robert Walsh

After he had been incarcerated for a while, the governor of the Bastille came to Robert Walsh with a proposition, obviously prompted by someone else. It was that he could obtain release from the Bastille if he would consider destroying him, 'that hath destroyed my Religion, King and country' – that is, Oliver Cromwell.[54] Walsh would be set to work with another in the business and would have money and liberty if he agreed to kill Cromwell. At first, or so Walsh later said, he refused to go along with any scheme for killing Cromwell, simply seeing such an act as murder, but later he began to see the scheme as an opportunity to at least get out of prison and return to England. There, he thought, he could tell all to the Cromwellian government and thereby curry favour with the Protector's regime. Beyond this Walsh's plans seem to have been rather vague. He was later to claim that the idea of playing the double agent was one he had in mind, but at the time he might not have been so sure of this, seeing as he really was down on his luck. Eventually Walsh did manage to get out of the Bastille under terms, including being barred from carrying arms against the French king for five years, and he then thought perhaps it was best to tell someone in authority in the Royalist camp of his schemes, lest he be thought an actual traitor to his king, or so he was later to claim. Moving on to Rouen, he approached James Butler, marquis of Ormond, with whom he had had previous dealings. Walsh was later to claim that Ormond actually advised him to go to England, having consulted Charles II about the plan, but that he was to use his discretion. Whatever the truth of this Walsh did set off for England, without a pass.[55] Conversely, this tale of Royalist sanction for his actions should be contrasted with Walsh's actual letter to the Lord Protector sent around this time, which is revealing, if nothing else, of Royalist *ennui*:

> I am soly come in to this country, with an absolute beleefe, my indeavours may appeer condusing unto your highness interest, and so consequently may hope, that my owne may be therein involved. My intentions shall beare noe maske in sheowing their cleernes unto your highness. I shall not dissemble. I most humbly beg the grace to be admitted the honour of waiting upon your heighnes, having some things of consequence, which I hope your heighnes wil fiend soe to bee; two offer onto your heighnes. God Almighty hath blessed and invested your highnes in the place you are inn; and had not his holy will soe decreed, doubtlessly you had not beene. This is my beleefe, as allsoe that I may prove instrumental unto your heignes continuance and interests. If that upon good grounds you may please to admit mee the honor of your commands, their shall be a reall obbeysance given by [&c].[56]

Here, it might be noted, Walsh doesn't offer himself as spy or agent. Indeed he avoids the word. Walsh claims only that he will endeavour to be 'instrumental' to Cromwell's interest and he will, he says, 'beare noe maske in sheowing their cleernes', nor will he 'dissemble', but will show 'things of consequence'. We can also perceive his very practical view of the Protector's government in that God set it up or else it would not be there, but he now wants to join and continue it and therefore will ask to have the 'honor of your commands'. Walsh, as we shall see, would continue to re-write his history, but at the time he was seeking to work his passage.

When he arrived at Rye, Walsh immediately contacted John Thurloe to let him know he was in the country and was now hoping to help the government. On reaching London Walsh did indeed have an initial meeting with John Thurloe, and in this he told the secretary that 'he 'founde myselfe very ill rewarded, yt my king never looked upon mee, all the while I lay prisoner in the Bastille'.[57] Some time later Walsh came back for a second interview and the pair then discussed foreign affairs, particularly those of France and Spain. Walsh was asked directly if he would take employment in the state's service.[58] He was also asked whether he preferred to serve at sea or on land and promptly demurred on naval service for, as he said, he knew little of it. Thurloe then went on to interrogate Walsh further in order to find out what the Irishman's estate was; Walsh replied that he had been 'outed of all'. To which the secretary claimed that he knew that Cromwell had actually seen Walsh's property in southern Ireland and hinted it could all be returned to him: 'you shall be taken

Arrest of Guy Fawkes in the cellars of Parliament, 1605 (19th century)

Nathan Hale Led to His Execution: 'I only regret that I have but one life to give to my country'

RIGHT. *The Unfortunate Death of Major André.* Goldar (engraver), after Hamilton (painter). Mixed method, 1783

BELOW. *John Thurloe, Cromwell's spymaster.* From an illustration on the front page of T. Birch's *A Collection of the State Papers of John Thurloe* (7 vols, London, 1742)

Venice: The Upper Reaches of the Grand Canal with S. Simeone Piccolo by Canaletto

View of Piazza San Marco, Venice (1723) by Canaletto

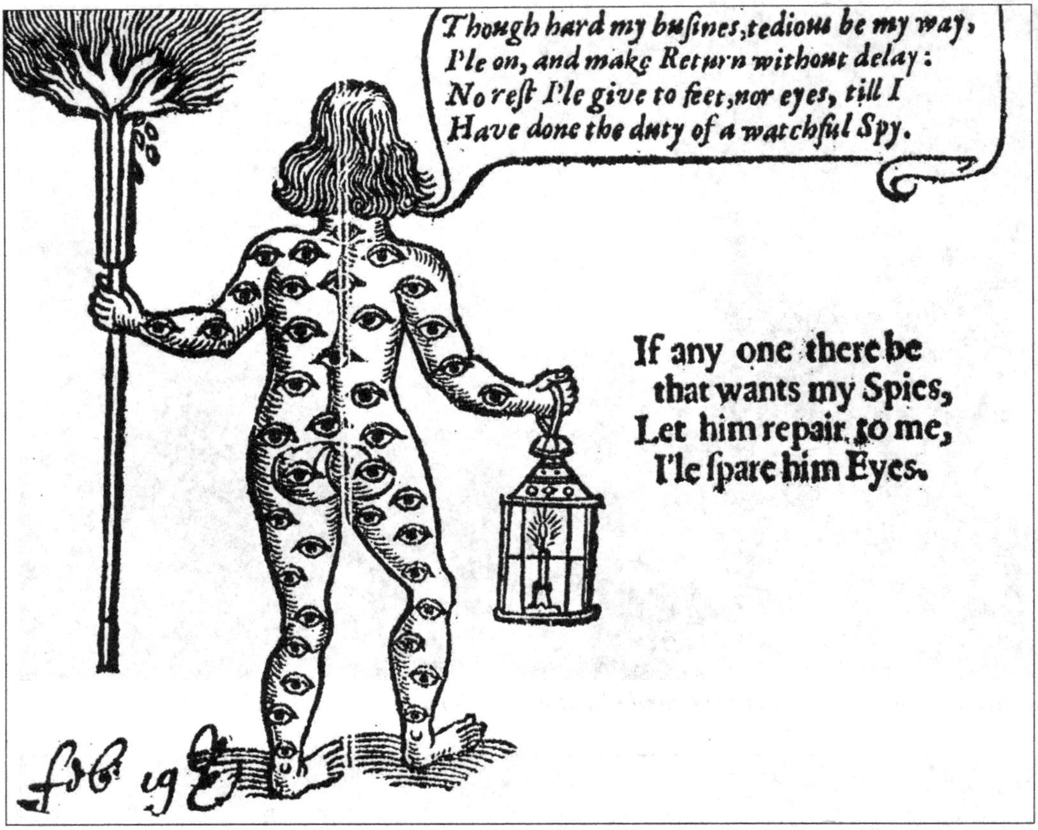

An illustration on the front cover of Henry Adis's *A Spie, sent out of the Tower-Chamber in the Fleet* (1648)

The Assassination of William the Silent of Orange at Delft. The killer fires at point blank range into the chest of his victim

Philippe, Duc d'Orléans, Regent of France (1674–1723) by Jean-Baptiste Santerr

Giacomo Casanova

King Charles I of England (1600–1649) from the workshop of Anthonis van Dyck (c. 1632)

ABOVE. *King Charles II of England, 1653* by Philippe de Champaigne

LEFT. *Gustavus Adolphus, King of Sweden* (Gustav II Adolf)

King James II of England by Sir Godfrey Kneller

King James I of England (1566–1625) by Paul van Somer (c. 1620)

Louis XIV, King of France, 1701

Doge Alvise Mocenigo of Venice by Tintoretto (Jacopo Comin, 1518–1594)

Count Axel Oxenstierna of Södermöre, 1583–1654

Philip II of Spain by Titian (Tiziano Vecellio, c. 1488–1576)

ABOVE. *Philip V, King of Spain* by J. Ranc

RIGHT. *Equestrian Portrait of Sultan Selim II.* Engraving 1566

ABOVE. *King Sigismund III of Poland (1566–1632)* by Martin Kober (c. 1590)

LEFT. *Jean-Baptiste Colbert,* Marquis de Torcy

Queen Anne by Michael Dahl

care of, and if yow bee for his H[ighness] you shall have a better revenue and estate then ever'.[59] Thurloe's techniques in dealing with this potential agent may thus be perceived: a mixture of carrot and stick; a subtle questioning to find out what Walsh knew, if anything, and whether he could be of any value. And behind Thurloe, of course, lay the Lord Protector, whom he had kept fully informed of the affair.

As a result of the interviews, Walsh now began to think himself well in with the secretary, but a few days later he found to his surprise that Thurloe had turned cool towards him. This, Walsh later claimed, was mainly due to the fact that Thurloe had been making enquiries and as a result he had obtained more information about Walsh. Both Cardinal Jules Mazarin and Sir Kenelm Digby now proffered their knowledge of Walsh. Indeed Digby's letter on Walsh, which survives, damns the Irishman beyond repair, noting Walsh's 'venome' and 'Malitious Tongue' and how, 'forging of Letters, and doing Treacheries . . . hath bin his Ordinary Course'. This in itself was perhaps no bad thing for the potential spy's curriculum vitae, if suitably controlled. That he was a, 'wretched creature . . . an Irish papist . . . and because I [Digby] have heretofore shamed him and have broken some cheating Designs of his by making publique some of his Infamous Villanies', was another matter.[60] Nevertheless, Thurloe decided to try Walsh once more. In this further interview Thurloe now directly asked Walsh: '[w]hy did . . . [Digby] think this'? Walsh blustered through his answers, but also began to offer some intelligence on the exiles. However, by now Mazarin had also intervened and indeed the Cardinal had written directly to Cromwell that Walsh was, 'a most dangerous person'.[61] The secretary thus dropped, or was ordered to drop, Walsh. When Walsh did finally get another interview, Thurloe told him to his face that he was a 'suspitious person' and wanted to know what intelligence he had of the king's court. Walsh's reply, that he'd had no real contact with the king abroad, was met with a withering response: 'you cannot serve us, for we must be served by them who have a power and [an] interest there'.[62] Walsh hoped, he told Thurloe, that he could obtain such a connection. In that case, said the secretary, write to Ormond, and when Thurloe actually saw a letter in Ormond's hand, he just might be able to use him. Even though Walsh apparently did this, Thurloe seems to have been inclined to let go of Walsh anyway, feeling perhaps he was of little value and too untrustworthy. While Walsh had word he was to be allowed to stay in England, the prospective agent was soon baulked in any further plans. He lapsed into old habits, was kept hanging on by Thurloe and John Barkstead, who ran intelligence affairs from the Tower, and then Walsh found himself under arrest and incarcerated in the Tower itself, where he languished for some time. In the course of this he, 'sent and sent to Thurlo: but not a worde could I ever heer from him'.[63] His new career seemed to be over before it had begun.

Three months later he had a new visitor: Lord Broghill. Broghill was by this stage high in the favour of the Lord Protector and he began to personally interrogate Walsh, asking him if he now repented his ways. Of course he did, so Broghill then put a new proposition before him. Broghill said that the government had now received information that there was a design contrived by Charles II to kill the Protector, and he asked Walsh what he knew of this. Of course, Walsh now denied any knowledge of such a plot, even though he had heard of one. Broghill then offered him the chance to go out to the king's exiled court and there act as an agent with his information being sent not to Thurloe, but directly back to Broghill. Walsh swiftly agreed to undertake the mission. Of his relations with Thurloe, Walsh told Broghill that he had written a letter to Cromwell, but this, said Broghill upon seeing it, 'clashed too much upon Thurlo'; Broghill then offered to mediate with the Protector himself and told him to leave out the attacks on Thurloe 'wch otherwise would undoubtedly retarde and cross my liberty'.[64] Rather than get lost in the by-ways of the Council of State's rivalries, Walsh now agreed to follow Broghill's instructions.

Two days later Broghill, with the lieutenant of the Tower John Barkstead alongside him, came into Walsh's cell with his discharge. The Irishman was swiftly removed out of town and transferred to Broghill's own house and there, in a closed room, they devised a cipher for the communications they soon hoped to have. In the course of this, Broghill revealed that, building on his Scottish experience, he had already managed to obtain an intelligencer situated about the king, and afterwards he also revealed that he had a third man located at court. Broghill even flourished a letter from one of these men which had much intelligence in it.[65] This, of course, may have been a subtle means of telling Walsh that his information, when he eventually began to relay it, could be compared and checked, or that he would have to compete for the right to supply information and should think of performing as well as possible.[66]

Walsh then made ready for his journey and took to coming back at night for further instructions. He was initially given £50 at which he immediately began to raise objections, telling Broghill it was not enough. This apparently annoyed Broghill who told Walsh that this was in fact his own money and he couldn't get any money out of the state at present as he had already had enough difficulty with members of the Council who didn't trust Walsh in the first place. In any case there were others in the Tower who were perhaps equally useful or even better suited for the business at hand for they had been used before. At this, Walsh hastily backed down. With this hint of limited funds from his new master he instead turned to private enterprise: 'I was necessitated to take up

Forty pounds worth in silk stockings, to carry me into Flanders'.[67] In the meanwhile, Walsh later claimed that he had secretly communicated with Ormond, via Lady Ormond and her son, about the whole affair and told him what he was doing. If true, and there are doubts about Walsh's later version of events, by now he was probably speculating about trying to play both his new and old masters off against each other.

Soon afterwards, short-changed or not, Robert Walsh rode off towards Gravesend under orders to take a ship to the Continent. This proved abortive and instead he decided to ride on to Dover, where he planned this time to take the packet boat to Dunkirk. On the way, while at Canterbury, he was arrested by a warrant under a law suit of Mr George Paule and was promptly taken back to London and thrown into the debtor's prison of the Fleet. He managed to get a note out to Broghill, who told him severely that Cromwell wouldn't intervene in private law suits about debt, but had asked Broghill to write to Barkstead, and try to get the debt cleared. If this did not transpire then Walsh should, 'set your wits to work to get out, and when you have done any service, you shall see my affection by its effects'.[68] Ever hopeful, Walsh also tried Thurloe again, but this time with the plaintive but not untruthful line: 'Yow see I am no sooner out of one prison, but that I gett into another'.[69] In fact Walsh's new enemy proved to be the Warder of the Fleet who played him 'many prankes': Sir Jeremy Whichcote. Although the debt was eventually settled for the moment and Walsh did manage to get out of prison, the actual arrest was not an accident but deliberate, and this time it was not Thurloe or Broghill's doing, but the Royalists'.

In fact Sir Jeremy Whichcote later claimed that he had actually bought up the office of warden of the Fleet, 'in order to serve the King', and to give the exiled monarch's agents a safe haven. Whichcote had uncovered Walsh's intrigues with the regime, not too difficult as he said some at Cromwell's court had told him that Walsh had a design to seize the king and bring him back to England with Walsh as the principal man in that affair. Once more we see the rivalries in the regime. Fearing the worst and knowing of Walsh's reputation, Whichcote immediately asked the agent's creditors to put in a claim against him and thereby ensure that Walsh's design of going abroad could be stalled.[70] This done, officers from the Fleet prison were ordered to apprehend Walsh. With Walsh in the Fleet, Whichcote was soon called before the Protector's council to answer for his actions. According to him, he was also ordered to bring his prisoner with him, but he demurred at this. When finally he came before the council board Oliver was sitting there with a letter Whichcote had actually written to Sir Richard Willys about the business. Fortunately it had been written in a disguised hand and Whichcote recognised it.[71] A stern interview followed, with the Lord Protector asking where his prisoner was and how he could hold a, 'person imployed (to use his words) in our service'. Whichcote bluffed his way through and blithely claimed that Walsh's debts were so great that if he had taken him out of prison for any reason at all he would be forced to pay them himself.[72] The Protector then grimly told Whichcote that, 'he lookt upon him as a suspicious person', but dismissed him after noting that, 'he should observe him a little more narrowly', in the future.[73]

Despite being compromised, Walsh now managed to raise enough money to pay his creditors and once again set off for Europe. When he eventually got to Gravesend and went aboard ship there was a chance the ship would be searched (it was a regular practice), so he hid on board, as best he could, alongside the Royalist Sir James Bridgeman. As it happened, the latter did have a pass from Cromwell to travel, but when the ship was eventually boarded he foolishly managed to give the searcher an old letter from Charles I to him by mistake. Naturally the officials couldn't understand this and dragged Bridgeman ashore. Walsh, in the meanwhile, attempted to hide in some straw, only occasionally popping his head out to see what was going on. Eventually he was rousted out and asked for his pass. The pass he handed over was then found to be two months old. He was once again detained. He swiftly sent his servant off to Broghill to try to obtain a new pass, but in the meanwhile managed to persuade the officer that he should stay on board ship. Shortly afterwards a letter from Thurloe arrived. In the course of the discussions Walsh managed to pocket this and, the wind getting up, the ship set sail before further enquiries could be made. Walsh claimed that Broghill was still working independently of Thurloe at this point and it was he rather than Thurloe who had directed him.

Once landed, Walsh soon went to ground in his former Royalist haunts. He was then asked to carry a letter to Bruges, but instead he first went to Ghent to see a friend who had carried his own letters out of England to Ormond. At Ghent he became aware that Ormond was actually in the city. When Walsh tried to see the marquis, however, the latter turned him away. It was only after some delay that he finally got to see Ormond and then told the marquis that he had all the time been working to obtain the good opinion of the regime and related to him how Broghill had got him released after he had agreed to work for him. Walsh said that he had then been sent over on the condition that he investigated the potential assassination plots against the Protector. He handed over the cipher he had received from Broghill and also said that he had got in with some Baptists in London who were planning a rising and that there was a design for surprising three or four of the richest city merchants to bring them into Flanders for ransom. He also claimed that he had seen letters from some of those near the king who were obviously traitors. Indeed he claimed to have been told if he had any difficulties to contact one person in particular and he would be protected. This man had sent letters out to Cromwell and Walsh offered to have them intercepted and so entrap the traitor, but an angry Ormond refused to hear any more of his tales and soon afterwards told Walsh he should leave the country. The thwarted Walsh drifted towards Bruges, but while there he was seized by the local authorities and told he was accused of coming into the country to kill the king on Cromwell's orders. They once more threw him into prison. Walsh now had no money and no pen, ink or paper to write to anyone. He later discovered that Broghill was furious at his actions and the suspicious Royalist exiles sent John Digby, earl of Bristol, and Henry Wilmot, earl of Rochester, to interrogate Walsh. In the course of this questioning Walsh speedily accused Sir Edward Hyde of being the traitor around the king. Hyde was outraged (Charles didn't believe the tale), and Walsh was left to languish in gaol, where he amused himself by composing (he had eventually scrounged some writing materials), various versions of his tale that he proposed to send to all and sundry, denying all accusations against himself and blaming Hyde for his fate.[74]

Walsh's failure leaves us wondering who exactly he was working for and whether this whole series of events had been a double bluff all along. Why was the Lord Protector so obvious with Whichcote that Walsh was an agent? What was Thurloe's part in all of this? Was this a venture by Broghill alone, or was Thurloe in agreement? Was the use of Walsh really to spread disinformation and disarray amongst the Royalist exiles, rather than for any real intelligence he might gather? Or did his employment go wrong because of an internal rivalry between Thurloe and Broghill? Or, finally, was he merely so incompetent that the mission had little real chance of success? The ground is so obscured that ultimately no real answers to these questions seem possible.

In fact Robert Walsh was to languish in gaol for some time and this temporarily put an end to his usefulness for all sides. On his eventual release he remained in Flanders, distrusted by all. It was not the end of his career, however, but when the Restoration finally came in 1660, it represented for Walsh not another chance at redemption, but a disaster, with him scrambling in exile for any new patronage he could get. Nevertheless, this brief journey into the heart of the Cromwellian intelligence system can allow us some insights into this world, its operations and its difficulties. As we have seen it leaves many questions unanswered, but it does show some of Thurloe's techniques and the division of labour in gathering intelligence and other operations in this regime. More significantly an analysis of Walsh's personality can give us a reading of some of the spy's own motivations for his actions.

Walsh, social caste and honour

It is relatively unusual to get the agent's side of affairs in these cases, for mostly they are locked into brief manuscript letters that all too often begin and end abruptly. This case, however, allows us to begin to interrogate and to perceive motivation in both the public and private spaces. While it is not unique (Joseph Bampfield and Henry Manning are two prominent cases), it does allow for some insight into the mind of the early modern double agent.[75] In this instance, certain themes do stand out: Walsh's social caste, his 'Irishness', the idea of honour and the public and private faces he evidently sought to project.

There is little doubt that despite all his travails, Walsh thought of himself as a gentleman with 'quality and title', however underhand his dealings had been with both sides of the political divide.[76] Indeed, while many of the men employed in the profession of espionage had similar pretensions for themselves (often seeing others as lesser beings), in this at least Walsh had some claim. His background was that of a gentleman. He was also distinctive in being an Irish gentleman. Walsh noted of his nativity that, 'being born in Ireland, I hope may not pass for a crime', and that he was a Catholic of sorts and of 'Old English' descent.[77] Later historians have described this particular ethnic grouping in early modern Ireland as one of 'peculiar ambivalence' in their, 'temporal and spiritual allegiances', with respect to the pope and Stuart dynasty. It may be that this makes Walsh's confusions of loyalty in this case slightly more explicable.[78]

On the other hand, Irish links with espionage of this period were inevitably associated with military life. A number of Irishmen of the day, of varying social degrees, became routinely associated with espionage activities and this led them into a bewildering pattern of loyalties. They also gained a reputation for being useful in the world of political violence.[79] Furthermore, as an Irish gentleman, while Walsh obviously felt able to talk to Broghill on more or less equal terms, and responded to Ormond ingratiatingly; with John Thurloe, an Englishman, who may well have been prejudiced against the archetypical down-at-heel landless Irish gentleman he saw before him, he behaved somewhat differently and less successfully. In addition, as a gentleman, Walsh was able, during his Royalist interrogations, to become equally assertive and even try to undermine his supposed 'lordly' interrogators' social status. Cross-examined by Bristol, Walsh spoke thus: 'if it please yor Excellence, yor Lord shpp, yor honnor, or what you please[,] as knowing it displeased him not to give him his titles'.[80] This was a deliberate slight on a man who had the power to release him and smacks of someone who had a high opinion of himself.

Secondly, it is also clear that Walsh's persona, or at least that persona which he projected in his texts, revolved around his views of 'honour culture'. This type of worth lay both in internal virtues, but also in the external perceptions of the deeds of individuals and in the appreciation of those deeds by others. It was, as some historians have noted, often more of a vulnerable concept than might be thought; it also needed to be frequently defended in terms of masculinity and responsibility. Honour could not be left stained, for if it was, the audience to which it was directed would never respect the individual. Respect, of course, related to many social values, but also to the ability to use violence by word or deed if necessary.

Aspects of this gentlemanly honour are seen in Walsh and included: his use of arms, his knowledge (secret knowledge especially), his access to power (however measured), his wealth (or lack of it), and his dogged clinging on to his social status whatever his actual position at the time. Some of these assets, of course, were measured in the eyes of those below and those above him. The obverse of honour was shame: 'a psychological and social state' of 'collective disapproval'.[81] That masculine honour could be easily lost and was difficult to regain, was a, 'source of jeopardy, one of several that were central to exchanges involving trust'.[82]

Of course Walsh in these years found himself in a nether world where honour could be regularly bought and sold. As a soldier of fortune, naturally he had frequently sold his services, but never, or so he said, his honour. In the espionage world he was trying to enter, however, he took care to deny this possibility by attributing his outward actions to a deeper allegiance, a deeper cause, not just to the base selfishness of which others accused him. Of course honour amongst spies is, 'a difficult notion to define, since honour consists in the public recognition of a publicly valued role'.[83] So ultimately, could the spy ever really have honour? Can an incompetent spy have any chance of honour at all? It is unlikely that even Walsh believed at bottom that what he was doing was anything but a series of continual betrayals, but he made a great deal of effort to undertake the later re-organisation of his deeds and actions, and took a great deal of care to avoid the label of traitor: a word, of course, that provided an immediate and direct contrast with any notions of honour.

There is little doubt that Walsh continually sought to reshape his honour through manuscript or printed texts. In turn, these documents shape our knowledge of his life and they entailed an often detailed reconstruction by him of both the public and some of the private events in which he was involved, as well as giving the world, or his particular audience in the case of the manuscripts, a relation of his adventures as *he* saw them. Frequently, the resulting texts were repetitive, fragmented and confused, with appeals made in plaintive prose, or an equally sneering tone against any opposition, while at the same time being equally fearful of being caught out. Were anyone to critique his view of himself then his response was naturally to turn towards violence:

> my credit being thus trampled upon, by Fobbs, Rascals and Villains, that never dar'st appear to lay anything to my charge, face to face or before justice, but still like a Parator falsly informing behind my back . . . O what a pitty it is, that the noble law which was allowed of to the Lord Rea, and David Kamsy should not again be permitted; which was to fight *lespee a la main* on a publick stage, to maintain the Truth, which would give an Allaye unto impostory and false accusations.[84]

His other intentions were undoubtedly more practical. He wished to return from his exile to obtain land to give him respectability and bolster his claims to gentility and thereby to regain some power and security in what had otherwise become a dismal round of prison and exile. That he never really achieved this in the 1650s was not for want of trying.

It was the print culture of the day that finally allowed Walsh to reassert his public face, despite his private textual face being already all too well known amongst his masters and peers as one who was completely untrustworthy. In fact the public face allowed Walsh an opportunity to rewrite his life story in a new form: the fragmented biography. An apt form, perhaps, for a man who tried to play on both sides of the divide. Such writings now allowed Walsh to dramatise his life and recreate his narration in actual texts that were always, or nearly always, about himself; *he* could now be the continual object of his writing, and he was continually reassured that the reader would agree with this basic fact of life. Other individuals in these works were shaped to revolve around him and *his* knowledge of the secret history of the times. In short, it was a claim to his audience that you once thought my story was like this, but it wasn't really, in fact it was *really* like this. In doing so he gave the 'Noble reader', time to reflect on Walsh's dealings while still pleading his cause for: 'As truth is truth, those who persist therein are the Sons of God'.[85]

Any related actions given in such texts were to be read by his audience through Walsh's own self-image. So, in the course of this, we gradually see his recreation as the loyal, but essentially misunderstood secret servant of the crown. He was neither in the wrong nor really working for the rebel republic, he was a double agent, but in the best sense. Walsh also tried to do this by striking or undermining other forms of loyalty, that of Broghill, Bristol, Hyde, or Ormond. In the end all were occasionally disloyal and his was but one form of it, and then not the grandest or most wicked of disloyalties.

Lastly, Walsh frequently wrote in the third person. This signifier occurs in both manuscript and printed texts. In them he often refers to 'RW' or 'Sir Robert Walsh'. This implicit distancing of himself from his actual deeds enabled him as an author to use factual evidence which he could then mix together with fantasy; this was then repeated, exaggerated or plainly just re-written.

The chaotic agent and his Royalist identity

It has been argued that the idea of the early modern self-image can be seen as a:

> relation between those dimensions of experience that people describe as *internal* (conscious or unconscious thoughts feelings, beliefs, emotions, desires) and those they describe as *external* (speaking or writing, hating or loving, praying or blaspheming, laughing or crying, stealing or buying, and so on).[86]

This self-image was also linked to social groups and networks. Early modern identity therefore was ultimately the, 'self-conscious awareness of the complexity of community'.[87] Added to this was the early modern predilection for 'performance and rhetoric'.[88] A predilection which was a valuable asset for any spy.

Walsh's self-image was undoubtedly a chaotic and selfish one. We can find it in both manuscripts and public texts. In many senses Walsh was performing all of the time and, as we shall see, performing poorly for the most part. One view of himself, for example, is in a petition sent to Charles II in August 1658. Here Walsh lays stress upon 'zeal and innocency', his 'honour and honesty', as well as his loyalty. 'Some', noted Walsh, 'will say I am bold, but I have a clear conscience and perfect loyalty. . . . Pray consider me as a man and a Christian'. He is also clear that he was never self-serving and was not seeking absolution for 'Grace belongs to rogues and traitors and is not requisite to me'. He tried to situate himself as part of, 'a most perfect truth'.[89] Yet in his religious life, the mark of a seventeenth-century man, Walsh continually threw up a clouded image: 'I tould him [Thurloe] I was bred a papist, yt I had seene and heard of many religions, and was not for altogether as thereto resolved, wch to take'.[90]

If in his published texts Walsh took to creating self-images for a broader readership; what were his ultimate aims? In fact, Walsh's public text creation represented an attempt not just to create a more coherent narrative of his own rather incompetently managed life, but also a personal explanation – a publicised *mea culpa*. His texts of late 1679 and 1687 are undoubtedly attempts to enter this re-varnished public self into the public space and to provide support for his personal concepts of loyalty and honour. Context was also important in this case: one text emerged in the course of the Popish Plot and the exposure of Walsh's obscure double dealings with the informer Edmund Everard, the other in the reign of James II when he once again sought redemption with the Stuart regime.[91] Walsh was also keen in 1679 to reject the name of 'informer' by paying homage to the 'true liberty of a subject' to loyally enter into such discourses.[92] Ironically the books themselves, 'were taken in the Binder's House (about 2000 in number) and there held by the local constable of St Martins one Grey'. The latter, grumbled Walsh, sold, 'several of them for 3s a piece, without my privity, consent or order'.[93] Once more he had lost control of his history.

In 1687 Walsh's history was re-written yet again. In this case the events of 1655–57 were now re-orientated to enable Walsh to claim that in fact Ormond was always under the exiled king's orders in asking Walsh to, 'venture himself into England, and there use his Endeavour, in relation to what may be of use unto his Majesties interest and service'.[94] Nor was Walsh ever, 'pretending to Sollicite', for the lands he had lost, but in fact Cromwell, hearing he was actually working for the king, sent, 'four files of Musqueteers', to arrest him.[95]

Walsh re-casts his entrance into Cromwell's service by now relating the tale that it was rumoured that the Royalists had planned to assassinate Cromwell and the Protector had looked to some of those in the Tower to go undercover into Flanders to uncover the truth of the matter. Only now did Broghill come in to recruit Walsh and the latter only reluctantly agreed to go. It was then that other Royalists spread the mistaken rumours that Walsh had in fact been sent to Flanders to kill the exiled king. Walsh the undercover Royalist agent is thus created and presented to the public.

By this stage Walsh's shaping of his materials and his endless construction of versions of his past were solely for public consumption and interpretation and thereby he seems to have thought lay salvation.[96] Yet the preoccupations in his texts continue to show how much the text is, throughout, actually a performance. Walsh was continually acting the part of a loyal, but misunderstood subject and they constitute, through the language used, and through a negotiation of his troubled identity, a new image of this 'woeful knight'. We can, however, finally see Walsh in performance as others actually saw him by reflecting upon a manuscript text from 1679, which relates to events that occurred in December 1676, and in which he appears as a very 'woeful knight' indeed.[97]

We find Robert Walsh in 1676 in his declining years, lurking in public spaces such as the Blue Post Ordinary in Haymarket and the Starr in Fenchurch Street.

It may be argued that his views and techniques as a spy had not really changed from his earlier days discussed above. A government clerk called Lewis, who worked for the Treasury at Derby House, is the narrator of the events in this case. Lewis fell in with Walsh seemingly by chance. Yet it is a Walsh we recognise; one whose character traits John Thurloe may long ago have guessed at and which may well account for the secretary's ultimate rejection of the Irishman from his service. While Lewis gives us a somewhat melodramatic viewpoint, he does catch for us a final vision of the failed double agent in action. At times Walsh becomes almost a parody of himself: a roaring, rambling, whispering Irish gamester; sly, loquacious, pompous, and very untrustworthy. By this period the somewhat elderly blade, akin to other Restoration stage Irishmen of the day had apparently taken to crashing about the London scene with ever more unsuccessful plans from an ever fertile brain. At this stage it is not that clear who he was actually working for, but his methods in 1676 had clearly remained little changed from the earlier years of his career.

Lewis' tale begins in a public house, a regular haunt of spies, where Walsh with, 'much wine and wily caresses, pulling out a Purse full of Guinneys out of his fob', and, 'calling for fresh bottles of wine', took to indulging his victim with laughter, jokes, good fellowship and a promise of further meetings, hoping that he would be a suitable mark for his schemes.[98]

Moving on to the Starr inn a few days later, the drama continued with Mr Clifton, the owner of the pub or the 'Man of the house', innocently asking Lewis in front of his new friend: 'how the Little women did? 'Wheat, 'the knt startleing what, he maryed? Pox take you, blaming one for not telling him sooner'. Yet despite this miscalculation that Walsh was going to have his victim to himself, he was not dismayed: 'Come, said he, send for her'.[99] Lewis was eventually persuaded to do so and Walsh now found himself meeting Lewis's wife and mother. Walsh loudly swore he would be as a godfather to the young couple, 'Wherat my mother thanked him'. 'Judge the power of his badge' as Lewis later ironically pointed out.[100]

Of course more compliments followed from the Irishman and one suspects, as did Lewis at first, that perhaps Walsh was simply suggesting an assignation with his mother. 'Well Madam, quoth he to the mother, you & I must be better acquainted'.[101] Yet his plan seems not to have been so simple, for afterwards, taking Lewis 'aside', Walsh declared boldly, 'I doe be franck', and then he mentioned 'a piece of land in Ireland', talked of 'settleing . . . in England after all my Travells', and of 'marrying with some rich widow'. Lewis naturally demurred, for he was not, he said, 'a matchmaker' or a pimp! "Oh" sd . . . [Walsh] "you mistake me I mean your *mother*, to whom communicate the thing" . . . to recommend him to someone of her acquaintance instancing ye Lady Dawes'.[102]

Naturally the 'old woman' on being told this 'piece of folly' was angry, or having herself been mistaken with the previous flattery, had apparently thought she was on to a good thing and 'with indignation enough bidd me [Lewis] tell him [Walsh] that she scorn'd the Employ either on his or any others behalfe'; 'shee would not speak wth him, for she had heard he was a Cheat etc'. So even at this date Walsh's reputation and singular honour still preceded him. Sir Robert, however was nothing dismayed and was 'impatient "till he heard from ye old woman". "What good Tideings from my mother?", he called out to Lewis at yet another inevitable tavern meeting. Lewis' reply was that: "Shee seemed much concern'd at the vanity (as she tearmed it) of his desires, and withal bidd one tell him in as cleare and tart words as I could, that shee looked upon him . . . as one notorious dangerous by what she heard. At wch he dams & sincks her saying 'pox take ye old Presbyterian Judas, shee does me a kindness if she listed . . . hang her' " '![103]

Nevertheless, the tables began to turn as Lewis sought now to play Walsh along to find out what he really wanted. For after a while in their talk, Walsh at last came to the point. He wanted to know of Lewis' wages at Derby House: 'could you live upon it' he asked, 'I told him I made a shift'. 'then . . . [he] glides slyly upon an enquiry into the nature of ye Trust of our office; desiring to knowe how farr it, and that of the Treasury' went. Later still, in other meetings arranged between the pair at the Rhenish Wine House, or in his own lodgings near the Savoy, Walsh attempted to discover what Lewis knew of the 'secrets of the Nation' and how he could get him a better place, but Lewis eventually became troubled and baulked at this and finally ended the acquaintance with a knowing phrase: 'what you designe thereby aire at noe lesse then the leading one unto destruction'.[104]

Whereupon Robert Walsh, clumsy as ever in his dealings, drifted off to his next adventure. If this was really the level of his espionage technique then it is no wonder he faced continual failure. As Theophilus Lucas was to say ever 'since gaming is become a trade . . . adventurers thereat do not all ply upon the square' and Lewis's encounters with Walsh in the end merely finally confirm his inadequacies as a double agent.[105] Yet, for all of this, perhaps Walsh, because he fought so hard to do so, may still have the last word:

> Enemies enviously and ungroundedly he hath had, who are now disbanded into the other world, yet if any particular man carry any animosities against him, he knowing not of any ground or Subject he hath given, he is ready to satisfie any that may pretend to the contrary, leaving those who read this, to judge the hardness of the measure he hath met with.[106]

CHAPTER FOUR

Nathaniel Hooke and the Dynamics of Covert Operations in Eighteenth-century France

Daniel Szechi

Late in the evening of 11 March 1708 the inhabitants of the little Fife fishing port of Crail were confronted by a spectacle Scotland had not witnessed in over fifty years: an invasion fleet anchored in the Firth of Forth.[1] Three years of plotting, negotiations and covert preparations had finally come to fruition and nearly 5,000 heartily seasick French regular troops stood ready to land. The news spread like wildfire, and all over the country Jacobite nobles, lairds and gentlemen sharpened their swords, loaded their pistols and prepared to call out their tenants. The moment they had been waiting for, to strike a blow against the Union with England, and for King James 'VIII', the exiled Stuart claimant to the throne, had finally arrived.[2]

Or so it briefly appeared. For a Royal Navy squadron under the command of Sir George Byng was close behind the French fleet, and its admiral, Claude de Forbin, comte de Forbin, knew his ships, most of which were fast privateers conscripted for the mission and stripped of their heavy armaments to make room for the troops and supplies they were carrying, were not capable of fighting Byng's squadron. Forbin effectively had two choices: he could take his ships further up the Forth, beach them and add his crews to the invasion force, or he could run for it in the hope that his ships, heavily laden as they were, could still escape. He chose to run and successfully extracted all but one of his ships from the jaws of defeat. While Byng was busy capturing the *Salisbury*, an English prize taken by the French some time before, the rest of Forbin's fleet fled north.[3] There, off Aberdeenshire, Forbin, the army commander, Charles Auguste de Matignon, maréchal de Gacé, and the twenty-one year old Jacobite King James considered what to do next. Forbin's orders were to coordinate his landing of the troops with the Jacobites onshore, but he detected no friendly signals, which was not surprising given the filthy weather prevailing at the time and the fact that the Scots Jacobites expected him to land in the Forth or at Inverness. James begged to be landed under almost any circumstances, if necessary alone but for a small retinue of exiled Jacobite noblemen. Forbin, who well knew how fond his master, Louis XIV, was of the young Stuart prince, point blank refused and instead insisted on sailing north to attempt a landing in the Moray Firth. Bad weather prevented a landing there and a storm swept the French fleet back out into the North Sea.[4] By that point all hope of surprise was lost, the troops were in a wretched condition and the French and Jacobite officers were thoroughly demoralised. Without further argument Forbin took the fleet back to Dunkirk where the soldiers gratefully disembarked and the expedition was formally abandoned.[5] James VIII consoled himself by going off to campaign in Flanders with the main French army, while Forbin and de Gacé threw themselves into furious dispute with each other as to whether the army or the navy was to blame for the failure of the *Entreprise d'Écosse*.[6] The fallout from the interservice dispute was so bad that it was to be thirty-six years before the French military was willing to mount another attempt to invade the British Isles.[7]

Yet for all its last-minute failures of execution, the basic structure of, and preparation for, the Enterprise of Scotland were very well done indeed.[8] In 1708, in the opinion of at least some well informed historians, the Jacobites had a very real prospect of seizing control of the country.[9] This would probably have had a disastrous domino-effect from the point of view of the British state. French-backed Jacobite seizure of power in Scotland would immediately have derailed the British war-effort in Flanders (potentially opening the way to a French victory there), very likely have plunged the British Isles as a whole into civil war and in Scotland at least could have resulted in the restoration of the main (exiled) line of the Stuart dynasty – though how long it would have lasted is an open question. Not bad for the investment of less than 5,000 troops, some stripped-down privateers and a few shiploads of munitions. And the key protagonist in putting the whole operation together was a secret agent named Nathaniel Hooke.

In many respects Hooke was the archetype of the classic professional spy-cum-secret-agent of the age. Not only did he serve multiple masters at different times in different kingdoms, he did so with remarkable fidelity. More unusually, he managed to make his fortune while doing so. The French military may have come out of the '08 with its reputation in tatters; Hooke never looked back and he ended his life wealthy and full of honours. The story of how he got there is an epic and fascinating tale which will hopefully be told in full elsewhere; this essay will look in detail at the operation that made his fortune.[10] For there is much that the plotting, negotiation and politics behind the '08 can tell us about the problems of organising covert operations in the early modern era, and the conduct of Nathaniel Hooke well illustrates the way a resourceful agent could use even unsuccessful operations to advance his own career.

Nathaniel Hooke began his life in a place and at a time that was spiritually a world away from where he ended. He was born in 1664 in Dublin, the third son of John Hooke, a Nonconformist Protestant minister in Drogheda. His grandfather, Thomas Hooke, was a Dublin merchant and alderman and, more importantly from the young Nathaniel's point of view, a classic hard faced man who had done well out of the war. In Thomas Hooke's case this was the Great Civil War that wracked the British Isles from 1640 to 1653. As a strong Protestant, Thomas Hooke seems to have had no problem transferring his allegiance in the course of the war from Charles I to the king's rebellious Parliament and thence to the Lord Protector Oliver Cromwell. In the process he made a great deal of money supplying the Protestant forces fighting the Catholic Confederate rebels in Ireland, rose to the mayorality of Dublin and, as a zealous servant of the victorious cause, in the aftermath of the war was able to buy a goodly estate out of confiscated Catholic lands. The restoration of the monarchy in 1660 slowed, but did not halt, the rise in the family's fortunes, and despite occasional anti-monarchical grumblings the old man retained his aldermanic status and remained prosperous up to the time of his death in 1670.

Nathaniel's father was a minister of the Cromwellian state church, and refused to conform to the new (Anglican) religious establishment after 1660. He duly lost his benefice, which obliged him to abandon his vocation and set up as a merchant back in Dublin. John Hooke nonetheless seems to have passed on his strong religious convictions to his son Nathaniel, who was first educated by Nonconformist associates of his father's, and then more expensively at Kilkenny Grammar School (where he may have known Jonathan Swift) and Trinity College Dublin, emerging with a strong commitment to (Nonconformist) ministry. To this end, Nathaniel's family paid for him to transfer to Glasgow University in 1680, presumably on the assumption that he would find its strict Protestantism more congenial. The Bothwell Brig Covenanter/Presbyterian rising took place in southwest Scotland while he was there, and though we have no direct evidence of Nathaniel's involvement, he left soon afterwards to throw himself into radical English politics.[11]

By 1680 in England the Exclusion Crisis was at its height. Mass demonstrations, nationwide petitions and political confrontation between the king and his Parliaments were creating an explosive mix that appeared close to precipitating renewed civil war. This all stemmed from widespread apprehension in the political nation at the growing likelihood that Charles II, who was at least publicly an Anglican Protestant, would be succeeded by his openly Catholic brother James, duke of York. The Exclusionists (who were to transform themselves into the 'Whig' party in the early 1680s) were opposed to the supporters of the crown, who increasingly became known as the 'Tories' as the crisis unfolded. Both parties were anti-Catholic, but whereas the Tories believed the line of succession was sacrosanct and that the future James II could be effectively limited by laws and Parliaments, the Whigs contended that a Catholic king would soon find loopholes in any legal sanctions and would then dismantle the religious settlement and bring back popery (Catholicism). The only sure way to safeguard Protestantism in the British Isles, according to the Whigs, was to exclude all Catholics from inheriting the crown. Because the king had no legitimate children, however, in making this argument the Whigs opened up another question: if the future James II and VII was excluded, who should be next in line for the crown? James had two surviving Protestant daughters by his first marriage, Mary and Anne, and Mary was married to her cousin, William of Orange, but both daughters were (at this stage) resolutely standing by their father and his right of succession. Furthermore, William of Orange, *Stadthouder* (military commander in chief) of the Netherlands, who would also have been included in Mary's succession, had a bad reputation for authoritarianism which made many Whigs fear he might be as much of a threat in his own way as his father-in-law. By 1683 many Whigs were, therefore, looking to more radical alternatives: either the re-establishment of an English republic or the legitimation of Charles II's charismatic and ambitious bastard son, James Scott, duke of Monmouth.[12]

Nathaniel Hooke's role in all this is obscure and was undoubtedly marginal, but he was sufficiently committed to the Whig cause to leave Cambridge (whence he had moved from Glasgow to continue his education) to join other leading lights among the Whigs in exile in the Netherlands some time after 1682. His conduct there is again obscure, but he certainly drew sufficiently favourable attention among his fellow exiles and co-conspirators to attract the patronage of none other than Monmouth himself, who had appointed Hooke his personal chaplain by 1685. Hooke was accordingly a significant participant in the conspiracy underpinning Monmouth's rebellion, which broke out when the duke and a party of Whig exiles landed near Lyme Regis on 11 June 1685. As far as we know, Hooke had had no military training up to this point in his life, and he certainly played no part in the military events of the rising. Instead, he was secretly dispatched to London to prompt the Whig underground there to rise against the newly crowned King James II and VII. Meanwhile Monmouth and his army were totally defeated at Sedgemoor on 6 July, and the authorities were soon interrogating rebel prisoners with a view to unraveling the entire plot and rounding up the key conspirators. As a particularly well-placed, and probably very well-informed survivor, Hooke was hurriedly obliged to go into deep hiding, and we again lose sight of him for some time.[13]

Life underground, however, did not suit Hooke and he was soon looking for a way to make his peace with the government. After a brief, cruel period of exemplary retribution, James's government backed away from further persecution of the Whigs, and by 1687 had, indeed, reversed its former alliance with the Tories and the Church of England and was looking to the Whigs and their Nonconformist allies for help in packing a new Parliament.[14] James hoped to use such a compliant Parliament to pass a raft of legislation allowing religious toleration for all Christian confessions in England, an objective shared by many Nonconformists and Catholics. This eventually opened the way for Hooke to emerge from hiding, and on 13 July 1688 the government formally published his pardon. What happened next was much more unexpected than the timely submission of a former rebel plotter and Nonconformist minister: shortly after he was pardoned, Hooke converted to Catholicism.[15]

Hooke's reasons for such a *volte face* have been the subject of some debate. Was he sincere, or just looking to boost his career prospects under the Jacobite regime? He never suggested anything other than a genuine change of heart, though his new faith certainly did further his career under King James. Perhaps the proof of his sincerity is that while he was a prisoner of the Williamite regime in the early 1690s (at a time when the Jacobite and Catholic cause was doing very badly) he was given ample opportunity to recant his Catholicism, and promised patronage and favour if he did so.[16] Yet Hooke spurned the offer. Though he was apparently never a loud or particularly zealous Catholic, he was content to live and die in his new faith. In the short term this immediately benefited him: the same month as his pardon he was appointed a King's Messenger, which is to say an official courier and executive agent of the crown. William of Orange's invasion in November 1688, however, soon put an end to Hooke's career as a civil servant. James suffered a mental collapse in the face of widespread betrayal both within his cherished army and the royal family and fled to France in December.[17] There he recovered his equilibrium sufficiently to be able to go to Ireland to lead a Jacobite fightback against the Williamite revolution, and in his train came the former King's Messenger, Nathaniel Hooke.

Given his experience of conspiracy, knowledge of how to move around the country undetected and how to survive underground, Hooke was the obvious choice to undertake secret missions back to England, and he apparently initially acted as a courier between James and John Graham, viscount Dundee, the leader of the first Jacobite rising in Scotland. By June 1689, though, Hooke was back in England conveying a bundle of secret commissions to James's supporters in the northwest. Unfortunately for him, however, we know about this particular mission because he was detected and arrested by the authorities at Whitehaven. His next stop was the Tower of London. Once again Hooke was regarded as a potentially high-value source of intelligence, and had the honour of being questioned not just by his immediate captors and other magistrates, but also by Secretary of State Charles Talbot, duke of Shrewsbury, and King William himself. He did not break and he refused to defect to the Williamite side, and in January 1690 his elder brother John, a successful lawyer in London, successfully filed a writ of *habeas corpus*. Released on bail, Hooke took the first opportunity to return to his master in Ireland. There can be no clearer indication that, as far as he was concerned, his die was cast.[18]

It was apparently at that point that Hooke moved over from the civilian to the military side. By mid-1690 he was being described as 'Major' Hooke of the Queen's (Piers Butler, viscount Galmoy's) regiment of horse, though, as far as can be made out from the available evidence, he was still mainly working as a Jacobite envoy and secret agent. Hooke nonetheless fought at the battle of the Boyne on 1 July 1690 and remained behind in Ireland serving in his military capacity after James fled back to France.[19] Under the articles of Limerick, which negotiated an end to the fighting in Ireland in autumn 1691, all serving Jacobite officers and men still in the country were offered a choice: they could accept amnesty and swear an oath of allegiance to the Williamite regime. Thereby they would regain both their property and the right to return peacefully to their pre-war lives and occupations throughout the British Isles. Alternatively, they could forfeit all of the above and be conveyed, under flag of truce, to France to continue the war there. Such agreements were not uncommon in contemporary European warfare and were known as 'granting the honours of war'.[20] Despite the fact that relatively few of the Jacobite troops were professional soldiers before 1689, the majority – some 14,000 men – opted to go to France in the confident expectation that they would soon be returning to the British Isles in the triumphant van of a Franco-Jacobite invasion, and among their number was Major Nathaniel Hooke.[21]

In France the unit in which Hooke was an officer saw extended military service in Flanders between 1691 and the war's end in 1697, though we know little of Hooke's part in those campaigns apart from a mention of his having been one of the Jacobite officers assigned to the invasion force for England gathered in northern France in 1692, at which time he watched from the cliffs above La Hoogue as the Royal Navy and its Dutch allies comprehensively defeated the French navy. Hooke was, though, apparently still episodically ordered away from his military duties to undertake secret missions to the British Isles. In 1695–6 he was one of several Jacobite agents involved in setting up the Fenwick Plot, a conspiracy for a rising in southern England which was to be supported by a sudden French invasion of the Channel coast. This was the heart of the whole project, but his centrality was obscured by the government's discovery of a side-plot hatched by a marginal group among the conspirators which aimed at kidnapping or assassinating King William. As far as is known, Hooke was not privy to this side-plot, but he was nonetheless named by the English government as one of those involved. In any event, he was either already back in France, or successfully evaded capture and returned there shortly afterwards, because he saw out the rest of the war on active service with his regiment.[22]

The Peace of Ryswick, completed and signed by the warring parties in 1697, immediately brought on a savage retrenchment of French public financing, and expensive luxuries like King James's 'English' (actually overwhelmingly Irish) army, which was entirely dependent on French subventions, were natural candidates for the cuts. Louis XIV kept the nucleus of an Irish brigade on the regular strength of the French army, but the bulk of the Jacobite soldiery was forthwith discharged, including, it would appear, Nathaniel Hooke.[23] Like many other Irish officers and soldiers he seems to have been reduced to hanging around the exiled court at St Germain-en-Laye for several years, surviving on whatever pittance James II and VII's shadow government could spare him.[24] There was little or no activity in the Jacobite underground over the same period, so his services as a secret agent were no more required than his abilities as a military officer. The net effect of these dreary interwar years seems ultimately to have been to push Hooke towards seeking his fortune elsewhere. He obtained his formal release from James's service in August 1701, shortly before the king's death, and by October was in the Netherlands on his way north to look for employment, presumably of a straightforwardly military kind, in Scandinavia, where war had recently broken out between Sweden and a coalition of its regional enemies. But then a better opportunity beckoned. For there he encountered an old friend and relation, John Cutts, Lord Gowran, who was busy organising the recruitment of foreign troops suitable to make up the English contingent in any renewed war between France and the Grand Alliance.[25]

Hooke shrewdly perceived that he might be able to use the well-connected Cutts to establish a back channel to the upper levels of the English political and military establishment which might be useful for French diplomacy during the gathering crisis over the Spanish Succession.[26] In particular, Cutts was close to John Churchill, at that point earl, soon to be duke, of Marlborough and one of the so-called 'Duumvirs' (the other being Sidney Godolphin, earl Godolphin) who were to dominate England's government in the early years of Queen Anne's reign. Hooke, who ran a nice line in plausibility, affability and charm, also managed to ingratiate himself with Alexander Stanhope, the English Ambassador to the Netherlands, and sundry lesser figures associated with the government at Westminster who were passing back and forth between England and the Netherlands at this time. He then carefully compiled a long, thoughtful memorandum on what he had discovered and the potential opportunities it offered and sent it off to Jean-Baptiste Colbert de Croissy, marquis de Torcy, Louis XIV's secretary of state for foreign affairs. Torcy was impressed, and encouraged Hooke to develop his connections further, with a view to scouting the possibility of secretly negotiating a deal that would avert the coming war. Hooke diligently obeyed, and by the end of 1703, when he and Torcy deemed it necessary he extract himself before he was compromised or apprehended, he had won the confidence and approval of the French minister.[27]

This was to prove the making of Hooke's fortune. For a foreigner to rise high in the service of France at the beginning of the eighteenth century he had to have a well-connected patron and come from a suitably noble background. Winning Torcy's favour gained Hooke the first of these, and he subsequently manufactured the second.[28] Thereafter, given that in his own way Torcy was something of a meritocrat, as long as Hooke served his master diligently and well he could expect a steady improvement in his fortunes, as in fact proved to be the case. In the first instance Torcy's influence secured Hooke promotion to the French equivalent of the Lieutenant-Colonelcy of the Regiment de Sparre.[29] This was originally a unit raised in Sweden for French service, but by the early eighteenth century had become primarily a repository for adventurers, deserters and cutthroats of all nationalities. As such, it was a relatively low status, second tier regiment, yet that does not diminish its importance for Hooke. Despite the fact that he was not yet a French subject or recognised as a nobleman (that was not to come until 1706) he was henceforth on the regular French army payroll and promotion ladder. As long as he well minded who he now served, his prospects were far better than they had been in the service of King James – something Hooke was never to forget.

His mission in the Netherlands had also brought Hooke into contact with a number of Scots officers in English and Dutch service and he appears soon to have recognised that in the gathering political crisis brewing over contemporary Anglo-Scots relations lay the seeds of his further advancement.[30] Hooke, like many others, such as the Jacobite Regent, Queen Mary of Modena, and the papal nuncio in Paris, Cardinal Filippo Antonio Gualterio, was taken in by the cunning and plausible Simon Fraser, Lord Lovat, a rogue of the first water, and seems like many of his contemporaries to have initially accepted Lovat's account of the state of Scotland as gospel.[31] Hooke, however, had the sense to gather information from other sources to add to whatever Lovat could give him, and thus by the time Lovat was exposed for the villain he was and incarcerated in the Bastille,[32] Hooke had built up a relatively solid basic understanding of the political situation in Scotland and could present himself (at least to Torcy) as something of an in-house expert on the subject.[33] This was particularly important given the situation in which France found itself in 1704. By then the War of Spanish Succession, which had formally broken out in 1702, was already going badly. France had not recovered economically from the huge effort necessary to fight the previous war to a draw, and went into the new war with the additional burden of having, effectively, to prop up the enfeebled Spanish empire, now ruled by Louis XIV's grandson, Philip V (whose succession to the Spanish throne was the ostensible cause of the war).[34] To add to France's woes, in Flanders the French armies had found themselves struggling to hold back a large Allied army commanded by Marlborough, who was a much more formidable opponent than his predecessor, the at best average King William, and in Italy the French armies and their allies were being trounced by Habsburg forces led by the talented Prince Eugene of Savoy. Rounding off this sombre picture, Portugal and Savoy had defected to the Allies, leaving France only one substantive ally of its own beyond Spain: Bavaria, and revolt was flaring up in the Cevennes region of southern France among the savagely persecuted Huguenot (Protestant) community.[35] During the campaigning season in 1704 the situation further worsened when Marlborough invaded Bavaria, decisively defeated a Franco-Bavarian army at Blenheim in August and drove the Elector of Bavaria, Maximilian II Emmanuel, and the survivors of his army into France as penniless refugees.[36] In such circumstances Louis XIV and his ministers were likely to be interested in any proposal that might release France from the strategic vice in which it was trapped and the concomitant threat of a comprehensive military defeat in the war as a whole.

Enter Nathaniel Hooke. He first penned a long memorandum proposing an invasion of Scotland in late 1703.[37] This was read to Louis and the royal council, and seems to have made a good impression, in that it was remembered in the following year as France's military situation worsened. Hooke, though, faced a structural problem. Information from, and invasion projects targeting, the British Isles were de facto not part of the remit of any French ministry, but instead of a French ally: the exiled Jacobite court at St Germain. The exiled Stuarts had, moreover, been exploring the possibilities of a rising in the British Isles since the outbreak of hostilities, and by the time Hooke was handing in his memorandum to the royal council, already had agents assessing the situation in England and Scotland.[38] St Germain's problem in a French political context was that the Jacobite government in exile had built up a reputation among Louis XIV's ministers for being run by pathetically incompetent second raters and for being riddled with spies and traitors.[39] All that kept it on the

French payroll was Louis and the royal family's fondness for the exiled Stuarts and the lingering hope that the Jacobite connection might come in useful some day.[40] It is worth noting in this context that while there were inevitably security breaches and failures in the underground movement directed by St Germain, these were no worse than might have been expected given its need to operate using zealots, enthusiasts and volunteers who were under constant, vigilant surveillance by the post-revolutionary regime in the British Isles. Even the security surrounding the most successful conspiracy of the age, that leading to the revolution of 1688, was breached on more than one occasion, and thus it is not surprising that the Jacobite underground likewise suffered episodic penetration and failures.[41] The Jacobite court had also regained some of its fire following the death of James II and VII, whose never more than mediocre abilities had declined in his final years and who had become more and more focused on his religious duties and the need to make his peace with his God.[42] The regent for the new Jacobite king, James III and VIII, was his mother, Queen Mary of Modena, who had matured into a shrewd politician well able to handle both the political factions at St Germain and the French court at Versailles.[43] She also gave renewed purpose and direction to the Jacobite movement as a whole. Hooke thus faced a major obstacle: how was he going to make Scotland his special project when in French institutional terms it already belonged to someone else?

Hooke's major advantage here was that by 1704 he was very clearly Torcy's man and a senior field officer in the French army.[44] He traded this up by turning his old Jacobite connections and background into a French asset. Thus he (not necessarily insincerely) pandered to the French ministers' suspicions of St Germain by endorsing their misgivings about security at the Jacobite court, while deliberately and regularly emphasising his own loyalty to France and Louis XIV in his letters and memoranda.[45] Hooke also successfully petitioned to become a naturalised French subject in 1706 and made sure that his undoubted courage, diligence and efficiency as the field commander of the Regiment de Sparre became well known. He was still casually referred to as 'English' by French ministers and courtiers, but by 1707 it is fair to say that he had built up a reputation for being trustworthy, effective and above all loyal to France.[46] At the same time, Hooke was well aware that he needed the approval of St Germain.[47] Unless France launched a massive invasion of the British Isles, with an army of upwards of 20,000 men – a virtual impossibility during the War of Spanish Succession – any French landing needed the support of the Jacobite underground, in the shape of not just thousands, but tens of thousands, of Jacobite volunteers. And the Jacobite court would only deliver the support of its adherents (the only military asset it possessed) if it agreed with the plan for the invasion and was persuaded there was a real prospect of success. More immediately, if Hooke was to move around unnoticed in the British Isles and expected to meet and negotiate with the potential leaders of any rebellion there he needed St Germain's co-operation and endorsement. He had, therefore, to play a careful game, convincing both his French masters and the Jacobites that in his heart of hearts he was their man and worth supporting.

Hooke managed this with aplomb. While he was lobbying influential bureaucrats and generals to support his Scots project, the Jacobite court was making its own proposals to the French government.[48] Charles Middleton, earl of Middleton and the senior Jacobite Secretary of State, in June 1704 submitted a proposal for a French invasion of England and/or Scotland based on multiple agents' reports and a careful assessment of the situation.[49] But it got nowhere. None of the French ministers were willing to take it up. When Hooke, however, proposed an exploratory mission to Scotland by someone whose judgement the French government felt it could rely on, he met a much more favourable response.[50] Circumstances had admittedly changed for the worse since the Franco-Bavarian defeat at Blenheim in August, but approval of the mission was relatively quickly forthcoming. The only question remaining was who would be the best man for the job? The mission obviously required someone who could speak fluent English, knew how to move around the British Isles undetected, was senior enough in the French military or government hierarchy to be taken seriously by the leaders of the Jacobite underground and yet was felt to be absolutely sound by Louis XIV and his ministers. To succeed, the mission also needed the full co-operation of St Germain, and while they were undoubtedly happy to find the French showing any interest in a Scots project and were bound to help facilitate the operation, they were much more likely to exert themselves if they believed the envoy was secretly one of their own. The pool of potential candidates accordingly cannot have been large; indeed, it probably consisted of just one man: Nathaniel Hooke, and he duly departed for Scotland in June 1705.[51]

What he found there was from his point of view a frustratingly fluid situation. There were two opposed political coalitions: the 'Court' and the 'Country'. The Court party had one clear objective: to persuade the Scots Parliament to accept the Hanoverian succession. To this end it was willing either to do deals within Scots politics that would leave Scotland nominally independent, but tied to the same succession as England, or take a more radical approach and negotiate a Parliamentary Union between the two kingdoms, which would achieve the same end in terms of the succession, but was seen by many Scots as something greatly to be desired for religious and economic reasons. The Country party was loosely composed of magnate factions, principled individuals primarily motivated by patriotic principles and Jacobites who saw the crisis as both symptomatic of everything they hated about the post-Revolutionary world and as a golden opportunity for a counter-revolution.[52] Scotland was also riven by deep religious divisions, not just between the Protestant majority and the tiny Catholic minority, but within Protestantism, and this was in many respects the key to Scottish politics in an age where religion and politics were inextricably intertwined. The Jacobites were overwhelmingly Episcopalians, who believed in a hierarchical church similar to the Church of England. This was the form of Kirk government that had prevailed in 1688, and was overthrown as part and parcel of the Revolution. The Court and proponents of the Union were mainly Presbyterian in religion, adhering to the new order in the Kirk imposed in the 1690s. Yet some Episcopalians were pro-Union for economic or personal reasons, and some Presbyterians were bitterly opposed to any closer union with England, fearing the purity of the Kirk might be compromised by association with the Church of England's 'white popery'.[53] To best serve France and himself, Hooke needed to persuade sufficient elements within this mix to take up arms against the Scots government and/or the possibility of union with England to make their rebellion a major problem for the English government at Westminster. France's situation, however, meant that there were few military assets that could be redeployed to support a Scots uprising. His instructions from the king and his ministers, indeed, were absolutely clear on this score: once he established that there was a body of Scots genuinely in a mood to rebel he was to work on reducing their demands, 'by degrees', to as little as France could get away with.[54] This effectively left Hooke playing not just a double, but a triple or even quadruple game, though the central thrust was clear: for strategic reasons a Scots rebellion would be very helpful for France, and engineering one would be very helpful in advancing the career of Nathaniel Hooke.

The corollary was that throughout his negotiations with various Scots political leaders in 1705 Hooke was looking for commitment to the proposal for a rebellion from as many of them as possible on any grounds whatsoever. Thus he was willing several times to go through the tedious rigmarole of meeting James Hamilton, duke of Hamilton, late at night in a pitch-dark room in Holyrood Palace (so the duke could swear that he had never seen Hooke), to explore the possibility that the ambitious Hamilton might be willing to take up arms to put himself on the throne of Scotland.[55] In like fashion, he was very interested in Presbyterians who might be persuaded to oppose a union of the kingdoms in arms for religious reasons, despite the fact that such extreme elements within Presbyterianism were as hostile to the exiled dynasty as they were to the idea of closer association with England. To make himself acceptable to these Presbyterians Hooke even ensured that his accreditation nowhere mentioned the exiled Stuarts, only claiming that Louis was sympathetic to proposals for restoring the liberty and independence of Scotland.[56] Predictably, however, Hamilton proved to be a broken reed. What he was primarily interested in was securing French money to fund his political manoeuvring (and pay off some of his huge debts) and for France and St Germain to instruct the Scots Jacobites slavishly to follow wherever he led, thus aggrandising himself politically (and raising the price Westminster would have to pay to buy him off, assuming that was his hidden intent).[57] The extreme Presbyterians Hooke was never able to sound out himself because he became in effect a prisoner of the Jacobites.

This is not to suggest that brevet Colonel Nathaniel Hooke of the army of the Most Christian King of France, Louis XIV, was incarcerated in chains in a cell. But he was without doubt closely trammeled throughout his time in Scotland. The Jacobite underground had a number of different strands, but the most important at this time was a Lowland network organised and directed by a group who styled themselves, 'the Juncto'. This consisted of Anne Drummond, dowager countess of Erroll, her son, Charles Hay, earl of Erroll, William Keith, earl Marischal, David Murray, viscount Stormont and Charles Home, earl of Home.[58] It was this network that arranged for Hooke to be guided in disguise from place to place, and arranged for him to stay in safe houses in Edinburgh and elsewhere. They were the ones, too, who set up meetings with both members of their own network and other Jacobite groups outwith it. They were also the ones who negotiated with him at length while they had him under their control.[59] The upshot of all of which was that they convinced him that they, and the real, committed Jacobites more generally, were the only ones worth doing business with.[60] This was not deceiving Hooke. Hamilton and the extreme Presbyterians were highly unlikely to deliver the result that Louis and his ministers wanted, and in Hamilton's case Hooke soon recognised that.[61] Despite their differences the Jacobites were the best prospect for a revolt. Yet acceptance of this put the Juncto and its adherents in a stronger bargaining position. If they were the only game in town, Hooke, France and St Germain had to be prepared to accommodate their aspirations and objectives. The Juncto, moreover, recognised this, and though they sought to persuade Hooke that they were definitely willing to rise, they committed themselves to nothing in terms of times and places. Detailed negotiations were left to the envoy they agreed to send to France in the autumn of 1705.[62] In effect, the Juncto kept its options open. They proved to Hooke that they could rebel if they reached a sufficiently good deal with France, but implicitly left open the possibility of continuing to battle any union with

England by conventional politics. France, in other words, was not going to get what it wanted for nothing. Hooke now had to sell the need to make a deal with the Jacobites to his masters back home.

Never a good sailor, Hooke returned to France after another miserable voyage and set about composing a report on his mission.[63] The final result was a carefully crafted and highly informative memorandum directed to Torcy and Michel Chamillart, the Minister of War, but ultimately intended for the king and the royal council (to whom it was read on 8/19 October 1705).[64] Hooke's trademark as a French secret agent was always his dispassionate and careful analysis of the people and situations in which he found himself, and his memorandum was a *tour de force* in this respect.[65] Suffice it to say that it would have been difficult to have read and understood it and not be convinced that the only option left was to deal with the Juncto Jacobites rather than Hamilton or anyone else. The only questions were the price and the timing. Which was where the project went awry. Contemporary armies usually suspended military operations between the months of November and March. This was for purely practical reasons to do with the fact that troops camping out under canvas at that time of year tended to die in droves, of sickness and cold, and their horses needed to be moved closer to stockpiles of hay lest they starve to death in the open country. During this closed season the governments of Europe typically recruited their military units up to strength, replaced lost or damaged equipment and moved them to winter quarters in towns and cities close to where they would be campaigning next season. This meant that strategic decisions as to where to launch major offensives the following year were usually made the preceding October or November. But Hooke arrived back only in mid-September,[66] the Juncto Jacobites had not yet reached a firm treaty with the French and would not do so until their emissary arrived in France and there were many other pressing calls on France's military planners. Hooke did his best to get the Juncto to hurry up, but as Anne Erroll explained in a letter to Queen Mary of Modena: 'where many is to be managed, the slow must in some things be humoured as well as the forward encouraged.'[67] The Juncto's envoy, Charles Fleming, brother of the earl of Wigton, at last fully instructed by his principals, only finally set sail from Aberdeen for France on 9 November.[68] Cross winds, further delays and, finally, interception by a Spanish privateer out of Ostend meant that he did not arrive in a French-held port until 19 December. By then the window of opportunity had closed. There would be no Enterprise of Scotland in 1706.

To make matters worse, fearing that the privateer about to intercept his ship was an Allied vessel, Fleming had dumped his formal accreditation and papers from the Juncto into the sea.[69] Hooke could vouch for him, but it cast a shadow over Fleming's *bona fides* that those who were sceptical about a Scottish expedition were happy to exploit, and though Fleming did his best to convey his friends' good intentions and get things moving, the whole project stalled.[70] The fundamental political problem facing Hooke and Torcy was that the army and navy did not want to mount a Scottish expedition. By 1705 Louis and his ministers all recognised that France was facing catastrophic defeat. Despite their best endeavours the French army could only muster about three quarters of the strength it had deployed in the Nine Years War, it had already been driven out of southern Germany and Italy, was on the defensive in Flanders and was fighting against a wave of major revolts convulsing Spain.[71] The navy had been defeated in two major battles and was so short of funding that its capital ships could afford only limited operations. The upshot was that the Allies dominated the sea lanes.

All of which might seem to suggest that the French government had no choice but to commit itself to some kind of radical military venture that might turn the situation around. And a successful Scots expedition would almost certainly have done so. If, say, the French invasion had triggered a rising by 20–30,000 Scots it would have produced a credit crisis in England (as actually happened in 1708), forced the withdrawal of most, if not all, of the English contingent in the Allied army in Flanders and probably the recall of Marlborough to command a new English conquest of Scotland.[72] Even if the Scots were promptly defeated, the English war effort would have been profoundly weakened and dislocated and France's armies would have had the advantage in Flanders for at least one campaigning season. If the Scots managed to avoid defeat for a year or two, diverting England's military resources to the extent of effectively eliminating the English contribution to the Grand Alliance, there was a distinct possibility of France triumphing so far as to be able to dictate a peace to its enemies. So why were the French army and navy opposed to the Enterprise of Scotland projected by Hooke?

As far as Chamillart and the army were concerned it was foolhardy adventurism. The army already had insufficient men to maintain its field strength, never mind its garrisons, in the major theatres of the war. The likeliest outcome of the Enterprise of Scotland was that the troops committed to the expedition would be lost. Worse, if it succeeded for a time, reinforcements would very likely be demanded by the field commanders in Scotland and thus it would become yet another theatre of war draining France's non-existent reserves. For sure the Scots rebels' need for modern armaments would put a fresh strain on France's war industries, which were already straining to meet the demand.[73] Better, in Chamillart's opinion, to stick to conventional, lower risk operations. In the final analysis, defeat in Scotland would be the end for the troops concerned, who would have nowhere to escape to; (another) defeat in Flanders or Spain at least left the possibility of rallying the survivors, reforming the units and eventually retrieving the situation.

For the navy and its minister, Jérôme Phelypaux, comte de Pontchartrain, a Scots expedition was equally unwelcome, though for very different reasons. By 1705 the French war at sea was for the most part already being carried on by the private sector, in the form of syndicates of merchants who financed commerce raiding by French privateers because they could no longer trade overseas owing to the Allies' naval supremacy.[74] Many members of the French nobility, including Pontchartrain, also invested in this *guerre de corse*.[75] Hence, if the navy was obliged to put together an invasion fleet, it would have to conscript privateers to carry the troops and their supplies. Most of the big warships had been laid up and there was not the money, men or resources to make them seaworthy in time. Not only would the conscription of the privateers disrupt the profitable operation of the *guerre de corse*, it would also destroy the internal credit of the privateering system.[76] Pontchartrain had in effect licensed merchant syndicates to wage war on behalf of France. If he confiscated their prime assets, their warships, and – even worse – they were lost or damaged (not at all an unlikely prospect during landing operations off the coast of Scotland), the syndicates would be very loath to renew their commitment to the war even if they could afford to do so.[77] Again, for certain, if the expedition succeeded for a time it would require the constant diversion of Pontchartrain's scanty naval assets to convey reinforcements and supplies into Scotland. Unsurprisingly, neither the army nor the navy was at all enthusiastic about the Enterprise of Scotland.

Thus the project stalled in 1706 and there was nothing Hooke, Fleming, St Germain or the Juncto Jacobites could do to get it moving again until the end of the campaigning season. Hooke gave up and rejoined his regiment in Flanders.[78] Perversely, however, the course of events in 1706 made a Scottish expedition considerably more likely. In Flanders Marlborough was smashingly victorious at Ramillies and followed up by capturing a clutch of major fortresses, thereby knocking a major hole in France's northern defences, and in Italy Eugene routed the French at Turin and drove the remnants of the Franco-Spanish army out of Italy.[79] There was now a distinct possibility that France itself might be invaded in both north and south. The wave of revolts in Spain had also been incorporated into a major Allied effort to dethrone Philip V, who was only sustained by draining French troops from other theatres and pouring them into Spain. Now more than ever France needed something dramatic to retrieve its military fortunes, and the royal council seems naturally to have gravitated back to the Scots project. Reports out of

Scotland also looked promising. When they were revealed late in the summer of 1706, the terms of the proposed union with England gave rise to anger among large and important sections of the Scots population. When the Scots Parliament met and it became apparent that the terms themselves (which, despite the popular protests, had a substantial body of support in the country), a bit of judicious bribery and some old-fashioned political arm-twisting were likely to deliver a Parliamentary majority in favour of the Union, there was a surge of anti-Union rioting in Edinburgh, Glasgow and other major towns.[80] Which all seemed to suggest that the Scottish moment had arrived. Hooke, who had spent the campaigning season in Flanders and been wounded at the siege of Menin, was to head a military support team to be thrown into Scotland in early 1707 in advance of the French invasion.[81] This was to consist of a handful of native Scots officers seconded from their French regiments and a couple of shiploads of arms and ammunition.[82] It was hoped that Hooke could use these to precipitate the Scottish rising that France and the Juncto Jacobites had been negotiating for over a year, and open the way for a follow-up French invasion of the country.

There might even have been some prospect of success (at least in terms of getting a rising going), given the mood of much of the Scottish population in early 1707, but Hooke then ran into two major roadblocks: Chamillart got cold feet again and St Germain became suspicious of France's motives. As we have already seen, Chamillart was never keen on a Scots operation, and he now chose to demand verification of the details of what the Jacobites had promised in terms of support. Another envoy was to be sent to Scotland to look into the matter before any final decision about the Enterprise of Scotland was taken.[83] Hooke was unhappily pressed into service, only to find that St Germain feared there was a secret plan to use the Scots Jacobites as a diversion and then abandon them to the tender mercies of the incoming British government. Queen Mary of Modena and her ministers promptly warned the Scots Jacobites not to stir unless they were assured of French support, and refused to give Hooke their authorisation to set off, command or in any way precipitate a Scots rising while on his 'fact-finding' mission.[84] Hooke did his best to get out of the job, but when directly ordered to undertake it he once again threw himself into making it a success.

This was the genesis of his second visit to Scotland, the mission that resulted in the attempted invasion of March 1708. In many respects it took the same form as his first mission in 1705, but the dynamics on both ends of the negotiations were notably different on the second occasion and therein lay its more positive outcome, from the point of view of France and the Scots Jacobites. At the Jacobite end, the Union that they had so feared and opposed had actually come to pass. They were accordingly angry and, to a certain extent, embarrassed.[85] Over the autumn and winter of 1706–7 they had been comprehensively outmanoeuvred by the Court and the Scottish Whigs, betrayed (again) by Hamilton and had signally failed to capitalise on popular outrage against the Union to stop it in its tracks.[86] A French invasion allied to a Jacobite rising was, they believed, their last chance to retrieve the situation. On the French side the campaigning season had begun well, with a great victory over the Allies at Almansa in Spain in April.[87] Prince Eugene was, however, poised to invade southern France and besiege the French naval base at Toulon (an operation that eventually resulted in the destruction of the French Mediterranean fleet), and the dearth of military manpower and economic resources to support the war was steadily growing worse.[88] Both sides thus had considerable incentive to reach an agreement, and Hooke was well placed to broker it.

Hooke nevertheless did not want the job by this stage, and it is, perhaps, a mark of his professionalism that he carried it off as well as he did. Once again, what the French government was principally interested in was as much rebellion as they could get with as little investment of resources on their part as possible. Hooke was also instructed to assess the military and logistical infrastructure of Scotland with regard to the degree of opposition a French-backed Jacobite revolt would face, the number of men it could mobilise and whether or not it could be self-sustaining economically.[89] He fulfilled his remit on every count. Landing at Slains Castle on 10 April after a frustrating month at Dunkirk waiting for contrary winds to change, Hooke appeared to entrust himself once again to Anne Erroll and the Juncto.[90] They received him warmly, apparently assuming that he was sympathetic to their plight and would be willing to enable them to subvert the intent of his mission, i.e. that he would simply go through the motions and return a warmed-over version of his previous report. Hooke, however, took a much more hard-headed approach. He accepted a briefing from Anne Erroll, then proceeded in effect to check what she had told him through antithetical sources. The Juncto Jacobites were not the only strand to Scottish Jacobitism. There was also Hamilton, who claimed to be a Jacobite, and his connection of kinsmen, clients and friends, and, too, there was a parallel, but associated, Catholic Jacobite network.[91] The Hamilton connection was quickly exposed as a broken reed from a French point of view. The duke claimed to be too ill actually to meet Hooke, and when Hooke sent him Chamillart's list of formal queries, Hamilton deliberately tried to sabotage the negotiations by demanding so many troops and other resources as effectively to block further progress. Hooke's response was forthright: 'I treated this response with ridicule,' he coolly recorded in his final report.[92] Hooke also established that Hamilton's connection was in disarray, and that individuals within it, such as William Livingstone, Viscount Kilsyth and George Lockhart of Carnwath were prepared to commit themselves to the Juncto's plan even if Hamilton refused to participate.[93] He then wrote Hamilton off and moved on.[94] Travelling around Scotland, Hooke also took a close look at both the Catholic Jacobite network and – albeit indirectly – at the extreme, southwestern Presbyterians whom Elizabeth Howard, Duchess of Gordon, had been sounding out with a view to an alliance in the event of a national rising against the Union. The Catholics he found to be fully committed to the Juncto's plan, but too few to be more than an adjunct to a larger uprising.[95] The extreme Presbyterians of the southwest he (probably mistakenly) believed to be similarly committed, but again too few to go it alone or even take the lead. In the end to, 'make the design more general', and bring in, 'the most powerful lords in Scotland,' there was no alternative to dealing with the leaders of the Episcopalian Jacobites.[96] In the course of his travels he met eight noblemen specifically committed to the Juncto, saw pledges from others and was introduced at various points to many more, who did not know specifically who he was or the remit of his mission, but expressed their willingness to rise against the Union, and he was assured by intermediaries that the Highland clans were on board.[97] Having thus established beyond doubt that the Juncto was the dominant strand in the Scots Jacobite movement, Hooke cautiously moved into the negotiation phase.

This was always going to be difficult. For professional and personal reasons, Hooke wanted the negotiations to be a success. Yet he was well aware that Chamillart and Pontchartrain would seize on any concession or demand that might be viewed as 'excessive' to sink the whole project. His instructions also indicated he should again beat down the aid the Scots Jacobites could expect to the absolute minimum France could get away with.[98] The Juncto Jacobites had also been forewarned by St Germain to be sure that France was truly committed before they acted (an injunction of which Hooke was aware by the time of the negotiations), and had a good sense of France's dire strategic situation, notwithstanding recent successes in Spain. A good deal of verbal sparring duly followed. The Scots team consisted of two brothers of John Murray, duke of Atholl: Lord James Murray of Dowally and James Murray, baron Nairn, who represented him throughout the process, plus Stormont, James Ogilvie of Boyn and Patrick Lyon of Auchterhouse. This core group at various times called in other respected figures within the movement, such as James Graham, James VII's former Solicitor-General, for consultation.[99] Technically, Hooke succeeded in committing Louis XIV to nothing specific; the final document signed by the Jacobite negotiators, representatives of the rest of the Juncto network and the Catholic Jacobite group leaves the actual numbers of troops and armaments the French were to dispatch to Scotland to the discretion of the French government.[100] The Jacobite team nonetheless made it manifestly clear that they expected about 5,000 men, arms for 20,000 more and a war treasury commensurate with the same. It does not take much parsing to get the hint that, if France could not provide that level of support, the Jacobites would have to reconsider their options. Interestingly, this was in the same region as proposals made by the same group as early as 1704.[101] Hooke presented it as a negotiating success to his masters, but de facto he does not appear to have moved the Scots Jacobites much from their original demands. Nonetheless, he returned to France in very good odour. He brought with him signed commitments to revolt from a substantial tranche of the Lowland Scots nobility, a similar commitment from the Jacobite Highland clans, and the bones of a plan that depended on throwing a relatively small invasion force into Scotland.[102] Dire as its situation was (and *pace* Chamillart), France could probably spare 5,000 troops – the *sine qua non* of the whole Enterprise of Scotland – and the likely strategic impact was full of promise.

Hooke got back to France on 6 June 1707, and quickly threw himself into composing his report for Torcy and the royal council, which he completed on 28 June. He was completely convinced of the viability of the project by this stage, and that it was a potential war-winner for France, as he indicated in the first letters he wrote when he arrived back in France.[103] To keep St Germain cooperative he presented his report with a covering note to Torcy suggesting that he should write a separate, redacted version for St Germain, for, as he delicately put it, 'there are many things [in the report] that are not of a nature to be communicated to the King of England [James III]'.[104] To reassure Chamillart, he wrote an accurate abridgement of the whole memorandum, but added a few lines to underscore the significance of what he had found in Scotland. The Scots were ready, had committed themselves, and if France backed them, 'in six months time England will be unable to supply troops or money to our enemies, and will accept peace on whatever terms it pleases his Majesty [Louis XIV] to prescribe.'[105] Hooke was also gathering influential backing for the Enterprise. At the end of July Hooke, Charles-Honoré d'Albert de Luynes, duc de Chevreuse (de facto minister without portfolio on the royal council), and the diplomatic expert François de Callières followed up his report with an outline plan for the invasion of Scotland.[106] The Jacobite Juncto's emissary, Ogilvie of Boyn, arrived in Dunkirk on 11 August, and Hooke promptly arranged for him to travel incognito to the French court.[107] Hooke's intent was clearly to keep the project in the forefront of the councillors' minds as they began to deliberate on France's strategy for the coming year. An interview with Chamillart was arranged for Oglivie on 31 August, and a week later

Hooke followed up with a series of extracts of letters from Scotland which were read in council.[108] He then presented Torcy and Chamillart with a second, revised plan for the Enterprise on 16 September.[109] Shortly thereafter Hooke achieved his political breakthrough: Ogilvie was given the singular honour of a secret audience with Louis XIV, who pledged he would lose no time in setting matters in motion.[110] The key to making the project happen, despite Chamillart and Pontchartrain's continued covert opposition, would henceforth be reminding the king of its existence and potential. By 12 October, Hooke felt confident enough to write to Elizabeth Gordon (in white ink in an apparently anodyne personal letter) that he now had authority: 'to assure you that, provided you keep up your hearts and be not disunited by hopes or fears from the British Parliament, you shall be putt in a condition to do your busyness effectually as soon as the violent colds are over [i.e. Spring 1708]'.[111]

The Enterprise of Scotland was now on track. Troops were quietly billeted close to their embarkation point in Dunkirk, fast privateers there were apparently laid up for the winter, but in fact stripped down and prepared to carry troops and equipment, St Germain was secretly notified to prepare the equipage James III and VIII would need for the expedition and security was tightened.[112] The Scots Jacobites were, nonetheless, getting frustrated and anxious, and Hooke and Ogilvie both had to reassure them that the expedition was definitely going to happen.[113] The final decision to launch the Enterprise was taken in mid-December: Ogilvie was instructed to alert the Scots to be ready before the end of March 1708.[114] Despite further foot dragging and complaints by Forbin and Pontchartrain, Hooke had achieved his objective: by dint of his astute and careful politicking, the project he had been working on for over four years was finally going to happen.

Unfortunately – from St Germain's and the Scots Jacobites' points of view – it of course all ended in tears. The failure of the Enterprise of Scotland, moreover, cast a long shadow. France's fortunes lurched from bad to worse until 1710, when a political upheaval in Britain culminated in the return of a Tory majority in Parliament pledged to end the war as soon as possible. Even so, France emerged from the conflict badly battered, and definitely the defeated power. The Scots Jacobites had to helplessly watch the gradual ebb of the national outrage on which they had hoped to capitalise, and when they tried going it alone in 1715, it all went disastrously wrong.[115] St Germain found itself once again marginalised, and was obliged to spend the years until 1715 trying to bring about a restoration through conventional British politics, an experience it found exceedingly frustrating and ultimately fruitless.[116] Forbin was never employed again by the French navy and Matignon sank back into obscurity.[117]

Only Hooke emerged with something to show for his involvement. He had made sure that everyone concerned was impressed by his professionalism, and pulled off the remarkable feat of convincing all parties that he was sympathetic to them and their cause.[118] In truth, he was Torcy and Louis XIV's man all along and he reaped ample rewards for his faithful service. In 1703 he was a penurious foreign half-pay Major attached to an Irish regiment in French service. By 1708 he was a Frenchman with a certificate that specifically recognised him and his heirs as noble (a crucial achievement in eighteenth-century France), Colonel commanding of the Regiment de Sparre and a Brigadier-General. James III and VIII also created him Baron Hooke of Hooke Castle, county Waterford, in the Jacobite Irish peerage, which might not sound like much but further advanced his status and importance in France, where Jacobite peerages were generally recognised. To round out his career, in 1712 Louis XIV awarded him a pension of 1,500 *livres* a year for his good and faithful services, in 1718 he was promoted to Maréchal de Camp (the equivalent of Major-General) and in 1721 was created a Chevalier of the Order of St Louis.[119]

Not bad, considering that none of the covert operations which were the basis of his spectacular advancement actually worked. More important by far than operational success was the fact that by the early eighteenth century he had matured into a very professional and highly effective secret agent. He matter-of-factly risked his life to carry out missions his superiors believed were of great import, and fulfilled his remit each time. Most notably in Scotland, he got the dissidents he was working with fully to commit to a rebellion that would have greatly served French interests and steered the project through the minefields of French interdepartmental politics. But his clearly intermediate status, and the fact that he was primarily working for the equivalent of the foreign ministry, i.e. Torcy, which could not be blamed for the army and navy's mistakes, enabled him to emerge from the embarrassing fiasco of the '08 smelling of roses. Hooke also shrewdly developed two strands to his career. Rather than remain simply a spy and secret agent, reliant for his living on the uncertain gratitude of his superiors and their continued tenure in office, he leveraged his usefulness as an undercover operative to advance his military career. Steady, rather than spectacular, reward duly followed, and, as a result, in the end, he retired full of days, honour and respect rather than as a despised, starveling operator from the grubby underworld of intelligence and secret operations. More than anything else, perhaps, the secret life of Nathaniel Hooke provides a benchmark on how best to make a successful career as a special agent in the early modern era.

CHAPTER FIVE

The Fallen Politician's Way Back In

Melchor de Macanaz as Spy and Secret Negotiator[1]

Christopher Storrs

Early modern Europe witnessed the development of an elaborate network of diplomatic representation, one which in the eighteenth century embraced most sovereign states. However, alongside this public, visible structure there grew a sort of parallel universe of covert agents of all types, engaged in many of the same activities as the formally accredited ambassadors and envoys, who often depended enormously on the inhabitants of this twilight world if they were to carry out some of their most important functions, including intelligence gathering and negotiation. Unfortunately, but by its very nature, this world and its occupants are often barely visible to us. If they emerge at all from the shadows it is only tantalisingly briefly. Tracing them is made more difficult by the fact that their names (often aliases or incognitos) are rarely known to us, disguised or suppressed in order to ensure their safety, while they themselves were rarely trusted by employers, who often suspected them of being double agents. Savoyard diplomacy, one of the success stories of the eighteenth century,[2] relied in part on such men, but the public representatives of the duke of Savoy (king of Sardinia from 1720) were by no means enamoured of those they had to deal with. Take, for example, the Bolognese Giambattista Mazzoni, who wrote from Madrid to the Savoyard representative in Paris, when there was no Savoyard minister in the Spanish capital, and who dealt from 1728 with Joseph Milliet, marquis d'Arvillars, Savoyard representative to the Court of Spain.[3] Arvillars distrusted Mazzoni, who claimed to be the agent in Madrid of the Italian prince, the duke of Guastalla, although not recognised as such by Madrid's diplomatic community, and he was determined to deal carefully with him, describing him as very dangerous and capable of double dealing.[4] A rather different character was one Forni,[5] the Milanese secretary of the Imperial minister in Lisbon in 1747. Forni revealed to the court of Turin, ally of Empress Maria Theresa of Austria, secret Austrian-Spanish negotiations in the Portuguese capital,[6] but although fearing an attempt on his life might be made by those he had betrayed, he wanted little more by way of material reward than a job in Piedmont near the border of his beloved Milan.[7] We know little more about either of these men, the one apparently more at home in the world of covert intelligence than the other, and both of whom came to light while the present writer was researching other topics. But it was men as varied as these who made up that shadowy world upon which all sovereigns and states relied in the international struggle.

This was as true of Spain as it was of Savoy. Spanish intelligence gathering in the 'Golden Age', broadly speaking the period of Spain's European and imperial hegemony, c. 1556–1665, is a topic which has been well-covered, since it was an integral part of Spain's success in that era.[8] The century or so after 1665 is less satisfactorily treated, reflecting a larger neglect of the era of the last Spanish Habsburg, Carlos II (1665–1700) and the first Spanish Bourbon, Philip V (1700–46), when Spain was, apparently, less important an actor on the international stage.[9] Nevertheless, the later period, and above all the reign of Philip V, offers great scope for the historian of secret negotiation and intelligence gathering during the succession struggle which followed Philip's arrival in Spain, the resurgence of Spain as a great power after 1713, and Philip's efforts to secure the French throne after 1715.[10] What follows explores this topic by focusing on the career of one of the architects of early Bourbon Spain during the War of Spanish Succession, but who almost immediately after its conclusion suffered a lengthy disgrace and exile, in which he entered the murky world of the covert agent, Melchor Rafael de Macanaz (1670–1760).

Having reached maturity in the Spain of Carlos II, during the struggle for the succession Macanaz emerged as one of Philip V's most important Spanish collaborators, playing a leading role in the overhaul of Spanish government. However, his championship of royal authority vis-a-vis the Church – regalism – brought confrontation with the Spanish Inquisition and, following Philip V's second marriage, to Isabel Farnese in 1714, and the fall from power of the reforming clique of which Macanaz was a part, exile in France and the Low Countries for more than thirty years. During that time Macanaz wrote voluminously and also, justifying his presence in the present volume, acted as a shadowy agent of Spanish policy in north-west Europe and as an occasional, unofficial, often uninvited, adviser to his sovereign. During the War of the Austrian Succession, following the death of Philip V and the accession of Ferdinand VI in 1746, Macanaz was given an opportunity to rehabilitate himself, by acting in an official capacity in the peace negotiations in the Low Countries. However, he was soon felt to have compromised Spain, and was finally recalled and incarcerated until 1760 when the newly-succeeded Carlos III ordered his release. He died soon thereafter.

Historians of Macanaz's dramatic career have seen him in various lights, some emphasising his ministerial career before 1714 and the confrontation with the Inquisition, others his brief but disastrous experience as a formally accredited diplomat in Spain's efforts to extricate itself from the War of the Austrian Succession in 1746–7.[11] What follows deals primarily with neither the earlier phase of Macanaz's life, except insofar as it triggered and explains Macanaz's subsequent exile and activity as agent, nor with his later diplomatic appointment. Instead, it seeks to throw light on Macanaz's role in the intervening thirty years or so, above all insofar as it illuminates Spanish politics and policy and the often murky world of the 'dangerous trade'. Macanaz's activities in that world are not always easy to pursue, not least due to the absence of sources, the fundamental obstacle facing all students of covert diplomacy and intelligence gathering, and the problems of verification which inevitably surround so many of the sources that are to be found. This applies to some of Macanaz's own writings.[12] Besides those writings, and a less than complete biographical sketch written within decades of his death,[13] the key sources are the political papers, advice papers and Spanish diplomatic correspondence in the Archivo Histórico Nacional in Madrid and the Archivo General at Simancas and the reports in foreign archives of the ministers of other states who encountered and/or observed Macanaz – often indirectly, through a third party – in exile.[14] One final issue by way of introduction. Macanaz was not a spy in the conventional sense. But in exile he did play the part of an unofficial agent, obtaining and transmitting intelligence and negotiating clandestinely; he also associated with others who inhabited that world. His activity and experience suggest that we need to understand the world of the 'dangerous trade' more broadly than we generally do.

oOo

Melchor de Macanaz, one of seven children (four sons and three daughters) of the lesser nobility, was born in 1670, in the town of Hellín, in Murcia, southwest Spain.[15] His great grandfather, grandfather and father were hereditary councillors, in effect members of the local oligarchy, of Hellín. At age 15, Macanaz began to study law at the University of Valencia, graduating in 1689. He then moved to the University of Salamanca, to study jurisprudence, before becoming professor of law, and subsequently of canon law; it was there that his regalism was formed. In 1694, aged 24, he removed to Madrid, to make a career in the capital of the global Spanish Monarchy. There he made the acquaintance of the man who would become his patron, Juan Manuel Fernández Pacheco y Zuñiga, 8th marqués of Villena and duque of Escalona. Macanaz became tutor to Villena's two sons, the conde of San Estéban de Gormaz, and the marqués of Moya. Macanaz also acquired other patrons among the ruling elite, including the duque of Montalto, an influential figure in Murcia following his marriage to the sister and heiress of the last marqués of Los Vélez and President of the

Council of the Indies. This resulted in Macanaz's nomination by the king to the post of oidor in the Audiencia of the island of Santo Domingo in Spanish America,[16] but he did not accept the appointment. This decision is generally attributed to the opposition of Macanaz's parents to his departure overseas, but the young and ambitious lawyer may have feared relegation to provincial obscurity in the Indies. Whatever the reason, Macanaz remained in Madrid, where he continued to forge useful connections; these included one of Villena's relations, Cardinal Luis Manuel Fernández de Portocarrero, archbishop of Toledo (primate of Castile) and a powerful political figure in Carlos II's last years.[17]

Portocarrero was an important power-broker in the first years of the new Bourbon monarch, Philip V, and Villena was promptly (1701) appointed viceroy of Sicily, Macanaz acting as his agent in Madrid. In 1705, Macanaz accompanied Villena's eldest son to Zaragoza, as secretary, when the conde of San Estéban de Gormaz was appointed Captain General of Aragon. The fueros, the distinctive laws, customs and institutions of the territories of the Crown of Aragon, had long frustrated ministers in Madrid.[18] Following the Bourbon victory at Almansa (April 1707) over the supposed Valencian revolt against Philip V in favour of his rival for the throne, the Austrian Habsburg archduke, 'Charles III', Macanaz along with the Jacobite exile and agent, (Sir) Toby Bourk, then in Spanish service, was sent to help the French supreme military commander, Claude François Bidal, chevalier d'Asfeld in a radical overhaul of Valencia's government, at the expense of the fueros. Among various other tasks, Macanaz oversaw the confiscation of 'rebel' property in Valencia. In 1710 Macanaz returned to Madrid, but following the second major Bourbon victory at Villaviciosa that same year he was appointed Intendant General of Aragon, playing a major role in the reshaping of that realm's institutions. In 1713, back in Madrid, Macanaz was appointed Fiscal General, or senior lawyer, of the council of Castile as part of a major reform of the latter, which was now the most important of the councils which constituted the core of Spanish government.[19] The following month, against the background of deteriorating relations with Rome following its recognition in 1709 of Philip V's rival for the Spanish throne, Macanaz wrote and presented to the council of Castile his most important regalist work – one which would dog him for the rest of his life. This was the so-called *Pedimento de las 55 parrafos*,[20] a devastating critique of Church–State relations in Spain and of the Inquisition, written in typical Macanaz style: cogently argued, energetic, with no punches pulled. A year later, in the summer of 1714, the Inquisitor General, the Italian Francesco del Giudice, then Philip V's ambassador to Louis XIV, published a condemnation of the *Pedimento* in Paris, though without naming Macanaz. At this stage,

Philip V, still at odds with Rome, effectively shielded Macanaz from the Inquisition: del Giudice was replaced as Grand Inquisitor. In the autumn of 1714, then, Macanaz was at the height of his fortunes. Along with Jean Orry and the king's confessor, Father Pierre Robinet he was one of a triumvirate of ministers who, with the support of the queen, Maria Luisa Gabriela of Savoy, and the royal favourite, Marie Anne de la Trémoille, princess Orsini, or des Ursins, were overhauling Spain's government, and targeting the Inquisition, as few had hitherto dared. Macanaz was now a patron, with his own clientele of creatures.[21]

Within a couple of years, however, Macanaz was being tried by the Inquisition, and in exile in France, where he would remain for more than thirty years. Macanaz had made enemies. This owed something to his rather abrasive manner, but also to fundamental disagreements over policy, including how to deal with the Inquisition. At the same time, widespread hostility in Spain towards the way French subjects, including Orry, Guillaume Daubenton and Ursins, were exploiting Spain's resources, not entirely surprisingly extended to their Spanish ministerial colleague, Macanaz.[22] But most important of all was the death in February 1714, of Philip V's queen, and his second marriage later that year to the Italian princess whose dynastic and maternal ambitions would shape the international scene, and Macanaz's fortunes, for a generation: Isabel Farnese, the 'termagant' of Spain.[23]

Philip V's reign was one in which women enjoyed an extraordinary influence on Spanish political life. The first Bourbon king of Spain was dominated by his two wives – whether due simply to a powerful sex drive, or to a recurring melancholy which found relief in the close companionship of a supportive wife is not entirely clear[24] – and the change of queen inevitably had an effect. In December 1714, en route to Madrid, Isabel had an explosive encounter with Ursins, whom she banished there and then from Spain.[25] The advent of Isabel Farnese also meant the triumph of a clique of Italians, headed by del Giudice, and with him, the Inquisition.[26] Macanaz, fearing the worst, wrote to Philip V's grandfather and mentor, Louis XIV, in January 1715, articulating his anxieties regarding the reform programme in Spain in view of the imminent return there of del Giudice,[27] as well as to Philip himself.[28] But neither approach did him any good. In February 1715, Philip, pressed by his new wife, dismissed both Orry and Macanaz.[29]

Philip V allowed Macanaz to retire to France, to secure him from the Inquisition,[30] but this was the limit of the protection he afforded his erstwhile minister. He also expressed surprise at discovering that the exile had headed for Paris. In March 1715 Macanaz was ordered to leave the French capital; he headed for the town of Pau, closer to the Pyrenees and to Spain.[31] In the meantime, del Giudice had returned to Madrid in triumph, and was reinstated as Inquisitor General; in this capacity in August 1715 he ordered the preparation of a case against Macanaz. In June 1716 Macanaz was formally summoned by the Spanish Inquisition, prompting him to write to the Pope defending his orthodoxy. However, in October 1716, following his failure to appear in Spain to answer the charges against him, Macanaz was condemned in absentia, a sentence which was confirmed a year later, following an abortive attempt to get Philip V to have the Inquisition suspend its pursuit of his former servant. The confiscation of Macanaz's property was already underway, although it was complicated by the fact that Macanaz, his brothers and sisters had inherited in common.[32] Del Giudice would not last long as de facto chief minister in Madrid. But neither his successor, Cardinal Giulio Alberoni, nor any of the others who effectively filled that role thereafter, including the Dutchman, Jan Willem, baron Ripperda and the Spaniard, Jose Patiño, thought fit to recall Macanaz as long as Philip V and Isabel Farnese occupied the Spanish throne. It would be more than thirty years before Macanaz saw Spain again. Like many others caught up in the 'dangerous trade', Macanaz came to it unwillingly, in maturity, and in exile.

In leaving Spain, Macanaz became part of a remarkable Spanish diaspora triggered by the War of Spanish Succession. The collapse of Spanish Italy and Spanish Flanders in the course of that struggle had been accompanied by a considerable migration of officials and others from there to Spain itself. Equally, the triumph of Philip V in the peninsula and the collapse of the regime of the Austrian Habsburg Archduke, 'Charles III', were followed by the exodus from Spain, above all from the territories of the Crown of Aragon, of those who had acknowledged Philip's rival as king. Most headed to Austria and to those territories, Flanders, Milan, Naples and Sardinia, which had once been part of the Spanish Habsburg Monarchy but were now under Austrian Habsburg rule.[33] Just like the exiled Huguenot and Jacobite communities, and for the same mix of reasons, this Spanish diaspora would produce its complement of agents, plotters and spies. But Macanaz did not join the 'Austrian' Spanish exiles. Instead, remaining loyal to Philip V whose favour he no doubt hoped soon to recover, he settled in neighbouring France, the state which, ruled by Philip's Bourbon kin, had been the king's greatest support during the struggle for the Spanish throne and to which Philip himself remained deeply attached. From here Macanaz could easily keep in touch with events across the border, and could easily be recalled to Spain and, within very little time, be in Madrid.

oOo

Macanaz spent the first ten years of his exile in Pau, in the territory of Bearn, a French frontier province which was the seat of an intendancy but which, like so many frontier territories, enjoyed a distinctive, privileged regime. From Pau, where Macanaz resided in a Jesuit house, he corresponded with his former colleague, José de Grimaldo, who, in the administrative reforms implemented in Spain after 1713, emerged as Secretary of State for foreign affairs.[34] In May 1717, for example, Macanaz informed the secretary about counterfeiters operating in or about Bearn who introduced coins into Aragon and Catalonia, with the name of 'Charles III';[35] the following month he reported on criminals who had broken out of jail (in Pau) and headed for Aragon, and who might enlist in the foreign regiments stationed there.[36] In the absence of clear documentary evidence, Macanaz's relationship with the authorities in Spain in this period must remain vague. But French officials in Bearn clearly saw Macanaz as a useful channel to Madrid: in 1720 he forwarded to Grimaldo representations by the Intendant about a French ship which had been seized in the Spanish northern coastal principality of Asturias, in the hope of securing the vessel's release.[37] Throughout, Macanaz, who was clearly seeking to maintain a connection with the royal secretary, and in this way a presence at Court, declared himself, and no doubt thought of himself, as a loyal subject of Philip V and a good Spaniard.[38]

Whether Macanaz renewed, or sought to renew contact with those French diplomats, officials, soldiers and others with whom he had worked in Spain – Michel-Jean Amelot, marquis de Gournay, James Fitzjames, duke of Berwick, René de Froulay, count and marshal de Tessé, Asfeld, Orry, and Ursins – is unclear. So, too, is Macanaz's role in the plotting in France associated with Philip V's designs on the French throne after 1715. The price of peace for both Spain and France in 1713 had included a formal renunciation by Philip of his claim to the French throne, to prevent a union of the two Crowns, a renunciation made before the Castilian Cortes, which had been specially summoned for this purpose. However, Philip continued to believe that he had a rightful claim to the French throne, and making a reality of it seemed a real possibility given that, following a succession of deaths in the French royal family between 1711 and 1712, Louis XIV's death in 1715 meant the accession of the Sun King's great-grandson, Louis XV, aged just five. In the event of the death of the child king himself and in view of Philip's renunciation, the throne would pass to Philippe de Bourbon, duke of Orléans, who acted as Regent for Louis XV. But Philip V believed he should succeed, and he found widespread support in France for his view, which he sought to exploit. The secret machinations this involved,[39] culminated in the so-called Cellamare conspiracy, when Philip V's eponymous ambassador to the French court plotted against the government to which he was accredited and was expelled from France.[40] There is no evidence of Macanaz's direct involvement in these machinations. He was far from the capital and the Court, and reported French troop movements in 1719 when French forces invaded north-west Spain, as the recently formed Quadruple Alliance sought to oblige Philip V to evacuate both Sardinia, which Spanish forces had occupied in 1717, and Sicily, which they had invaded in 1718. Macanaz certainly continued to correspond with the Spanish court from Pau throughout this period. But this seems to have been a largely one-sided correspondence. In the spring of 1723, Grimaldo claimed not to be responding to Macanaz's letters from Pau, when, in a move demonstrating the continued importance of the royal confessor in the reign of Philip V, he consulted the then holder of that office, Daubenton, on what to do with yet another missive received from the disgraced former minister.[41]

Soon thereafter, Macanaz, like all European politicians, was presented with the bombshell dropped by Philip V when in January 1724 the king abdicated. Whether Philip was driven by a continuing desire to make a reality of his claim to the throne of France, or by renewed depression, he surrendered the Spanish throne to his eldest son by his first marriage, Luis I.[42] Macanaz promptly congratulated the new Spanish Secretary of State, Juan Bautista Orendain (or Orendayn), on the young king's accession and, in a characteristic display of his great erudition, cited various examples from Spanish history of monarchs, including that of the Holy Roman Emperor, Charles V, who had given up the throne, contrasting them with Philip V to the latter's advantage.[43] More important, the accession of the son of Philip's first wife no doubt encouraged the exile to believe that his banishment might soon be over.

Perhaps taking advantage of the change of regime in Madrid, Macanaz, complaining that he had long been suffering from a kidney infection planned to have an operation for this in Paris,[44] where he arrived in early April 1724. Macanaz's presence in Paris also brought him closer, as he was surely aware, to the peace congress which was about to convene at Cambrai, in order to resolve the main causes of international tension, most notably the Spanish court's insistence that Philip V's eldest son by his second marriage, Don Carlos, succeed to his mother's claims to the successions of the duchy of Parma and the grand duchy of Tuscany in Italy.[45] Gatherings of this sort had long been an important venue for peacemaking, although the real work was often done privately between a few key negotiators. They were also an occasion at which agents and informants of all sorts flourished.[46] For his part, the Spanish king's representative in the French capital, the Jacobite exile, Patrick Lawless, was embarrassed by the appearance of the disgraced former minister in Paris and sought orders from Madrid on how to receive him; he was told to show himself indifferent.[47] But the opinionated Macanaz, not inclined to reticence, soon offered Madrid a critical assessment of Spanish policy at Cambrai.[48] His assessment may have been valued in the Spanish capital where Philip V's confessor, now father Bermudéz, advised Grimaldo that the king could give Macanaz financial aid, but unofficially, to avoid any suggestion that Macanaz was a minister of the Catholic King, or as if he were in Paris on the latter's orders.[49] By the autumn of 1724, if not before, Macanaz was writing to Grimaldo via a certain Don Joseph Ignacio Beret de Cortiada at Zaragoza.[50] He may have used this same route to forward letters for Isabel Farnese from the princess de Conti, one of Philip V's supporters at the French court.[51] Later that same autumn, by which time Luis I had died and Philip V had resumed the throne, Macanaz, having now recovered from the affliction which had drawn him to Paris, asked Grimaldo whether his king wished him to remain there.[52]

Just what reply was given to Macanaz on this occasion is uncertain, although the Spanish court was already beginning to consider a radical solution to the problem of its relations with its inveterate enemy, the court of Vienna, one which would render the congress at Cambrai redundant (below). Nevertheless, the evidence suggests that Macanaz remained in Paris, with or without the permission of his own court. He was thus on the spot when the next major crisis in relations blew up between the French and Spanish courts. Philip V's bitter rival, Orléans had died in 1723, and was succeeded as Louis XV's chief minister by Louis Henri de Bourbon, duke of Bourbon. But the (French) succession issue remained problematic. To resolve it, Bourbon decided to return the four-year old Spanish Infanta, daughter of Philip V and Isabel Farnese, who was betrothed to Louis XV but who would not bear children for many years to Spain in the spring of 1725, and to marry the French monarch to a bride who might soon produce an heir. Inevitably, the move outraged the Spanish court, which again broke off formal diplomatic contacts with France.[53] The episode allowed Macanaz to play a role, again. In the spring of 1725, Lawless commended Macanaz's zeal in the Spanish king's service in Paris, especially at that moment in looking out for the Infanta, adding that Bourbon had threatened to put Macanaz in the Bastille.[54] He ordered Macanaz to accompany the Infanta to the Spanish frontier, but also urged the Spanish court to consider what to do with Macanaz, especially as the disgraced former minister lacked means (below).[55] This appears to have been the first occasion on which the British secretary of embassy in Paris, Thomas Robinson, mentioned Macanaz,[56] although the former was not personally well acquainted with the latter. Robinson believed Macanaz to be of Irish descent, a pardonable mistake given the number of exiled Irish knocking about in Europe, many of them acting as agents and spies, many of them in Philip V's service.[57] Another

Spanish diplomat in Paris, Isadore Cassado de Azevado de Rosalez, marqués of Monteleon, went further on Macanaz's behalf: he suggested that Macanaz, whose devotion he too praised, be allowed to accompany the Infanta to the Spanish court, i.e. across the border and into Spain. This would mean an end to Macanaz's now ten years of exile. It also meant confronting the case against the former which the Inquisition still had open. Monteleon thought this an easy issue to settle: the king could simply impose eternal silence on the process, so that Macanaz could continue to use his great talents in the service of the Catholic King.[58]

The Spanish court paid some attention to these recommendations,[59] and in the spring of 1725, Macanaz accompanied the Infanta from Versailles to Bayona, but not before the Spanish court, in a move suggesting that Macanaz was in its employ in some loose way, had settled his debts. Lawless claimed to have paid Macanaz's creditors 11,000 *livres* and to have given Macanaz himself a further 4,000.[60] Macanaz continued to send intelligence to Grimaldo en route: from Poitiers, for example, he reported the dispatch of French troops to the Spanish frontier, as the breach between the two courts continued to deteriorate.[61] He had also arranged for intelligence to be sent to him along the way from Paris by an Irish banker there, one Carol, who had apparently grown up in Madrid and whose relation and business partner in the Spanish capital Grimaldo was advised to contact.[62] Besides exemplifying the Irish diaspora, Carol also typified the extent to which Europe's developing financial and commercial networks facilitated the gathering and transmission of intelligence, underpinning the 'dangerous trade'. In the meantime, Lawless and Monteleon continued to press Macanaz's case with the Spanish king. Lawless noted the danger for Spain of the disgraced former minister's remaining in France, or travelling via that country to Italy; French awareness of the importance of Macanaz might prompt an attempt to seize him. He therefore suggested that Macanaz might reach Italy via a different route, or that he might be sent instead to Portugal.[63] Initially, the Spanish court appears to have been happy to allow Macanaz himself to choose between going to Italy, the main focus of Spanish ambitions in the generation after the conclusion of the War of Spanish Succession as Philip V sought to reconstruct old Spanish Italy and as he and his second wife asserted her claims there on behalf of their sons, or to Cambrai, where the congress had yet to conclude.[64] However, at Bayonne, where the Infanta's entourage arrived in May 1725, Macanaz received the king's order to go to Cambrai;[65] he was still not to be allowed to re-enter Spain. Philip remained reluctant to confront both the Inquisition, and perhaps also his queen, on behalf of his former minister, though he was ready to make use of Macanaz's abilities outside Spain.

Nor was Macanaz to play any part in the Cambrai congress. Frustrated at the lack of progress there, the Spanish monarchs had sought instead to do a separate deal with the Emperor, an initiative which culminated in the conclusion of the extraordinary peace treaty of Vienna between Spain and Emperor Charles VI in the spring of 1725. This 'diplomatic revolution' undermined the negotiations at Cambrai. Macanaz therefore headed instead for Brussels, capital of what had been the Spanish Low Countries, or Spanish Flanders, and what were now the Austrian Netherlands, the possession of Philip V's former rival and new ally, Charles VI,[66] and a territory with whose elite the Spanish court continued to maintain links.[67] In June 1725, Macanaz arrived in Brussels, where Philip V had no resident minister, although the Italian, Lorenzo Verzuso, marchese di Beretti Landi was there, about to depart to take up his post as Spanish ambassador in Venice. Just as earlier, in France, Macanaz received representations from the agents of other powers who clearly regarded him as a channel whereby to communicate with the Spanish court, and very probably as its agent. Thus, the Dutch resident in Brussels complained to Macanaz more than once that the trade agreement which was part of the recently concluded treaty of Vienna, and which gave the Emperor's subjects, in the form of the Ostend Company, commercial privileges in Spain and its empire, breached the terms of the peace of Munster of 1648, which had granted similar trading rights to residents of the United Provinces.[68]

The same thought, that Macanaz might have clout in Madrid, undoubtedly attracted others, including members of what might be thought of as a residual local hispano-flemish community. In the summer of 1725, Macanaz forwarded to the Spanish court the request of one Joseph Carlos Brambilla, whose father, he claimed, had served for fifty years in the Spanish armies in Flanders, Catalonia and Italy, to be appointed to the vacant post of consul of the Spanish nation in Bruges.[69] However, Macanaz's days in Brussels were numbered. Already, in September 1725, Philip V had ordered, in response to further letters from Macanaz, that his former Fiscal General be thanked for his zeal but that he should not do anything which would commit the king without royal order.[70] Clearly, Macanaz enjoyed some leeway from the Spanish court, but was exceeding the powers allowed him; indeed, in November 1725 he was peremptorily ordered by Madrid not to interfere further in negotiations and, in part to free him from temptation, to depart for neighbouring Liège.[71]

On 3 December 1725, Macanaz arrived in Liège.[72] The prince-bishopric of Liège, largely dominated by the Wittelsbach family in this period, was of little independent importance, but, tucked between the Dutch Republic, Flanders, France and the Holy Roman Empire, was a strategic (and hence intelligence) nerve centre. Macanaz spent two years in Liège. It was there that he wrote his

Defence of the Inquisition, surely in an attempt to gain credit with the Inquisition in Spain. It was here, too, that he married a Flemish woman of Spanish origin, Maria Maximiliana Cortes (or Courtois), the sister of Jose Cortes, whom Macanaz had known in Madrid.[73] Macanaz subsequently sought to press the interests of his new connections in Madrid. In November 1728, Macanaz forwarded to Madrid a memorial from Don Jacobo and Don José Cortes, explaining that they were natives of Liège who wished to enter Philip V's service, as junior officers, and that they hoped for some financial assistance to enable them to maintain their quality, or rank, suggesting that he at least believed he still had some credit with the Spanish court.[74]

Macanaz did not confine himself to writing of this sort. In December 1725, within weeks of arriving in Liège, which was an industrial area of some importance, and having read about efforts to exploit the mines of Guadalcanal in his native Spain, Macanaz sent to Madrid details of a machine to pump water out of mines.[75] Obtaining and dispatching information of this sort, which was often a closely-guarded secret precisely because it might help a competitor state, represented a sort of industrial espionage, as useful in its way as military and political intelligence.[76] But Macanaz also seems to have meddled in the recruitment of the Walloon Guards, an elite unit which was one of the enduring links between the Spanish court and the Flemish elite; and was in effect again told not to interfere in January 1726.[77] Macanaz also continued to watch developments in Spain, no doubt with a view to his own reinstatement there. In May 1726, Macanaz congratulated Orendayn, who had been rewarded with the title of marques of la Paz (the peace) for his part in negotiating the treaty or peace of Vienna, on having replaced Ripperda as Secretary for Finance: Macanaz declared it a subject that the latter understood rather better than the Dutch adventurer.[78] Macanaz's evaluation may have been well founded but it also has to be said that Ripperda, like Alberoni before him, had not used his authority to Macanaz's advantage. Macanaz may also have been flattering Orendayn in the hope that the minister might use any influence he had on the exile's behalf.

In the meantime, Macanaz continued to send intelligence to the Spanish court, which otherwise had no agent or representative in Liége. In the tense 'cold war' atmosphere which followed the conclusion of the treaty of Vienna, dominated by the formation of two armed camps in Europe, each of the rival alliances – Vienna on the one hand, Hanover (Britain and France at its core) on the other – was seeking allies in the expectation of renewed war. In July 1726, for example, Macanaz sent details of the armed forces, fortifications and finances of the Dutch Republic,[79] whose adherence to one of the rival leagues would, whatever the Republic's real weakness after 1713, be a major prize.[80] Not only that, but Macanaz's assessment of the state of European affairs was clearly valued by the Spanish court: that same summer of 1726, he was asked for his assessment of the international situation.[81] At the end of the year, with war apparently imminent, his sovereign ordered Macanaz, in that event and if Liège itself was threatened, to remove to the neighbouring Rhineland electorate of Cologne; in the meantime he continued to report war preparations in the vicinity of Liège.[82]

This role, in which Macanaz was clearly filling a gap in Spain's intelligence network, soon led to another. By January 1727, if not before, and as relations between the British and Spanish courts continued to deteriorate, culminating in the opening of the siege of Gibraltar in February of that year, Macanaz was involved in negotiations aimed at detaching the French court from its British ally and bringing it into the Vienna alliance.[83] Significantly, in the spring of 1727, Macanaz submitted an advice paper on Spanish policy in Africa and the Mediterranean, which was well received by Philip V.[84] At the same time, too, and anticipating another peace congress, Macanaz wrote for the Spanish court another wide-ranging assessment of the international situation, of the interests, maxims and policies of the various courts, of the advantages he thought the Spanish king might seek in any negotiations, and of the representatives Philip V might send to the assembly.[85] Philip V finally agreed to another congress, lifting the siege of Gibraltar in June 1727. But this was not the limit to Macanaz's secret diplomacy. In the late summer and early autumn of 1727, Macanaz began a secret correspondence with prince Eugene of Savoy, one of the Emperor's most influential ministers, who had been (absentee) governor of the Austrian Netherlands until 1724. Prince Eugene oversaw a remarkable private network of agents and informants across Europe which ran parallel to the official Austrian Habsburg diplomatic network and which enhanced his position in Vienna, where, as at other Courts, foreign policy was one of the most contentious areas in the struggle between different factions for the sovereign's ear and for power. For his part, Macanaz sent to Madrid copies of this correspondence, which continued into 1728.[86]

In the meantime, in the autumn of 1727, Macanaz received orders from Madrid to abandon Liège, and go to Paris, as the Spanish court prepared for the peace congress, which was to convene at Soissons, again near Paris.[87] To cover his tracks, Macanaz intended to take advantage of the Spanish diaspora: he would go under cover of visiting a Spanish family of his acquaintance living between Namur and Brussels.[88] Macanaz anticipated that he would negotiate secretly while José Ignacio Barrenechea, one of the Spanish plenipotentiaries at the forthcoming congress would be responsible for the public negotiations, and asked for the necessary credentials.[89] In the meantime, he continued to offer his advice on what Spanish policy should be, sending yet another advice paper on this subject to Madrid in the autumn of 1727.[90] Macanaz arrived in Paris in mid-November 1727; he and Louis de Brancas-Cereste, marquis de Brancas, whom he had known when the latter served as Louis XIV's ambassador in Madrid in 1713–14, and who was now a confidant of the de facto chief minister of France, Cardinal André-Hercule de Fleury, were soon ranging over all relevant issues.[91] But Macanaz seems once again to have gone too far, or to have excited the suspicions of Philip V's ally, the Emperor. In early December 1727 Macanaz was ordered by Philip to leave Paris and return to Pau. Macanaz sought to justify himself, saying that he had acted so as not to give suspicion in his conferences with the French ministers.[92] The Spanish court then seems to have wanted Macanaz to carry on dealing with both the French ministers and Eugene, in order to ensure that Philip V achieved a good result at the congress, which was now about to open at Soissons.[93] But in February 1728 la Paz clearly felt obliged to explain what Macanaz was doing in Paris to the Imperial minister in Madrid, count Lothar von Königsegg, seeking to reassure him by sending him a copy of a letter from Eugene to Macanaz.[94]

Throughout this, Macanaz was acting for Philip V and the Spanish court, and, like so many of those engaged in the 'dangerous trade', expected some material reward (see below). However, and again like a number of others who inhabited that world, he had his own views, and was not simply a hireling or mercenary. Macanaz was clearly shaped in his thinking by having grown up under the last Spanish Habsburg, when the global Spanish Monarchy, although weak and not hegemonic as it – arguably – had been before 1665 was nonetheless still one of the major powers. Macanaz believed that Spain remained powerful, but that it could do much more to defend its empire, to prevent foreigners from accessing the resources of that empire, and to ensure that Spain was respected. Thus, he frequently asserted the need to enforce more effectively the laws against foreigners seeking to trade in and with Spanish America, carrying off its wealth.[95] On the whole, however, his focus was less on the Indies than on Europe, where his projects invariably aimed to restore to the Spanish monarchy what it had lost in the War of Spanish Succession. In 1728, typically, Macanaz's proposals for assuring lasting peace in Europe involved (1) establishing three new houses, or sovereignties, two from what was taken from the Spanish Crown in the succession struggle, in Italy and Flanders, and the third to be provided by the Emperor, in all three cases an Austrian Habsburg marrying a Spanish Bourbon (including Don Carlos and Don Felipe, the eldest sons of Isabel Farnese); and (2) an alliance between Spain, the Emperor/Empire, Muscovy and France.[96] Closer to home, that same year Macanaz suggested ways of putting pressure on Britain to return Gibraltar, noting the importance of strengthening the fleet, and using it against the coasts of Africa, so that the other European powers should properly appreciate, more than they had done in the past, the value of the Spanish alliance; Macanaz could not resist suggesting that, if Philip V and his ministers had carried out an earlier (1726) African project of his, rather than besiege Gibraltar, the surrender of the latter would have been facilitated at much less cost, a proposal which suggests Macanaz was capable of a broad strategic vision.[97]

In December 1727, Macanaz, in another bid to return to Spain, perhaps even to office, offered to come to Madrid incognito to give his views, but while he was encouraged to continue to give advice nothing was said about his coming to Spain.[98] He therefore continued to advise from a distance and unofficially, enjoying a background role in the congress of Soissons.[99] Macanaz was frustrated by his lack of an official character and subordinate role, but in early 1728 was overjoyed to receive a cipher for his correspondence.[100] Nevertheless, Macanaz could still miscalculate in the eyes of the Spanish court. In the spring of 1728, Macanaz was effectively reprimanded by la Paz for reporting and apparently sharing the views of French ministers and others about divisions at the Spanish court between Isabel Farnese and the prince of Asturias, the future Ferdinand VI, and between Isabel and the Spanish people at large.[101]

Macanaz may have hoped the congress of Soissons would succeed,[102] but in June 1728 he feared it would be as disappointing for Spain as the earlier gathering at Cambrai, above all because Spain was the only power dissatisfied with the status quo. He therefore urged that the Spanish fleet be strengthened, that Spain's forces in America be increased to 6,000 men, and that Philip be ready to send help anywhere it was needed and/or to attempt an armed landing somewhere, keeping up to 210,000 troops on Spain's Mediterranean coasts for just such an adventure.[103] The following month, July 1728, Macanaz was in Paris, gathering together all he had written on Gibraltar for Fleury and the Keeper of the Seals, Germain-Louis de Chauvelin.[104] Macanaz's efforts may have brought some personal reward. At the end of 1728, Macanaz thanked the king for granting his nephew, D. Rodrigo Macanaz, a cadet in the royal bodyguard, a company of horse in the Calatrava cavalry regiment. However, in true Macanaz style, he was not entirely satisfied, pointing out that Philip V had originally granted the young man a company in November 1711, but that D. Rodrigo had been prevented from taking it up by the opposition of the conde of Aguilar. Macanaz therefore requested for his nephew either the rank of colonel, or that his captaincy be dated from November 1711.[105] Macanaz's pessimistic assessment of Spain's prospects at the congress of Soissons proved well founded, as it soon failed.[106] In response, Macanaz urged Philip V to simply ignore the other powers, who should, he thought, do Spain justice, and go his own way.[107] That Macanaz and his advice continued to enjoy some standing in Madrid at this time was clear to some observers, including the British minister, Benjamin Keene. In reply to a query from another British diplomat, one of the plenipotentiaries at the congress of Soissons, Stephen Poyntz, Keene wrote in the spring of 1729:

> It is certain that Macanas [sic] in spite of the Clergy and the Inquisition has all along preserved a credit with the King of Spain. . . . ; their project of regaining the lost Provinces, is what they have in common with all those who pique themselves upon being true Spaniards, and I doubt not but the same notion is cultivated and cherished in the Prince [of the Asturias]. . . ; it is also, what in all probability the King himself would heartily come into: But as the Queen's views would be entirely subverted by such a scheme, Macanas . . . [is] sensible, that she must loose her power, before any thing of that nature can be attempted or even proposed, and their fondness for this project makes them too easy to believe, thast that period approaches.[108]

There was the rub, for, as Keene continued, describing relations between the Catholic Kings:

> What indeed they advance of the King's natural passion being abated is true, and that his commerce with her is not as frequent as formerly; but no one could ever remark that her power was any wise diminished on this; for he is a Man of habitude, his custom of living and conversing with her and seeing her daily, continues the same influence over him that any other passion might have begun, and his indolence and irresolution will always subject his actions to be modelled and controlled as she thinks fit.

Some, particularly those who thought the forward policy in Italy pursued by Philip V and Isabel Farnese's claims neglected, even sacrificed, genuine Spanish interests, pinned their hopes on the heir to the throne, the Prince of the Asturias, the future Ferdinand VI, the younger son of Philip V and his first wife. Many believed that Ferdinand should have succeeded Luis I on the latter's death in 1724, and that Philip's resumption of the throne on that occasion was a usurpation. Ferdinand's court was, potentially at least, an alternative centre of power in Spain, although despite his resentment of his stepmother, Ferdinand lacked the character to turn his resentment into a serious bid for power. But all – foreign diplomats and policymakers and Spanish courtiers and ministers – had to tread carefully in view of these tensions in Spanish political life, as did Macanaz.[109] It was clear from Keene's account that, in the rather simplistic language of some contemporary commentators Macanaz was a 'good Spaniard' at odds with Isabel Farnese's policy objectives. In early 1729, Poyntz, reported that Macanaz and Álvaro José de Navia Osorio y Vigil, marqués of Santa Cruz, another of the Spanish plenipotentiaries at the congress of Soissons, were working together, encouraged by the king of Spain himself, and in direct, secret correspondence with the prince of Asturias's Court. Apparently, they were hoping that Philip V would abdicate for a second time, on his return from Badajoz where he was attending the marriage of the prince of Asturias with the daughter of the king of Portugal, Barbara of Braganza, and Isabel Farnese's influence would then collapse; apparently, too, they hoped to unite the allies of Hanover with Spain against the Emperor, and to recover Spain's lost province. It seems that Philip Wharton, duke of Wharton, and other Jacobite exiles encouraged them, with talk of the state of affairs in England, saying that Britain would have to join Spain and its allies.[110] Not surprisingly, Macanaz was critical of the treaty of Seville which followed in 1729, and which saw Philip striking a compromise deal with Britain and France to secure his and his wife's ambitions in Italy.[111] The succeeding years were spent by Macanaz in Paris with his wife and young daughter.[112] The former minister continued to be kept at a distance by the Spanish court. Not surprisingly, Macanaz was not favoured by Isabel Farnese's favourite and Spain's de facto chief minister, Jose Patiño,[113] whose brother, Baltasar Patiño, marqués of Castelar, a former protégé of Macanaz, arrived in the French capital in 1730 to press the execution of the Seville accord.[114] Macanaz promptly visited Castelar, offering his help, and continued to forward to Madrid letters from Philip V's supporters in France, including for example Louise-Françoise de Bourbon, duchess of Bourbon,[115] but Castelar had orders to have Macanaz quit Paris for Pau, to which Macanaz replied that he could not go, having no money.[116]

So Macanaz remained in the French capital. And although Isabel Farnese may have wanted little to do with the disgraced former minister, those acting for her were readier to deal with him. Thus in the spring of 1731, Macanaz was apparently contacted by the widowed duchess of San Pietro, sister of Louis XIV's former foreign secretary, Jean-Baptiste Colbert, marquis of Torcy, and a close confidant of Isabel Farnese. The duchess had recently arrived in Paris on a special mission, to gain the support of the French court in the Spanish queen's efforts to obtain as bride for her eldest son, Don Carlos, an Austrian archduchess. Whether at Isabel Farnese's suggestion or not is unclear, the duchess asked Macanaz's advice on how she should proceed. Macanaz apparently promised to consider what was clearly an opportunity to ingratiate himself with Isabel Farnese. However, the Emperor's aversion to such a marriage undermined Macanaz's prospects, and in September 1731, after repeated orders to abandon Paris he was ordered to leave for Pau immediately.[117] In face of his continued obstinacy, in December 1731, Castelar was ordered to take whatever measures he thought best to remove Macanaz from the French capital.[118] But as late as October 1736, Isabel Farnese attacked the French court for, among other things, its toleration of Macanaz; and in 1737 the new Spanish minister to the French court was ordered to watch Macanaz, and even to request his expulsion, although he dismissed the possibility that the former minister constituted any sort of threat[119] even though enquiries in the wake of the so-called Champeaux affair, in 1738, when a French diplomat was expelled for stirring things up against Philip V and his queen, apparently led back in France itself to Macanaz.[120] Macanaz remained in Paris between 1730 and 1746, but was largely excluded from public affairs, which may explain why he erred so spectacularly in his later negotiations (below) at Breda.[121]

In Paris, which had long been a magnet for exiles, agents and informers of all sorts, Macanaz had associated with at least some others who fell into these categories.[122] His relationship with the two so-called Sicilian abbots, Giambattista Platania and Giuseppe Caracciolo, who typify the distinctive role in the 'dangerous trade', particularly in continental, Catholic Europe of the lesser clergy, the itinerant Abbé and so on, as well as of Italians, was exemplary.[123] Just how these two men, sometimes referred to as the Sicilian priests or simply as the Sicilians, came to be in Paris was, like so much in this twilight world, unclear.[124] According to one version, they were consulted secretly on political matters by Philip V, to the disgust of others at Court, including Isabel Farnese, who had them secretly arraigned before an ecclesiastical tribunal and expelled from Spain before Philip could intervene. An alternative had it that Philip had let them see the secret articles of the treaty of Vienna (1725, above), but was upset by their reaction, and himself had them ejected from Spain.[125] For the next twenty years the two Sicilians supplied successive British diplomats in Paris with intelligence about Spain,[126] at a price,[127] although not all British ministers agreed with Horace Walpole, brother of Robert Walpole and British ambassador in Paris, as to the value of what they were buying.[128] The Abbés' source, or sources of intelligence in and about the Spanish court and its policy, lay within the circle of the heir to the Spanish throne, the future Ferdinand VI. They also included Macanaz.

The Abbés were clearly in contact with Macanaz. In the autumn of 1728, the British ministers, having suborned the secretary of Barrenechea, were able to send to London a copy of draught articles, prepared by Santa Cruza and

Barrenechea on the basis of the negotiations at Soissons and taken to Spain by the third (and chief) Spanish plenipotentiary, Miguel José de Bournonville y Sainte-Aldegonde, duke of Bournonville, which they had received from the secretary. The British ministers did not doubt that the project would succeed as long as Isabel Farnese was satisfied, as the Sicilian Abbés had long assured them of this, they having it from Macanaz, although this was hardly secret intelligence: as has already been noted, most policy-makers in Europe at this time thought Isabel effectively made Spanish policy.[129] The British ministers subsequently received from the same source the substance of a dispatch sent from Spain to the Spanish plenipotentiaries also noting that Macanaz had told the Sicilian Abbés that Barrenechea had consulted Macanaz about getting a letter from the Spanish court to the Genoese minister in London, Grimaldi.[130] Macanaz was becoming a thorn in the side of Cardinal Fleury, and increasingly bitter towards Britain.[131] In early 1729, the British minister reported that Fleury had long been pressing the Spanish court to recall Macanaz, as an opponent of peace and a meddler in French domestic affairs, saying that Isabella Farnese had agreed on condition that the two Sicilians were expelled from France.[132] A few weeks later, Poyntz noted that the Sicilian Abbés, who had now been ordered to leave Paris, had re-affirmed the contact between Macanaz and Santa Cruz and the circle of the prince of Asturias.[133] Macanaz continued to associate with the Sicilian Abbés (who did not leave the French capital). In August 1729, Walpole's secretary was informed by the latter, who had dined that same day with Macanaz, that Macanaz had learned, by private letters, that on the vexed question of the troops to be sent to the Italian duchies to guarantee the succession there of Don Carlos, the Spanish court would be satisfied with Swiss garrisons in Spanish pay.[134] In March 1731, the two Sicilians informed the British minister in Paris that Macanaz had told them of information he had received, indirectly, from Castelar's embassy secretary.[135]

To monitor the activities of the Sicilian Abbés, and the many other agents in Paris, Fleury resorted to the police authorities, headed by the Lieutenant General de Police, an official first appointed in 1667.[136] From 1725 until just before his death in 1739 this post was occupied by René Herault, who oversaw a re-focusing of its activity. The responsibilities of the police included the suppression of disorder, the execution of orders for arrests or intimidation, and the collection of information which could be useful to the cardinal and his government in enabling Fleury to maintain his grip on power.[137] During Herault's tenure, the nature of the reports on the population of Paris changed from being principally a record of the 'menu peuple' to one which incorporated detailed descriptions of the political gossip from the promenades and cafes. Daily reports were sent or given personally to Fleury. The contemporary ecclesiastical controversies which divided France were one reason for this: in February 1728, Herault visited the Jacobite exile, Francis Atterbury, bishop of Rochester, in Paris, following Atterbury's dabbling in French ecclesiastical politics.[138] Individuals were not only watched and spoken to: their papers might be seized, as were those of Atterbury in 1732 following his death.[139]

The Paris police authorities also, not surprisingly, monitored the activities of Macanaz. In March 1729 the British minister reported that the Lieutenant General de Police, having been employed by Fleury to discover where the two Sicilians were living, had informed him that they frequently visited Macanaz.[140] Later that same month, Poyntz assured Fleury that Vienna had assured Spain of its support in the event of war between the alliances of Hanover and Vienna, finding proof of this in a paper he had received from the Sicilian Abbés. When Fleury produced Herault's police reports of their frequenting Macanaz as evidence that the Abbés were rogues, Poyntz replied that the priests had never made a secret about their dealings with Macanaz.[141] Despite attracting the attention of the police authorities, Macanaz was not, as were some other participants in the 'dangerous trade', expelled from Paris.[142]

From at least 1743, with France and Spain at war with Britain, Austria and their allies in the War of the Austrian Succession, Macanaz was again sending intelligence reports to Madrid, from the French capital.[143] But by this time, Macanaz, now aged more than 70, was less of a concern to ministers in Madrid. Indeed, some were increasingly preoccupied less with the man than with his papers, and what would happen to them when he died, as he soon must. In 1745 the fear that those papers – on the one hand so valuable to the Spanish Crown, on the other hand so (potentially) embarrassing to it – was raised, and the need to avoid their falling into the hands of the French authorities should Macanaz die in Paris; the man and his papers must be secured. Unfortunately, the case before the Inquisition had still not been settled, although Inquisitors were less pressing on this after Giudice; this ruled out the return of Macanaz to Spain. But there was an alternative. Macanaz could retire to the kingdom of Naples (or the Two Sicilies) which, following its conquest by Spanish troops in 1734–35, during the War of the Polish Succession, was ruled by the very dutiful son of Philip and Isabel, Don Carlos (or Carlo di Borbone) the future Carlos III of Spain.[144] The business took some sorting, but by January 1746 Don Carlos had agreed and all was set for Macanaz and his books to go to Naples, where Macanaz would receive a pension for life of 500 *doblones* from Philip V, and where, the Spanish Secretary of State, Sebastian de la Cuadra, marqués of Villarias hoped, Macanaz would be treated with the distinction he deserved and that he would be able to conclude his work without the risk that his writings would fall into the hands of those who would use them to the prejudice of the Spanish Crown.[145]

The arrangements for Macanaz's journey to Naples were still being finalised,[146] when, in July 1746, Philip V died, to be succeeded by Ferdinand VI. This changed everything: Ferdinand had no time for his hated stepmother or her Italian ambitions, and wished to end a war which, after successes in 1745–6 which had promised to make the (Spanish) Bourbons dominant in Italy, had turned sour for Spain. Suddenly, the prospects of Macanaz, the fervent champion of Spain and Spanish interests, seemed to improve. As soon as Macanaz learnt of the change of monarch in August 1746 he sent one of the two Sicilian Abbés, Caracciolo, to Madrid, to negotiate his own return there,[147] which his sympathisers at the Spanish court were also pressing.[148] However, at the end of 1746, it was decided to involve Macanaz in the peace negotiations to end the War of the Austrian Succession which were taking shape in the Low Countries. It has been suggested that Macanaz was used on this occasion in part at least because his reputation was such that he could make extravagant demands which could be simply disowned if they proved unwelcome to the other side, but followed up if they were acceptable.[149] But his activities and his writings had also revealed his firm attachment to Spanish interests, and a hostility towards France at a time – 1746 – when the Franco-Spanish alliance was under strain and the two allies increasingly suspicious of each other.[150]

But first Macanaz's case before the Inquisition had to be resolved: this was done on 15 December 1746, when he was declared innocent,[151] demonstrating both the extent to which the Inquisition was in fact an instrument of state and what it had always been open to Philip V to do for his disgraced former minister. Macanaz's instructions for the peace conferences to be held at Breda, in the Dutch Republic, were prepared in December 1746.[152] Macanaz and his secretary left Paris in late January 1747, for The Hague.[153] There, in a series of meetings with the British representative, John Montagu, earl of Sandwich,[154] Macanaz outlined the bases of an Anglo-Spanish separate peace which emphasised 'Spanish' concerns – demanding the return of Gibraltar, for example – rather than 'Italian' ones. Macanaz and Sandwich then headed for Breda, where the Dutch-mediated peace conferences were to commence on 2 March 1747. In typically abrasive style, Macanaz demanded to be admitted to the conferences, which the French representative, Louis-Philogène Brulart de Sillery, marquis de Puysieulx, who claimed to speak for both France and Spain, refused to allow.[155] The confrontation was repeated two weeks later, after which the peace conference was adjourned, never to re-convene. English ministers did not know what to make of Macanaz, describing him, his extravagant claims for Spain, and his even more extravagant ideas of attacking France on all sides as some sort of Don Quixote, although the Savoyard representative in London, Giuseppe Ossorio Alarcon, urged them to surrender Gibraltar if it meant securing a deal with Spain which would isolate France.[156] The Imperial minister, count Ferdinand Bonaventura Harrach, was also dismissive of Macanaz. However, Ossorio's colleague, the Savoyard representative at The Hague, count Borré de la Chavanne, who claimed to have read some of Macanaz's earlier work, about which he was very positive, believed that Harrach's jaundiced view of Macanaz simply reflected the fact that the latter's policy was not that of the Imperial Court. Chavanne, who claimed to have been able to study Macanaz closely (at Breda and at The Hague, in 1746–7), found the Spanish minister's policy wholly intelligible: Macanaz wanted to get Spain out of a war that was ruining her using, as a 'good Spaniard', all possible means.[157] Nevertheless, Chavanne talked Macanaz, who was impatient to conclude a deal,[158] into modifying his more excessive demands.[159] Macanaz was perhaps too easily played on by Chavanne, who encouraged his obvious hostility to France and his commitment to narrowly Spanish interests, but he also exploited the former exile's desire to impress his own court with a diplomatic success.[160]

It was not to be. Not entirely surprisingly, these developments, and Macanaz's violent manner, caused concern at the French court,[161] at the Portuguese Court, where the British government was also hoping to negotiate a deal with Spain, through the agency of another Spanish exile, Jaime Velaz de Medrano, marqués of Tabuérniga, and consequently at the Spanish court, which could not afford a complete rupture with Versailles. Ferdinand VI and his ministers were obliged to backtrack at the expense of Macanaz, who was sidelined in the peace negotiations: these were removed to Aix, where a peace was finally concluded in 1748, after Macanaz had been replaced as the main Spanish negotiator. Macanaz, who continued to mobilise his friends in Madrid, was initially ordered from Breda to Ghent,[162] then back to Liège, a location which some of those friends contended, not entirely convincingly, indicated that he was not in disgrace.[163] From Liège, Macanaz immediately contacted Sandwich,[164] and vented his anger against one of his fiercest critics, the Spanish ambassador in Paris, Fernando de Silva Álvarez de Toledo, duque of Huescar.[165] In July 1747, Macanaz asked to be allowed to return to Spain, where he could correct and secure his writings, in order, he claimed, that all good Spanish subjects could enjoy the immense treasures given Spain by God.[166] But Macanaz still clearly hankered after a public role, offering to go as Spanish ambassador to Venice, where he hoped to promote a general peace settlement which would reverse – in favour of Spain, the sons of Philip V and Isabel Farnese, and Spain's princely clients in Italy – the territorial exchanges made since the death of Carlos II in 1700;[167] he also continued to correspond with Sandwich.[168] Macanaz continued, too, to seek places for those around him. Already, in May 1747, he had sought to secure a post in the bishopric of Liége for his longtime secretary.[169] Macanaz did not help himself by persisting in lambasting Huescar and other Spanish ministers he blamed for his recent misfortunes.[170] Increasingly, those ministers saw Macanaz as a liability and in March 1748, in a move designed to secure his person, he was at last authorised to return to Spain.[171] The fiasco at Breda also resurrected the question of Macanaz's papers, which were now, particularly his recent instructions, even more sensitive,[172] strengthening the case for his recall to Spain. The Spanish minister in the Low Countries was ordered to secure those papers left behind by Macanaz when the latter left for Spain.[173] As for Macanaz, once across the border in Spain, he was arrested in Vitoria in May 1748, and incarcerated briefly in the citadel of Pamplona, before being transferred to the fortress of San Anton at Coruna, where he remained until his release in 1760.[174] Understandably, Macanaz, who clearly did not anticipate detention, thought he had been badly treated.[175]

oOo

Macanaz is a fascinating character, but not necessarily – and despite a remarkable energy and optimism – a very attractive one, a man who lived the transition from late Habsburg to early Bourbon Spain and never managed to shake off the sense acquired in his formative years of being the subject of a great empire. Macanaz's hopes after 1713 of recovering what had been lost during the War of Spanish Succession suggest that Henry Kamen is not entirely right in arguing that Spaniards were happy to lose their European empire, in Flanders and Italy, during the succession struggle. One at least was not, and his belief that Spain should be restored to its former glory and respected by the other powers was perhaps the most important thread in his thinking after the War of Spanish Succession. Personally, Macanaz also experienced a dramatic transition in 1715 from being a leading minister to being an exile for thirty years, with the threat of the Inquisition always hanging over him. During his exile, Macanaz was not a spy, although the term's applicability might depend on the perceptions of others, many of whom did view him in this light and with suspicion. Nor did Macanaz see himself as being involved in a mercenary activity, although the allowance he received from the Spanish court was paid in part at least in return for the intelligence and analysis he provided. But Macanaz was not treated overgenerously, and like most recipients of pensions, salaries and wages paid by the Spanish court in these years payments were frequently in arrears, leaving him in real difficulties.[176] Nevertheless, as an exile like many of those who were engaged in the 'dangerous trade', he was involved in intelligence gathering and negotiation in a covert way which set him apart from the publicly acknowledged agents of the sovereign state who normally engaged in these operations, whose world he briefly entered in 1747, and whose eighteenth-century 'culture' has been surveyed so admirably by Hamish Scott.[177] Macanaz and his work were also the object of not always benevolent attention on the part of the authorities where he resided, and his material circumstances were rarely easy. His relations with his own court remain murky, but there can be no doubt that Macanaz was an agent of the Spanish court for most of his period of exile, and that at crucial times, notably during the 'Cold War' of the late 1720s, his activity was an invaluable supplement to Spain's intelligence network. In many other respects, too, and not least in being a man in what was a largely masculine activity and environment,[178] Macanaz was an appropriate and exemplary inhabitant of the opaque, twilight world in which the 'dangerous trade' was practiced. He also exemplified the way that that world provided a classic 'way back' for the disgraced statesman.

CHAPTER SIX

Giacomo Casanova and the Venetian Inquisitors

A Domestic Espionage System in Action in Eighteenth-century Europe

Paolo Preto

In Italian (as in English) the word *Casanova*, echoing the name of Giacomo Casanova, signifies a womaniser, indeed, a restless and insatiable seducer of women, lacking in any moral scruples, such as the Don Giovanni immortalised in the Mozart opera. And in fact it is highly likely that Casanova himself, while he was staying in Vienna in 1784–85, lent a hand to Lorenzo Da Ponte as he was writing the libretto for that operatic success. 'Adventurer', 'libertine', 'follower of the Enlightenment' and 'reactionary bigot' are among the many, often contradictory, definitions used by biographers and historians in their attempts to get the measure of the complex and shifting personality of this eighteenth-century man, even if the prevailing image in people's minds, recently revived in some successful films about his life, has become that of the 'great lover' to the point where it has swallowed up the other aspects of his career. Why not also 'secret agent', or 'spy' or 'informer' (the much commoner term used in the eighteenth century language of espionage)? It was, after all, a profession he followed for several years of his stormy life. The fact is that Casanova, as we shall see, was ashamed of this professional role and so in his *Histoire de ma vie*, the memoirs he wrote in his old age, he scarcely mentions it.[1] So, following the pattern of the *Histoire*, which for most of his biographical details is a valuable source and often the only one available (the latest studies have, moreover, revealed that it is substantially reliable apart from the blatant exaggerations of his amatory prowess), his biographers and historians have marginalised his career as a spy. Yet this was no marginal part of his life. Casanova was a prolific and lively writer of works of history, literature and social commentary, as well, of course, as accounts of his own fortunes as a lover, and the reports he wrote when he was a secret agent of the Venetian Republic provide us with a lively, precise and often well-written picture of an intelligent, cultivated, clever, and generally successful spy.

Moreover, the Venice where Casanova was born and where he spent a good deal of his life was the right place to become involved in the world of espionage. Indeed, ever since the later Middle Ages, but particularly in the early centuries of the modern age, Venice organised an efficient network of spies both abroad and at home to defend itself from its enemies, support its military actions and trade, and ensure the stability of its aristocratic-republican political system. The Council of Ten, within which from the first decades of the sixteenth century onwards worked the three specialist State Inquisitors, controlled a network of directly-recruited spies; other 'informers' (i.e. spies) were recruited by its ambassadors overseas and by the noblemen appointed to individual political, financial and military magistracies both in Venice and in its possessions. There was a whole diversified world of spies drawn from different social classes according to the needs of the tasks to which they were assigned. These included noble, or 'honourable' spies, when the spying was intended to penetrate foreign courts, or at home, to discover the vices and crimes of the noble ruling class, but also merchants; Jews; clergy (especially friars, who were valuable because of the social respect and relative immunity they enjoyed in Venice itself and the rest of Europe); commoners in their various trades and professions; and lastly large numbers of 'masterless men', or '*banditi*' (in both senses of the word, i.e. those banished because of some offence and therefore forced to leave the territory of the Republic, and in the generic sense of criminals, murderers and common delinquents), who were always ready for the riskiest actions.

The records of the State Inquisitors and of the Council of Ten, but also those of many other offices of the Republic have preserved a wealth of evidence of the activities of the Venetian secret services, of their personnel, of their methods (ciphered correspondence, sabotage, political assassination and poisoning, to name just a few) and even of their moral and political reflections on the craft of espionage and on the ethics of the spying profession. By the time Casanova became involved in the dangerous trade the general outline of the Venetian secret services had, though, changed somewhat from what it had been in the central centuries of the Modern Age. In the mid-eighteenth century Venice was in drastic decline in terms of its military and political power and had already lost many of its largest and most valuable possessions in the Levant. It had a considerably smaller navy and army and had diminished to the rank of a minor, marginal power in the Mediterranean and continental Europe. The parallel decline of its long-standing enemy, the Ottoman Empire, was matched by the rapid rise of Austrian power (not to mention that of Russia and France). Confined to a reluctant and powerless neutrality (which would not prevent Napoleon's invasion of 1796–97 and the final dissolution of the state), Venice appears to have been focused entirely on its still lively civic and cultural internal affairs. As the centre of a brilliant social scene including music, theatres, gambling dens, public and private festivities, and a fascinating – near mythical – annual carnival, eighteenth-century Venice attracted young aristocratic visitors from all over Europe who were taking the Grand Tour. But it was also the home of publishing houses, newspapers, and writers influenced by the French Enlightenment. In this Venice of *splendeurs et misères*, of entertainment, of cosmopolitan encounters between men and ideas, Giacomo Casanova spent some of the best, but also the stormiest years of his adventurous life.

Born in 1725, he claimed descent from a noble family, but this is very likely to have been one of his many fantasising boasts – probably, as his recent biographer Nicola Mangini reveals, he was the offspring of an adulterous affair between his mother and a Venetian nobleman. For certain he was registered as the son of Gaetano and Giovanna Faruzzi, who were both actors. Because of the premature death of his father and his mother's profession, which often required her to be on tour in Europe, he was brought up by his maternal grandmother, and received a good education in science and letters, nourished by his lively intelligence and cleverness. He was interested in every kind of experiment and experience, and attended the nearby University of Padua, where he received his degree in law. During these youthful years he was also admitted to a minor religious order. A career in the church was not, however, the focus of his ambition, though wearing ecclesiastical dress enabled him to gain easy access to Venetian high society. Casanova was far more influenced by the famously licentious and erotic, even bordering on the obscene, poetic inventions of Giorgio Baffo, than by any religious precepts. He soon began to travel widely: within the space of a few years he had been to almost all the major cities in Europe. Wherever he went Casanova managed to secure entrance into the most exclusive and lively circles of society, and everywhere he was the protagonist in amazing and risky love affairs that made him famous as a fascinating and successful lover, and impenitent libertine. Yet he was not wealthy, for he did not come from an established noble family, and so he had to find the means to live a spendthrift life. He did so by developing more or less legal expedients for making money. And in particular, when he was able to do so, he took service with influential persons and governments in order to get gainful employment. Thus it was in the midst of this whirlwind life of adventures and misadventures in love, business and politics that Casanova encountered the tempting, though unreliable and dangerous, world of espionage.

Between 1741 and 1746 his travels took him to Corfu, then to Constantinople, Naples, Rome, Ancona and back to Venice. At this point he ceased to be an *abbé*, and became a violinist, then an officer in the army, then a violinist again, and between one love affair and the next in 1746 managed to pull off a tremendous coup: he befriended the elderly Senator Matteo Bragadin. Casanova then cured him of a rare disease and convinced him that he brought about the cure through his skill in the occult and in magic (which he had learnt about during a brief childhood illness). Having thus gained the unlimited trust of the credulous senator he persuaded the old man to adopt him as his son and then tapped him for large sums of money with which he led a splendid life of parties and love affairs of every kind for the next three years. In 1749, however, the golden shower suddenly stopped and Casanova fled to Milan and then Mantua, where he tried to get a high price for a forged relic of St Peter. He then moved on to Cesena, then back to Venice.

In 1750 he left for Paris and Lyons, where he became a freemason, probably in a lodge of the Scottish rite. Paris at this time was the heartland of the Enlightenment and the *Encyclopédie*, but to Casanova it appeared above all to be the place where, 'impostors and charlatans can thrive better than elsewhere'. He met Enlightenment figures such as the novelist Claude Prosper Jolyot de Crébillon and the mathematician and encyclopaedist Jean le Rond d'Alembert, but was actually far more assiduous in frequenting theatres and high society, where between love affairs, balls and gambling, he hoped to make his fortune. Two years later he travelled to Dresden, Prague, Vienna and finally, in 1753, returned to Venice, where he opened a faro house (a form of gambling then very fashionable in Venice), which failed dramatically. Shortly afterwards he fell for a young nun who was already the centre of the French ambassador's attentions. For Casanova it was just one of many passing adventures, but for some members of the Venetian ruling class it was too bold a step even in the tolerant Venice of the eighteenth century.

The city was carefully watched by a massive network of 'informers' (i.e. spies) who reported everything to the State Inquisitors. Thanks to the massive documentation preserved in the Venetian state archives I have been able to retrieve the exact structure of the eighteenth century's domestic espionage services. One's first impression when you leaf through the thousands of almost daily reports to the Inquisitors and to the *Capitan grande* (chief of police) is of spying that is intrusive, thorough and all-embracing – of a society that watches everyone at all times of the day and night, almost in a preview of Orwell's Oceania in his novel *1984*, with the three Inquisitors taking the part of 'Big Brother'. Their remit ranged from the petty disputes and scandals of daily private life to their equivalents in public life, from thought-crimes to theft of property, from immorality to state security. Nothing seems to have escaped the eyes and ears of the spies and hence of the State Inquisition.

If, however, one turns from the huge mass of information flowing over the desks of the three Inquisitors to what was actually done by way of repression, the gap is so large that this harsh image of eighteenth century Venice, although apparently confirmed in the writings of followers of the Enlightenment and the Jacobins, turns out to be completely illusory. A few more or less gruff cautions to citizens and nobles about too disorderly moral and civic conduct, a few expulsions of undesirable foreigners, a few banishments of dissolute or politically restless noblemen to outposts in Dalmatia, a feeble campaign against 'enlighteners' and 'freethinkers', a very close watch on 'French mischief-makers' and 'Jacobins', but very few trials. This was the final balance-sheet of a century of close domestic surveillance. Complaisance, good-natured tolerance, cynical indifference, and perhaps, too, an awareness of the unavoidability of many civic and moral evils, characterised the conduct of the State Inquisitors. Thanks to their informers they knew almost everything about everybody, but against the misdeeds of most people they did not bother or did not wish, and perhaps did not wish because they were unable, to take drastic action.

The informers/spies were to be found everywhere in the city. They rummaged in every nook and cranny, they penetrated every social circle from inns of dubious repute to the luxury hotels frequented by leading nobles and foreign travellers. They went almost daily to the coffee houses where they picked up conversations, remarks and discussions about the events reported in the newspapers and about the petty and great events in the life of the Republic. They reported minutely and almost gleefully any disorder, restlessness, breaches of the peace or merely of current morality and manners, from the frequent presence of women of sometimes dubious character in theatre dressing rooms to businesses staying open too long or during Lent, to brawls, to misbehaviour of maskers during Carnival, down to snippets of daily gossip. They were out in force in the brothels to report public and private trouble, and also at the theatres, which were the Venetian social and cultural institution *par excellence* in the eighteenth century. There they secretly monitored the love affairs of the nobles, any heckling or shows of dissent during performances, and scandalous public displays ranging from protests against the extremely popular comedy by Carlo Gozzi, *Le droghe d'amore*, ('Love potions') that poked such fun at the poet Pier Antonio Gratarol as a libertine that he had to flee the city in disgrace, to the half-naked ballerina who outraged the respectable when she appeared in November 1791 at the San Samuele theatre. The surveillance network did not even overlook the great events in Venice's cultural life: the names of the librettist Carlo Goldoni, the writer Abbé Pietro Chiari and the playwright Gozzi often crop up in their reports. Religious life was also one of their favourite subjects: brawls and high life in the convents, love affairs between Venetian noblemen and foreigners with nuns, immorality and disorderly conduct by priests, strange sermons, churches reduced to salons for conversation and flirtation – these and similar episodes frequently recur in the spies' daily reports.

The unflagging zeal of the informers captured a wide spectrum of incorrect behaviours by nobles. These included the use of a *tabarro* (commoner's cloak) instead of the prescribed *vesta* (nobleman's robe), frequenting *malvasie* (malmsey shops) without a mask, homosexuality, brazen libertinage, to the point of openly living with prostitutes, conduct unworthy of noble rank (barkeeping, selling wine, smuggling, begging, shady activities), blatant lack of respect for religion, coarse and inappropriate remarks about government decisions in coffee houses, brawling, making a scene, riotous behaviour, gossip and spiteful comment about abuse of office, electoral corruption and other disorders. The informers also kept an eye on the life of other Venetians and they noted a surprising range of unruly and scandalous behaviour, oddities and weirdness. Sodomites and lesbians, women dressed as men, phoney 'beggars' at Carnival, brawls by day and night, outrageous Carnival masks, the secrets of alchemy and poisons, quarrels between neighbours, saucy tales of love, cuckoldry, jealousy and impotence. There was also popular disgruntlement at cheating toll-keepers and shopkeepers, at rising prices, desertions, robberies, theft, cutpurses, coiners circulating forged or 'clipped' coinage, and all the other daily infractions of the law and morals to which a great and busy city such as eighteenth-century Venice might give rise.

To begin with the structure of the surveillance network: the 'informers' were either 'occasional' (part-timers), recruited for particular political and social situations, or 'actual', i.e. tenured and employed on a permanent basis, with a regular monthly salary and sometimes, 'on their retirement, granted a pension'.[2] Who were these Venetian spies of the eighteenth century, whose ranks included for a while the notorious Giacomo Casanova, and what kind of a life did they lead – what was their moral and social profile? Some were petty criminals, mostly recruited by the *Capitan Grande* (responsible for a kind of municipal police force controlled by the State Inquisitors), who were used for investigations of petty and major common crimes. There were 'honourable' spies, of noble birth, a few desperate *barnaboti* (i.e. impoverished noblemen belonging to the ruling aristocracy) and other gentlefolk of good education, refined manners and a fair or even outstanding intellectual level. Also men from a wide range of professions and trades, both manual and clerical. Who were their targets? First and foremost they aimed at catching the political enemies of the Republic. There were spies who identified, watched, and caused to be arrested 'impostors' and 'trouble-makers' who threatened public order in Dalmatia (a region caught between the endemic threats and incursions of the Turks and the, by then far more dangerous, expansionist aims of the Russians and Austrians). Clandestine recruiting agents for foreign armies (Russia, the Austrians, the King of Naples, the King of Prussia) and emigrants were also kept under close surveillance. There were spies who shuttled between Venice, Trieste and Fiume, in order to keep careful track, however powerless they were to prevent, Habsburg steps to promote and strengthen the trade and economies of the two Austrian ports on the Adriatic, while other specialist spies, such as the Abbé Giovanni Cattaneo, watched foreign diplomats and other prominent foreigners staying in Venice in any capacity. Some 'informers' paid particular and growing attention, as France moved from discussions of Enlightenment to Revolution, to the 'clever folk', i.e. citizens who were a bit too curious about new ideas from abroad, the 'new sects and conventicles' of the 'disturbers' both real and potential of law and order and of civil and social tranquillity. Finally, of course, they were interested in freemasons and 'Jacobins' i.e. the real or supposed sympathisers with the hated French maxims of *liberté, égalité et fraternité*, and from 1796 onwards anyone favourable to the threatening enemy Napoleon Bonaparte, the commander in chief of the *Armée d'Italie*. Where, however, the Venetian 'informers' of the eighteenth century did their best work (and where Casanova himself excelled) was when they gleefully investigated in minute and penetrating detail the morals, i.e. the vices and virtues, of Venetian society in the final years of the century. Innumerable reports were delivered in which the spies discuss and characterise a host of 'courtesans', 'adventurers', 'women of easy virtue' (i.e. prostitutes – but the range of terms used by the 'informers' to denote the world's oldest profession is truly startling and amusing), their *magnamaroni* (pimps and madams), their *scolete* (brothels run by the prostitutes themselves) where they carry on their professional activities and their customers – who were often prominent members of the noble ruling class or famous foreigners in Venice as tourists. Other reports are full of detail about the world of the gamblers: in Venice you could gamble, win and lose almost anywhere, legally or, more often, illegally. Venice sustained a considerable number of cardsharps, among whom Casanova himself stands out. Massive yet elusive, Venice supported a world of swindlers and adventurers of every kind. *Stoccheggianti* (hitmen), impostors, *trappolatori* (confidence tricksters), 'scoundrels', 'skilled deceivers' were everywhere and provided daily grist for the spies' mill. The eyes and ears of the ubiquitous 'informers' would catch them in the act and report statements from witnesses and victims of their daring – and sometimes even amusing – swindles. There were impostors claiming to be the Tsar of Russia, others seducing innocent young men with promises of amorous adventures in order to rob them, still others hinting that they knew the secret of transforming base metal into gold. There were burglars, pickpockets, false priests and monks, clever cheats, letter of credit swindlers, coiners and lottery tipsters (crooks selling numbers supposed to win the lottery). In this Venice of 'women of the world', cheats and hitmen, Casanova was perfectly at home. The experience he had gained from many years of adventures of every kind in the great cities of Europe could easily be put to use. He was, too, not short of socially important acquaintances and therefore of opportunities to pull off coups such as the one he inflicted on the old senator Bragadin.

In fact, though, his first contact with the slimy world of Venetian domestic surveillance was neither straightforward nor favourable: it was not as an informer but as the object of an informer's unwelcome attentions that he appeared first among the reports sent to the State Inquisitors. Between November 1754 and July 1755 he was several times reported to the High Court of Venice by one Giambattista Manuzzi, one of the most perspicacious and able 'informers' available to the State Inquisitors and one specialising in politically sensitive social misconduct, for his dissolute behaviour and unconventional opinions regarding religion. Casanova's dissolute lifestyle, with its forbidden love affairs, gambling and – to say the least – dubious friendships, some remarks that went too far in relation to religion, his writings (or rather semi-clandestine manuscripts) that were rather too free on matters of religion and morals, plus some planned swindles like the one he had brought off against senator Bragadin, had caught the attention of some members of the aristocratic rulers of Venice, and they requested that the State Inquisitors watch him more carefully.

In two reports, of 11 and 30 November 1754, Manuzzi, who was a real master of such surveillance operations, sketched a brief but perceptive moral profile of Casanova. '[H]e is said to be a writer but of a fertile and scheming cast of mind', he obtained 'illicit advantages' by his acquaintance with gentlemen and ladies, he practised 'libertinage', he played cards, he was an 'impostor', a 'ne'er-do-well', an 'exaggerator' who lived off others, he had got a lot of money from the naïve Senator Bragadin, 'by making him believe that the Angel of light was about to come', and he amused himself together with a circle of friends by writing satires against the famous writer Chiari. On 22 March 1755, in another secret report to the State Inquisitors, Manuzzi depicted Casanova as a man of, 'secretive character who knows how to profit from people's gullibility', who associated with 'people of libertine morals', was a cardsharp and a member of a group of *Picurei* (Epicureans)'. On 12 and 24 of July in the same year Manuzzi revealed Casanova's membership of the Freemasons (he even got sight of his ritual garments) and discovered an openly blasphemous composition in verse Casanova had written, with open sexual allusions to the birth of Christ. The most complete portrait of Casanova as a libertine is in the report of 17 July 1755, which also marks the beginning of his adventures and misadventures in the world of Venetian espionage. Casanova knows 'the art of cheating', he practises, 'damnable impostures about the Rosicrucians, the Angels of light', he is a, '*picureo*, through his impostures and chatter he inveigles people into total libertinage of every kind of pleasure', he practices magic and soothsaying, and is trying to persuade a certain gormless 'Duke Grillo' (probably Scipione Grillo, duca di Monte Rotondo e dell'Anguillara) that he owns a universal powder that will obtain for him a serene passage from this mortal life to '*Addesi*' (it is not clear what this extra-terrestrial world might be). He talks with spirits, he is, 'a source of denial of the truths of religion', but he is very cautious in this respect, 'because this is a country in which Government and Religion may not be disputed except at great risk'. In any case Casanova protests, with other noblemen, that he, 'believes nothing of our Religion', and thinks that, 'those who believe in Jesus Christ are very deficient in their wits'. Manuzzi's definitive conclusion is that, 'one sees brought together in him irreligion, imposture, lascivious behaviour, and the pursuit of pleasure to a horrifying extent'. Because of some blatant cheating at the faro house, because of his satires against the Abbé Chiari, his deception of old Bragadin, his membership of the Freemasons, his blasphemous writings, even perhaps because of his too incautious wooing of the nun, or, more plausibly, for all these activities combined – and so well described by Manuzzi – on the night of 26–27 July 1755 Casanova was arrested by order of the State Inquisitors and sent to the political cells of the Piombi prison. He remained there for over a year, then made the astonishing escape described, with some exaggeration, in his *Histoire de ma fuite*, which made him a kind of celebrity, but was also indirectly the first cause of his future career as a secret agent.

After an exciting flight across Europe he reached Paris. In the meantime the Council of Ten banished him from Venice. In the French capital he set up a successful public lottery and resumed his acquaintance with the Abbé François-Joachim de Pierre de Bernis, who was the Secretary of State for foreign affairs 1757–8. It was the latter, guessing that Casanova's unusual abilities might make him a good spy, who entrusted him with his first delicate task. He was to travel incognito to Dunkirk to make a confidential reconnaissance of the situation of the garrison and the fleet there. The brilliant success of this venture, for which he was paid 500 *louis d'or*, earned him another mission in 1758: he travelled secretly to Amsterdam to exchange 20 million *livres* in French state bonds for others that had a higher yield. He was less successful, however, with an industrial mission to set up in France the manufacture of silk fabrics with French designs: he ended up in debtors' gaol. Meanwhile, he of course continued his incessant, and more or less successful, womanising. In 1759 he was in Holland, then in Cologne, in 1760 in Berne, then Ferney, where he visited Voltaire (who, however, did not welcome him), then Geneva, Avignon, Grenoble, Marseilles, Genoa, Leghorn and Florence. Between more or less successful seductions and business deals, he enjoyed some cultural interludes. Thus he went on a pilgrimage to Vaucluse as a grand act of homage to the poetry of Petrarch, and to Rome where he met and appreciated Raphael Mengs and Johan Joachim Winkelmann, masters of painting, sculpture and the history of classical art.

By 1761 he was back in Paris, where he brought off one of his most sensational swindles: he persuaded Jeanne Camus de Pontcarré de la Rochefoucauld, marquise d'Urfé, a gullible believer in the occult, that he possessed the philosopher's stone (for transmuting base metal into gold) and relieved her of a large sum of money. Between 1762 and 1772 he wandered round Europe: to London, Berlin (*chez* Frederick II), St Petersburg (*chez* Catherine II, whom he failed to persuade to reform the Russian calendar), Warsaw (expelled because of a duel with a nobleman), Vienna (expelled by direct order of Empress Maria Theresa), Paris (expelled again), Madrid (arrested) and Barcelona (expelled yet again).

Casanova's dearest wish during these years of wandering was to return to his beloved Venice with its brilliant and enchanting social life. In order to get his banishment rescinded, however, he had to curry favour with the omnipotent State Inquisitors, and so he began to offer to serve them on a voluntary, unrecognised basis, in ways that verge on working as a secret agent. Hence in November 1763, while he was in London, he offered the Venetian ambassador a trial of a new secret product for dyeing cotton fabric red, saying he would induce French and English craftsmen to produce handkerchiefs and other items of cloth in Venice, but the offer was not taken up. During the Carnival of 1769, while illness forced him to stay in Aix-en-Provence, he wrote his *Confutation of d'Amelot de la Houssaie's History of the Venetian State*. With this short polemic against the former French diplomat, who had harshly criticised the Republic, Casanova hoped to win the approval of the State Inquisitors. But no approval came. The favourable and decisive opportunity to move into the treacherous and exciting world so congenial to him finally occurred in November 1772 when he turned up in Trieste and at once unhesitatingly offered his services as a spy to the Venetian Consul Marco Monti, who – like all Venetian diplomats – combined political and economic espionage with his official activities and was in close touch with the State Inquisitors. His first mission was a hard one, but Casanova at once revealed his devilish ability as a tried and tested operator. Some Armenian monks from the Venetian monastery of San Lazzaro, after a quarrel with their superiors, emigrated to Trieste, planning to establish there, with the permission of the Empress Maria Theresa, a print works in competition with the one run by their brethren in

Venice. Casanova pretended to have been sent by a monk of San Lazzaro to offer 200 gold *zucchini* to an official if he would obtain in Vienna a ban on the Armenian print works, and intrigued to have the sacraments denied to the monks by insinuating that they had been excommunicated. In the end the monks returned to Venice and Casanova, as a reward for his success, was granted the longed-for revocation of his banishment. It is worth mentioning that in a letter to the Consul of 1 July 1774 Casanova called himself 'your secret agent', which was perhaps the first time this term, so familiar in the nineteenth and twentieth centuries, was used in Italy.

In September 1774 he was finally back in Venice, but life was far less fun than he had expected. His friendships with men of power and, correspondingly, their protection, were no longer there. No crafty schemes beckoned, so he tried to make some money by writing for newspapers and other literary activities, but he had little success placing two publications: an unfinished *History of the troubles in Poland from the death of Elisabetta Petrowna down to the peace treaty between Russia and the Sublime Porte*, which he had actually written while living in Trieste, and a poor quality translation of the Iliad. Facing poverty, but armed with his one successful trial as an agent, he decided to take the big, but as we shall see, bitter step of applying formally to become an 'informer-spy' for the State Inquisitors. His first approach to them, on 18 December 1774, was not clearly answered, but during 1775 he volunteered a number of reports in order to demonstrate his ability, describing a midnight scuffle over a woman between some noblemen, a scandalous breach of the peace in some alleys, gambling in some brothels and seditious remarks made by a lawyer about some of the laws of the Republic.

Casanova's most successful coup during his apprenticeship in spying on the secret weaknesses of Venetian society concerned a daring fraud attempted during 1778. Having learned of the illness of the ninety year old Pietro Zardi, a former wigmaker, some 'bright sparks' went to the Mint (i.e. the State bank) with another old man who claimed to be Zardi and collected his savings of 4,000 ducats. The sudden appearance, however, of the sprightly Zardi, unexpectedly recovered from his indisposition, foiled the robbery and the guilty men hastened to return their loot. Casanova, who had ample experience of tricking rich old dolts (as in the case of Senator Bragadin), promptly informed the State Inquisitors, not forgetting, in order to ingratiate himself and also perhaps to cancel out his own murky deeds in the past, to end his report with a moralistic broadside: 'if such shysters as these are allowed to flourish, no one will feel able to entrust his capital to the Mint', and declaring, 'there are no laws that address such secret and astute intrigues: the Inquisition alone can weed them out and swiftly put a end to them'.

From February 1776, though still not officially appointed as such, his activity as an 'informer' to the State Inquisitors, under the pseudonym Antonio Parolini, became regular and paid. Some of his reports dealt with trivial matters of breaches of the peace and immorality, while others reveal that this educated man was aware of contemporary social and political problems: the conspicuous consumption and loose morals of women (a subject he knew about from personal experience!) were leading to many annulments of marriages, and the problem was compounded by the greed and corruption of ecclesiastical lawyers. In Trieste, where he was sent on a secret mission, he discovered the Austrians' plans to increase the trade and to improve the harbour at Fiume, and he predicted that they planned to invade Dalmatia. He kept a close eye on the Consul of the Papal State, Agostino Del Bene, and tracked him to the Romagna, where he uncovered agents recruiting soldiers for the king of Prussia. He frequented theatrical performances and thus discovered that in the first masque in Campo San Beneto, entitled the *Ballo di Coriolano*, the director Giuseppe Canciani sowed, 'in susceptible minds a certain spirit of rebellion', and hinted to the audience, 'that it was possible to be disobedient'. The Inquisitors promptly suspended the subversive masque. Some of Casanova's reports merely mention petty day-to-day breaches of the peace such as, for example, a wrangle in a coffee house. His spying activities met with the approval of the Inquisitors who, on 3 October 1780 appointed him a *confidente attuale*, i.e. an official spy with a monthly salary of 15 ducats. Casanova took his duties as an informer very seriously and by the 28 October had submitted a far-reaching mission statement under four headings. With respect to religion, he would keep watch for anyone who, 'violates the respect due to it', and watch out for, 'the rise of abuses that may damage it'. As regards morality, he would keep an eye on 'novel luxuries', on, 'the libertinage of individuals', and on theatres and gambling dens. As far as law and order was concerned, he would check up on roughnecks, tramps and strangers, and on, 'private gatherings where it is important to know their plans, machinations and exploits', and especially on, 'seditious, scandalous and libellous writings and all the dangerous books belonging to that category'. Finally, he would watch out for fraud in trade and manufacturing, and specifically for, 'abuses of privileges, and exporters of raw materials for industry', and, too, for 'secret importers' of forbidden goods. And as the 'crown of every secret inquiry' he would, in addition, watch for, anything that appears to be a 'novelty' and 'suspect', without omitting or altering 'any particular'.

A few days later he assured his employers that he was, 'most scrupulously exploring the sources of secret crimes [. . .] designing to uncover their hidden plots'. He was, 'aware that ceaseless forgeries are being carried out', but regrets his inability to uncover them. And, in fact, during his first few hectic weeks of informing he only managed to discover that some noblemen were grumbling about a new law governing the *Quarantie* (the Council of Forty, Venice's Court of Appeals) and some excesses of 'whores and rent-boys' in the boxes of the San Cassano theatre. Perhaps his pen ran away with him as he composed such a far-reaching programme, which included in fact all the different branches of Venetian domestic espionage, or perhaps in Venice at that time there was a shortage of significant political news (the kind of greatest interest to the Inquisitors). At all events, only three months after his longed-for appointment as a 'tenured informer' the Inquisitors, dissatisfied with his reports, cancelled his salary and decided to pay him according to his performance.

Subsequently Casanova became involved with the notorious occult adventurer Giuseppe Balsamo (the so-called Count Alessandro di Cagliostro) whom he had met some years earlier in Aix-en-Provence, wrote a book criticising Voltaire, who had recently died (*An assessment of the book: eulogies of M. de Voltaire by various authors, 1779*) and in 1780 published a journal entitled '*Opuscoli miscellanei*' (Miscellaneous pamphlets). He also tried to become a theatrical impresario, with a plan to establish a *Comédie Française* in Venice. But all these initiatives in the world of culture met with failure. He was desperately short of money, even to finance his latest love affair with a commoner, so for almost two years he willingly went on accepting the few, but welcome, ducats with which the State Inquisitors rewarded his spying activities, some of which it must be said were of a high standard. Casanova's discoveries in the cafés, theatres, foyers, hotels and the streets of Venice were wide-ranging. He located the clandestine printing-press of a Spanish resident (Casanova knew some Spanish), who turned out to be an ex-Jesuit expelled from Paraguay. He revealed there was a theatre in the Hospital of the Mendicant Order. He reported a naked model at the academy of painting. He denounced a nobleman who, in violation of stern Venetian laws on the subject, was keeping company with a Russian diplomat. He uncovered an impotent husband who had agreed to take his separated wife back into his house. He informed on a quarrel in a shop involving the publisher and future informer Vincenzo Formaleoni. He notified them of the secret trading company set up in the Levant by a Venetian subject who had emigrated to Trieste. In October 1782 he carried out a new secret mission to Trieste where he gathered intelligence about the smuggling of olive oil from Istria, Austrian trade in the Adriatic, a plan to recruit two expert sugar-refiners and tipped-off the State Inquisitors about the emigration of a thousand Greek families secretly planned by a certain Giovanni Palatino of Cefalù.

The most significant and best-known of Casanova's reports as a spy is dated 22 December 1781 and has been frequently quoted by historians of

Enlightenment culture because it vividly illustrates the widespread readership of Enlightenment books in eighteenth-century Venice. 'Licentious books', wrote Casanova, 'were commonly to be found not only in booksellers' shops', 'but in the homes of educated people of every walk of life including noblemen who mostly keep them to satisfy their curiosity, being well aware of not being likely to morally corrupted because they are enlightened and armed with robust understanding'. The writings of famous *philosophes* such as Voltaire, Jean-Jacques Rousseau, Claude Adrien Helvétius, Jean-François Marmontel, Crébillon, Julien Offray de La Mettrie and Nicolas Antoine Boulanger were all circulating. Likewise, 'the epic poem by the impious Lucretius', the books of 'impious heretics', and 'the advocates of atheism Spinosa, Diagoras of Melos and Porphyry of Tyre'. And similarly, pornographic compositions such as the 'dreadful ode to Priapus by Alexis Piron', the 'impious' erotic verses of Giorgio Baffo and all sorts of other books, 'evil because blatant in their libertinage [. . .] deliberately written to excite with filthy voluptuous tales the waning and languid desires we must defy'. Casanova listed exactly how this wave of Enlightenment and licentious books was being brought to Venice to be sold secretly and also the names of certain noblemen who were particularly keen to acquire them. Casanova's reports, often with the annotations of the Inquisitors indicating the police measures to be taken against the victims of his delations, give us a clear picture of the social circles in which the 'informer' was acting and the numerous precautions and expedients adopted to conceal his trade while ensuring the secret and secure delivery of intelligence to the inquisitorial secretariat.

The amounts spies could earn for surveillance reports were modest, and, more importantly, came at irregular intervals, and so Casanova sought other sources of finance for his expensive lifestyle as a lover and libertine. He finally managed to find a good permanent post as secretary to the Marquis Carlo Spinola, but shortly afterwards a misadventure occurred that marks the final turning point of his turbulent life: in response to an insult aimed at him by Count Giuseppe Carletti and the Venetian nobleman Giovan Carlo Grimani, he published a satirical pamphlet (*Neither lovers nor women: the stables cleaned up* (Venice, 1782)) which, beneath a transparent and allusive veil of mythology, poured unvarnished scorn upon the two wretches. There was a huge scandal because it was easy to identify the victims of his libel, and Casanova found himself facing an inglorious return to the Piombi prison he so hated. Forewarned by a powerful nobleman of imminent measures against him by the very State Inquisitors he was faithfully serving, Casanova promptly fled to Trieste and then to Vienna. In June 1783 he made a fleeting visit to Venice, realised the way the wind was blowing and left again, this time for good. He travelled round Germany and Holland and tried another stay in Paris but had no luck there. In February 1784 he was hired by Sebastiano Foscarini, the Venetian ambassador in Vienna, to be his secretary, and resumed his journalistic activities, among other things with some articles published in the 'Trieste Observer' in defence of the position of the Venetian Republic in a dispute with the Dutch Republic because of a fraud by some adventurers from Venice upon Dutch traders. Perhaps he was hoping to repeat his previous experience in Trieste and ingratiate himself once more with the State Inquisitors in the hope of yet another return to Venice, but the sudden death of Foscarini ended any such hopes and left him unemployed and penniless. During this brief interlude in Vienna he again befriended Lorenzo Da Ponte, who had also fled hastily to Vienna to avoid his own arrest (ordered by the State Inquisitors on account of a bawdy secret and anonymous denunciation). It has been suggested that Casanova may have collaborated with Da Ponte on the libretto for Mozart's *Don Giovanni*. There is no proof of this, but who better than Casanova to provide lively ideas from lived experience about a successful womaniser and impenitent libertine?

But Casanova's career as an adventurer, lover and spy was nearing its end. Without the means nor, by this time, the inclination for further adventures and affairs he accepted the post of librarian to Count Karl von Waldstein, chamberlain to Emperor Joseph II, and moved to Dux (Duchkov), near Teplice in Bohemia, a dismal and isolated place where, as his biographer Mangini writes, 'boredom, melancholy and rebellion invade his spirit'. The only consolation in his dull, dismal life was his constant correspondence with many of the friends he had made in his wanderings and especially his interest in literature and history. It was in this period that he wrote his *Histoire de ma vie*, and, too, *The Soliloquy of a Thinker* (Prague, 1786), a harsh condemnation of impostors (a subject all too familiar!) aimed especially at Cagliostro, *The Icosameron, or tale of Edward and Elizabeth* (Prague 1788), a moralising, utopian and strongly anti-Enlightenment novel, and other less important pieces, some of which he did not finish. Although he was far from the cockpits of European politics Casanova, thanks to his correspondence with old and new friends and his reading of newspapers and pamphlets, followed with interest (but also with repugnance and horror) the course of the French Revolution. Like many people in the eighteenth century he angrily rejected a movement that was ruthlessly destroying the aristocratic world into which, with varying fortunes, he had tried to insinuate himself for so long in order to gather its most tempting fruits.

Among the indirect consequences of the French Revolution was the disappearance of the Venetian Republic, invaded, humbled and then ceded to Austria by Napoleon Bonaparte (12 May–17 October 1797). Casanova's response to this event was ambivalent, like the rest of his love–hate relationship with Venice. On the one hand, according to a correspondent of his, he was upset, in despair, groaning because of the conquest of his 'ungrateful homeland', so powerful and glorious in the distant past. But on the other, in a fit of lucid political analysis well steeped in the unassuaged resentment he felt towards those aristocrats who more than once had made his life difficult and bitter, he admitted that the republic was sick and had been allowed to languish and die because of the dreadful but pointless avarice of an immoral and desperate political system, utterly lacking in foresight, which had avoided taking the necessary remedies. In matters of faith, in God and religion, too, his last years spent in the distant village in Bohemia reveal a definite about-turn compared with his youthful unbelief and 'Epicureanism'. Perhaps consciously accepting the wisdom of the Venetian proverb '*quando el corpo se frusta l'anema se giusta*' (When the body begins to fail the soul sets sail), Casanova, as he lay dying, received the sacraments and, in the words of one of his friends, declared: '*J'ai vécu en philosophe et meurs en Chrétien*' ('I have lived as an Enlightenment man, but I die as a Christian').

When he said these last words on 4 June 1798, Casanova had not completed his *Memoirs*, notably the *Histoire de ma vie*, which he had been revising since 1790 – they take us only up to 1774 and the eve of his return to Venice. His biographer Mangini has speculated that he may have wished to limit himself to the joyful golden years of his life as an adventurer, not wanting either his readers or himself to remember his failures and the physical and spiritual decline of his later years, but the common opinion is that illnesses and his death prevented him writing the second part. In any event, Casanova is lavish with the details of his amazing love affairs in the *Histoire de ma vie* as it stands, but as in all other aspects of his life, whether political, economic or cultural, he is reticent about his career as a spy and 'informer'.

As I wrote some years ago the debate about honour, or rather dishonour, has always accompanied the story of espionage down the ages:

> Useful, indispensable, practised by European states of the Modern Age, espionage has never overcome the strange anomaly of disapproval, dishonour, and even infamy being heaped upon those who carry it out. The end may be necessary, even praiseworthy; the man who achieves it, though keenly sought, is often despicable or morally ignoble.

Jean-Pierre Alem has rightly pointed out that even when, as in our own society, espionage is organised in complex multiple agencies, espionage never dares to call itself that without euphemisms, as is clear from the official titles of the secret services of the world's Great Powers.[3] Hugo Grotius (1583–1645), the father of the doctrine of Natural Law and the Law of Nations, considered that it was lawful to send men to reconnoitre in enemy territory, while Cristobal Benavente y Benavides, a seventeenth century theorist of the art of diplomacy, believed that though spies were, 'everywhere necessary, used, and allowed, they are always tainted by unworthiness'. Necessary for the good of the state, but nevertheless infamous, the spies of Europe have never shaken off this remarkable contradiction, which sometimes consumes their conscience, especially in the case of noblemen concerned for their personal and family honour. In the midst of the Enlightenment the infamy of a professional spy was reaffirmed by two great *philosophes*. For Voltaire the business of a spy was to, 'sell their friends' secrets and earn their living by informing and often by calumny'; for Charles de Secondat, baron de Montesquieu, 'Espionage might perhaps be tolerable if it could be done by honest folk, but the necessary infamy of the person may reflect upon the thing itself'.[4] In Casanova's Venice no one had published any treatise on the subject of the lawfulness and infamy of espionage, but from the reports of the informers who were more or less distinguished colleagues of our adventurer, one can glean valuable clues about the doubts and hesitancies that go with a profession that is scarcely ever a free choice, a 'chosen way of life', but rather is the outcome of economic, family or political needs.

> It is especially noblemen and other persons of social standing who are distressed to see their family's and their own reputation and honour labelled as infamous by their work as spies: they desperately insist on complete secrecy not merely so as not to put them out of the game but above all to avoid any stain upon themselves or their own family.[5]

Among the 'informers' of the State Inquisitors there were many 'honourable' spies, often the younger sons of Italian or foreign noble families who used their social status and their good standing in court circles, in diplomacy and in the army, to gather intelligence for the benefit of Venice. They included noblemen from Spain, Holland, France and almost all the Italian states (including Venice's own hinterland). But there were also a few who belonged to the impoverished noble *barnabots*, living in desperate poverty, whose only recourse was to deal cards and take wagers in gambling dens since their noble rank did not allow them to take other work. Casanova was not a nobleman, even if he did claim noble descent, but he was certainly at his ease among the 'men of letters', another category within which the State Inquisitors found it easy to recruit able and willing 'informers'. It was no accident that one of his most successful actions as a spy was, as we have seen, to report on the spread of Enlightenment books in Venice. When, on 1 July 1774 he decided to offer his services as a spy to the Venetian Consul in Trieste, he asked him to bear in mind the practical and moral risks of any discovery of his activities:

> [p]lease remember that one of my major concerns has to be that no one in this city ever manages to find out that I am one of your secret agents, not just because if I were discovered I would have no access to anyone and therefore would be of no further use to you, but for the further reason that I would risk being driven out in disgrace, a fatal misfortune for my poor honour even though I may flatter myself to think that once driven out from here I would be welcomed by the merciful embrace of the Prince I serve, whilst at present I am without this privilege enjoyed by so many others.

Six years later, as we have seen, Casanova was driven by need to offer his services as a spy to the State Inquisitors. In his mission statement as a newly-appointed full-time 'informer', written on 28 October 1780, there is of course no trace of moral scruples. Indeed, it emphasises how 'secret inquisition' is justified:

> Normally a criminal is punished only when the crime has been committed, while a pre-emptive action beyond normal rules, which are always weak, nips the crime in the bud. This in my humble opinion is why secret inquisition is sublime, and partly divine since it brings man a benefit that is no more than the opposite of the evil intended, of which he remains unaware and for which, no knowing how it has come about, can only thank eternal Providence from the bottom of his heart.

A few years later Casanova, now living far from Venice, old and tired in his hermit-like exile at Dux, reflects upon his parenthesis as an 'informer' and feels ashamed and so in his *Histoire de ma vie* he passes over this dishonourable stage of his existence. What he thought of it in his heart is, however, revealed in a passage of the *Isocameron*, devoted, in allegorical disguise, to Venice's spies, who are paid better the less they are seen. They are men, 'who are of good repute and wish the world to be unaware that their trade is to betray: it is punishment enough for them to know it themselves'. Truly, to Casanova in his last years, now sober, conservative, Catholic and the enemy of Enlightenment and libertines, the memory of his adventures as a secret agent seemed bitter and dishonourable.

Notes

Introduction

1. Jock Haswell, *Spies and Spymasters. A Concise History of Intelligence* (London, 1977), p. 8; Phillip Knightley, *The Second Oldest Profession: Spies and Spying in the Twentieth Century* (London, revised edn, 2003). The term: 'dangerous trade' used to describe espionage and covert operations is so ubiquitous as, apparently, to have no single source.
2. Rose Mary Sheldon, 'The Ancient Imperative: Clandestine Operations and Covert Action', *IJIC*, 10 (1997) pp. 299, 309; E. P. Thompson, *The Making of the English Working Class* (London, 1981, reprint of revised edn, 1968), pp. 90, 530, 637; 'Editorial', *INS*, 1 (1986) p.3; Alan Marshall, *Intelligence and Espionage in the Reign of Charles II, 1660–1685* (Cambridge, 1994), pp. 116, 117, 120, 168.
3. Alan Haynes, *Invisible Power: The Elizabethan Secret Services 1570–1603* (Stroud, 1994), pp. 52–3; Gary Kates, *Monsieur D'Eon Is a Woman: A Tale of Political Intrigue and Sexual Masquerade* (New York, 1995); Yuval Noah Harari, *Special Operations in the Age of Chivalry, 1100–1550* (Woodbridge, 2007), pp. 134–5.
4. Haswell, *Spies and Spymasters*, pp. 88–9, 101, 107, 126–8.
5. Tom Holland, *Persian Fire. The First World Empire and the Battle for the West* (London, 2006), pp. 85–6; Richard Bonney, *The European Dynastic States 1494–1660* (Oxford, 1991), pp. 276–7.
6. See, for example, M. R. D. Foot, *SOE in France: An Account of the Work of the British Special Operations Executive in France, 1940–1944* (London, amended edn 1968).
7. Peter Bondanella, ed., *Niccolò Machiavelli. The Prince*, trans. Peter Bondanella and Mark Musa (Oxford, 1985 reprint of 1984 edn), pp. xiv, 55–6. See also: Sir Samuel Morland's justification of domestic espionage, summarised in Marshall, *Intelligence and Espionage*, pp. 1–2.
8. This is in contradistinction to the more pacific activities of the artistic and business (and occasionally information-gathering) agents who are the subject of recent work by Hans Cools, Marik Keblusek and Badeloch Noldus (for which see: Cools, Keblusek and Noldus, eds, *Your Humble Servant: Agents in Early Modern Europe* (Hilversum, 2006)). See, too, the analysis of the difference between these agents and the spies and covert operatives dealt with in this volume in the essay by Steve Murdoch below.
9. Henry Kamen, *Spain 1469–1714. A Society of Conflict* (Harlow, 1983), pp. 38–44; Marshall, *Intelligence and Espionage*, pp. 144–5, 146.
10. Brian Champion, 'Spies (Look) Like Us: the Early Use of Business and Civilian Covers in Covert Operations', *IJIC*, 21 (2008), p. 543.
11. Though not always. In 1717 the British government scandalised Europe by raiding the Swedish ambassador's residence, arresting him and seizing his papers (Paul S. Fritz, *The English Ministers and Jacobitism Between the Rebellions of 1715 and 1745* (Toronto, 1975), pp. 22–7) and in 1718 the French government publicly intercepted the Spanish ambassador's courier to search his bags, and followed it up by arresting the ambassador himself and searching his residence (Simon Harcourt-Smith, *Alberoni, or the Spanish Conspiracy* (London, 1943), p. 191). Both ambassadors had, though, gone way beyond what was considered acceptable behaviour by actively plotting to overthrow the government to which they were accredited.
12. Geoffrey Parker, *The Grand Strategy of Philip II* (London, 1998), pp. 56, 169, 171, 191; Phyllis S. Lachs, *The Diplomatic Corps Under Charles II and James II* (New Brunswick, New Jersey, 1965), pp. 26–46; Christopher Storrs, 'Intelligence and the Formulation of

Policy and Strategy in Early Modern Europe: the Spanish Monarchy in the Reign of Charles II (1665–1700)', *INS*, 21 (2006) pp. 497–8.

13. A. J. Loomie, 'Wotton, Sir Henry (1568–1639)', *Oxford Dictionary of National Biography* (Oxford University Press, 2004) [http://www.oxforddnb.com/view/article/30001, accessed 18 Jan 2010].
14. Parker, *Grand Strategy of Philip II*, pp. 155–7.
15. Haswell, *Spies and Spymasters*, p. 52; Sean P. Winchell, 'The CDX: the Council of Ten and Intelligence in the Lion Republic', *IJIC*, 19 (2006) pp. 335–55.
16. Marshall, *Intelligence and Espionage*, pp. 3, 4, 161, 211.
17. Paula R. Backscheider, 'Defoe, Daniel (1660?–1731)', *Oxford Dictionary of National Biography* (Oxford University Press, 2004); online edn, Jan 2008 [http://www.oxforddnb.com/view/article/7421, accessed 15 Feb 2010]; Haswell, *Spies and Spymasters*, pp. 37–8.
18. Parker, *Grand Strategy of Philip II*, p. 56; Christopher Duffy, *Frederick the Great: A Military Life* (London, 1985), pp. 326–8.
19. Haynes, *Invisible Power*, pp. 1–8; Eveline Cruickshanks, *Political Untouchables: The Tories and the '45* (London, 1979), p. 50; Nicholas Rogers, *Crowds, Culture and Politics in Georgian Britain* (Oxford, 1998), pp. 38–9.
20. Paul F. Grendler, 'Giacomo Antonio Marta: Antipapal Lawyer and English Spy, 1609–1618', *CHR*, 93 (2007) pp. 802, 803; Lachs, *Diplomatic Corps*, p. 34; Storrs, 'Intelligence and the Formulation of Spanish Policy and Strategy', p. 500; Marshall, *Intelligence and Espionage*, pp. 140, 151, 153.
21. Haynes, *Invisible Power*, p. 49; HMC, *The Manuscripts of his Grace the Duke of Portland, Preserved at Welbeck Abbey* (15th Report, Appendix, Part IV, 1897), iv. 258–60: Captain John Ogilvie to Harley, Rotterdam, 12/23 October 1705; iv. 444–5: Defoe to Harley, Edinburgh, 11 September 1707.
22. Haynes, *Invisible Power*, pp. 114–15, 124.
23. Marshall, *Intelligence and Espionage*, pp. 277–8.
24. Marshall, *Intelligence and Espionage*, pp. 120, 132, 247.
25. HMC *Portland*, iv. 469: Greg to Michel Chamillart (French Secretary of State for War), Whitehall, 30 December 1707; 475: memorandum on French prisoners' letters, Whitehall, 18 January 1708; 480–1: 'K.O.' to Harley, [London] 13 March 1708.
26. See, for example, Peter Dixon and John Chalker, eds, *Jonathan Swift, Gulliver's Travels*, with an introduction by Michael Foot (London, reprint 1987 of 1967 edn), pp. 235–7.
27. For Cromwell, see Alan Marshall's essay below; for Walpole and Robespierre see Fritz, *English Ministers and Jacobitism*, pp. 59–108 and William Doyle, *The Oxford History of the French Revolution* (Oxford, 1989), pp. 178, 191, 202, 264, 267–8, 272–9.
28. G. V. Bennett, *The Tory Crisis in Church and State 1688–1730. The Career of Francis Atterbury, Bishop of Rochester* (Oxford, 1975), pp. 205–58; Michael Durey, *William Wickham, Master Spy: The Secret War Against the French Revolution* (London, 2009), pp. 51–3.
29. Geoffrey Parker, *The Dutch Revolt* (London, reprint 1988 of revised 1985 edn), pp. 133–6.
30. Harari, *Special Operations in the Age of Chivalry*, pp. 172–3; Mark Nicholls, 'Fawkes, Guy (bap. 1570, d. 1606)', *Oxford Dictionary of National Biography* (Oxford University Press, September 2004); online edn, May 2009 [http://www.oxforddnb.com/view/article/9230, accessed 16 February 2010]; Scottish Catholic Archives, Edinburgh, Blairs Letters 2/93/4: [Fr James Carnegy] to [Fr Lewis Innes?], 22 January 1704.
31. Cruickshanks, *Political Untouchables*, pp. 57–8.
32. See for example, Karl de Leeuw, 'The Black Chamber in the Dutch Republic During the War of the Spanish Succession and its Aftermath, 1707–1715', *HJ*, 42 (1999) p. 135, for the appointment of Abel Tasien d'Alonne (William III of England's illegitimate

half-brother) as Grand Pensionary Anthonie Heinsius's private secretary and chief cryptographer.

33. Victor L. Tapié, 'Louis XIV's Methods in Foreign Policy', in Ragnhild M. Hatton, ed., *Louis XIV and Europe* (London, 1976), p. 4.
34. Marshall, *Intelligence and Espionage*, p. 132.
35. Richard Garnett, 'André, John (1750–1780)', rev. Troy O. Bickham, *Oxford Dictionary of National Biography* (Oxford University Press, 2004); online edn, May 2009 [http://www.oxforddnb.com/view/article/512, accessed 28 January 2010].
36. Peter H. Wilson, *Europe's Tragedy. A History of the Thirty Years War* (London, 2009), pp. 537–41. See David Worthington, *Scots in Habsburg service, 1618–1648* (Leiden, 2004), for a more detailed account of this operation and the rewards its perpetrators received.
37. Marshall, *Intelligence and Espionage*, pp. 298–9.
38. Ragnhild Hatton, *George I: Elector and King* (London, 1978), pp. 58–60.
39. H. M. Chichester, 'Grant, Colquhoun (1780–1829)', rev. S. Kinross, *Oxford Dictionary of National Biography* (Oxford University Press, 2004); online edn, May 2006 [http://www.oxforddnb.com/view/article/11251, accessed 28 January 2010]; Chichester, 'Grant, John (1782?–1842)', rev. D. G. Halliday, *Oxford Dictionary of National Biography* (Oxford University Press, 2004); online edn, January 2008 [http://www.oxforddnb.com/view/article/11272, accessed 28 January 2010].
40. Alan Marshall would add duress to this: *Intelligence and Espionage*, pp. 122, 125.
41. H. T. Dickinson, *Bolingbroke* (London, 1970), pp. 142–4; Bolingbroke, *A Letter to Sir William Wyndham* (London, 1717), in Oliver Goldsmith, ed., *The Works of the Late Right Honorable Henry St John, Lord Viscount Bolingbroke* (5 vols, London, 1772), i. 3–98.
42. Haynes, *Invisible Power*, pp. 37–9.
43. James Hutson, 'Nathan Hale Revisited: A Tory's Account of the Arrest of the First American Spy', *Library of Congress Information Bulletin* (http://www.loc.gov/loc/lcib/0307-8/hale.html, accessed 19 February 2010).
44. Marshall, *Intelligence and Espionage*, pp. 261–2.
45. Lorenzino de Medici, *Apology for a Murder*, trans. Andrew Brown (London, 2004). I owe this reference to Alan Marshall.
46. W. A. Speck, *Reluctant Revolutionaries: Englishmen and the Revolution of 1688* (Oxford, 1988), p. 80 note 11.
47. Jonathan Scott, *England's Troubles: Seventeenth-Century English Political Instability in European Context* (Cambridge, 2000), pp. 20–65.
48. Carlo Ginzburg, *The Cheese and the Worms: The Cosmos of a Sixteenth-Century Miller* (London, reprint 1982 of 1980 edn), pp. 2, 4, 98–9, 102.
49. R. B. Wernham, *Before the Armada: The Emergence of the English Nation 1485–1588* (New York, 1966), pp. 264–5, 380–1; Richard Cust, *Charles I. A Political Life* (Harlow, 2007), pp. 51, 64, 68; Hillel Schwarz, *The French Prophets. The History of a Millenarian Group in Eighteenth-Century England* (London, 1980), pp. 22–7. See, in particular, Orest Ranum, *The Fronde: A French Revolution* (New York, 1993); S. A. Westrich, *The Ormée of Bordeaux: A Revolution During the Fronde* (Baltimore, 1972); and Timothy Venning, 'Stouppe, Jean-Baptiste (fl. 1651–1673)', *Oxford Dictionary of National Biography* (Oxford University Press, 2004); online edn, January 2008 [http://www.oxforddnb.com/view/article/71950, accessed 25 March 2010] for a notably well documented episode of English involvement with Huguenot resistance (I owe this reference to Alan Marshall).
50. Wilson, *Europe's Tragedy*, p. 462; Ragnhild M. Hatton, *Charles XII of Sweden* (New York, 1968), pp. 236, 526.
51. Parker, *Grand Strategy of Philip II*, pp. 154–5, 159, 160, 161, 191; T. W. Moody, F. X. Martin, F. J. Byrne (eds), *A New History of Ireland III: Early Modern Ireland 1534–1691*

(Oxford, 1976), pp. 591–9; J. F. S. Gordon, ed., *The Catholic Church in Scotland From the Suppression of the Hierarchy to the Present Time, Being Memorabilia of the Bishops, Missioners, and Scotch Jesuits* (Aberdeen, 1874), iii–xv.

52. Marshall, *Intelligence and Espionage*, p. 254; François Bluche, *Louis XIV*, trans. Mark Greengrass (New York, 1990), p. 402.
53. For Elbing see Steve Murdoch's essay on Sir James Spens, below p. 46, and for Ireland see John Childs, *The Williamite Wars in Ireland 1688–1691* (London, 2007), pp. 214, 216, 269, 274, 282, 286.
54. R. A. Stradling, 'Spanish Conspiracy in England, 1661–1663', *History*, 87 (1972) pp. 269–86; K. H. D. Haley, *The First Earl of Shaftesbury* (Oxford, 1968), pp. 443–5. See also Marshall, *Intelligence and Espionage*, p. 133, for the case of Henry de Buat.
55. C. V. Wedgwood, *William the Silent. William of Nassau, Prince of Orange 1533–1584* (London, reprint 1967 of 1944 edn), pp. 214, 230, 248.
56. Wedgwood, *William the Silent*, p. 249.
57. Parker, *Dutch Revolt*, p. 217.
58. James VI and I proclaimed the end of the war with Spain on 23 June 1603, and the treaty of London, which included a proposed marriage alliance between Henry, Prince of Wales, and the Infanta Anne, was signed on 18 August 1604; Mark Nicholls, 'The Gunpowder Plot', *Oxford Dictionary of National Biography* (Oxford University Press, 2005); online edn, September 2009 [http://www.oxforddnb.com/view/theme/92749, accessed 20 February 2010].
59. Parker, *Grand Strategy of Philip II*, p. 56, and cf. John Lambert's conduct, outlined in Alan Marshall's essay below.
60. Winchell, 'The CDX', pp. 341–55.
61. Winn L. Taplin, 'Six General Principles of Intelligence', *IJIC*, 3 (1989) p. 482.
62. HMC *Portland*, iv. 479: 'Gassion' (Ogilvie) to [Harley], [London] 6 March 1708.
63. Parker, *Grand Strategy of Philip II*, p. 25; Marshall, *Intelligence and Espionage*, pp. 165, 191; see also Marshall's description of John Thurloe's use of intelligence to further his own interests as well as those of the Protectorate p. 72.
64. Bonney, *European Dynastic States*, pp. 330–34.
65. See, for example, the structure and functioning of the Phélypeaux de Pontchartrain patron-client system: Sara E. Chapman, *Private Ambition and Political Alliances. The Phélypeaux de Pontchartrain Family and Louis XIV's Government, 1650–1715* (Woodbridge, 2004).
66. John C. Rule, 'Colbert de Torcy, an Emergent Bureaucracy, and the Formulation of French Foreign Policy, 1698–1715', in *Louis XIV and Europe*, pp. 277–82; for Prince Eugene see Christopher Storrs' essay on Macanaz (below).
67. Parker, *Grand Strategy of Philip II*, pp. 47–65; and see Christopher Storrs' description of Prince Eugene of Savoy's network in his essay on Macanaz (below p. 127).
68. Christopher Andrew, 'Codebreaking and Signals Intelligence', *INS*, 1 (1986) p. 1.
69. John Keegan, *Intelligence in War. Knowledge of the Enemy from Napoleon to Al-Qaeda* (London, 2004), p. 298; Rose Mary Sheldon, 'Intelligence and the Historians', review of N. J. E. Austin and N. B. Rankov, *Exploratio: Military and Political Intelligence in the Roman World from the Second Punic War to the Battle of Adrianople* (New York, 1995), *IJIC*, 11 (1998) pp. 110–11.
70. Viz: cyber-attacks by the Chinese security and intelligence services on US commercial and government internet sites in autumn 2009. In this context it is also interesting to note that even special forces operations are now heavily reinforced by sigint and surveillance teams who far outnumber the men at the sharp end. By the later stages of the war in Northern Ireland 1970–97, for example, each SAS four-man team was supported in the field by about sixty intelligence and sigint officers from a specialist unit known as 14 INT (I owe this latter information to Steve Murdoch).

71. Rule, 'Colbert de Torcy', pp. 275–6; De Leeuw, 'Black Chamber in the Dutch Republic', pp. 133–56.
72. See for example, Pierre Burger, 'A Study of the Papers of the Abbé Eusèbe Renaudot', in Eveline Cruickshanks, ed., *Ideology and Conspiracy: Aspects of Jacobitism, 1689–1759* (Edinburgh, 1982), p. 117.
73. Penry Williams, 'Babington, Anthony (1561–1586)', *Oxford Dictionary of National Biography* (Oxford University Press, 2004); [http://www.oxforddnb.com/view/article/967, accessed 9 February 2010]
74. K. H. D. Haley, *William of Orange and the English Opposition, 1672–4* (Oxford, 1953); Burger, 'Renaudot', pp. 119–20; Rule, 'Colbert de Torcy', pp. 267–8.
75. Parker, *Grand Strategy of Philip II*, p. 14; Bluche, *Louis XIV*, p. 81; Wolfgang Michael, *England Under George I. The Quadruple Alliance* (London, 1939), pp. 81–2; Henry Kamen, *Philip V. The King Who Reigned Twice* (London, 2001), pp. 123–4; Wedgwood, *William the Silent*, pp. 213, 230–1, 248; Marshall, *Intelligence and Espionage*, pp. 262, 268–70, 272–4.
76. Haswell, *Spies and Spymasters*, pp. 15, 144; Rose Mary Sheldon, 'The Ancient Imperative: Clandestine Operations and Covert Action', *IJIC*, 10 (1997) p. 299; Keegan, *Intelligence in War*, pp. 3–20.
77. Brown, 'From the Editor', *IJIC*, 1 (1986) p. 1.
78. Taplin, 'Six General Principles', p. 475.
79. See also, Grendler, 'Giacomo Antonio Marta', pp. 789–809.
80. Sir Samuel Morland argued that the fallen state of humankind made this essential: Marshall, *Intelligence and Espionage*, pp. 1–2.
81. See Thomas Birch, ed., *A Collection of the State Papers of John Thurloe, Esq. Secretary to the Council of State and the two Protectors Oliver and Richard Cromwell: to which is prefixed the life of Mr Thurloe, with a complete index to each volume by T. Birch* (7 vols, London, 1742).
82. Richard Horowitz, 'A Framework for Understanding Intelligence', *IJIC*, 8 (1995) p. 395.
83. Haswell, *Spies and Spymasters*, p. 142.
84. Herbert Harvey Rowen, *John de Witt, Grand Pensionary of Holland, 1625–1672* (Princeton, 1978), pp. 731–2, 734, 736–7, 742, 748, 750, 752.
85. Bluche, *Louis XIV*, pp. 80, 246–7, 400–1.
86. Rowen, *John de Witt*, pp. 874–82.
87. John Miller, *James II. A Study in Kingship* (Hove, 1978), pp. 193–5; Speck, *Reluctant Revolutionaries*, p. 80; John Childs, *The Army, James II and the Glorious Revolution* (Manchester, 1980), pp. 142–5.
88. Taplin, 'Six General Principles', p. 485.
89. See, for example, Marshall, *Intelligence and Espionage*, p. 232. It should be noted that this problem still persists: Horowitz, 'Understanding Intelligence', pp. 395–404.
90. Taplin, 'Six General Principles', pp. 486–7.
91. HMC *Portland*, iv. 464–7: 'Gassion' (Ogilvie) to [Harley], 25 December 1707.
92. John Sibbald Gibson, *Playing the Jacobite Card. The Franco-Jacobite Invasion of 1708* (Edinburgh, 1988), pp. 112–47.
93. Parker, *Grand Strategy of Philip II*, pp. 48–54. Timeliness is seen as crucial by modern commentators: Taplin, 'Six General Principles', pp. 485, 488.
94. Late seventeenth-century England, for example: Lachs, *Diplomatic Corps*, pp. 4–7.
95. As was the case with both the Republican and the Jacobite underground in the British Isles: Marshall, *Intelligence and Espionage*, p. 163; Edward Gregg, 'The Politics of Paranoia', in Eveline Cruickshanks and Jeremy Black, eds, *The Jacobite Challenge* (Edinburgh, 1988), pp. 42–56.
96. Stephen K. Roberts, 'Sealed Knot (act. 1653–1659)', *Oxford Dictionary of National Biography* (Oxford University Press, September 2009), online edn. [http://www.oxforddnb.comview/theme/98250, accessed 23 February 2010].
97. Taplin, 'Six General Principles', p. 490.

Chapter 1: Diego Guzmán de Silva and Sixteenth-century Venice

1. See Carlos Carnicer and Javier Marcos, *Espías de Felipe II: Los servicios secretos del Imperio español* (Madrid, 2005). Queen Elizabeth's England had the other most extensive spy network in Europe. See the recent works by John Bossy, *Giordano Bruno and the Embassy Affair* (2nd edn, New Haven, 2002) and *Under the Molehill: an Elizabethan Spy Story* (New Haven, 2001).
2. Parker, *Grand Strategy of Philip II*, pp. 47–65.
3. See Garrett Mattingly, *Renaissance Diplomacy* (reprint, New York, 1988), pp. 207–19; Donald E. Queller, *The Office of Ambassador in the Middle Ages* (Princeton, 1967), chapter 4; and M. S. Anderson, *The Rise of Modern Diplomacy 1450–1919* (London, 1993), pp. 12–13.
4. J. H. Elliott, *Imperial Spain 1469–1716*, 2nd edn (London, 2002), p. 132.
5. Parker, *Grand Strategy of Philip II*, pp. 80–5.
6. See the classic works by Fredric C. Lane, *Venice: A Maritime Republic* (Baltimore, 1973), and William H. McNeill, *Venice, the Hinge of Europe 1081–1797* (Chicago, 1974).
7. See Filippo de Vivo, *Information and Communication in Venice: Rethinking Early Modern Politics* (Oxford, 2007), chapter 2.
8. See Paolo Preto, *I Servizi Segreti di Venezia: spionaggio e controspionaggio ai tempi della Serenissima* (Milan, 1994).
9. Giovanni K. Hassiotis, 'Venezia e i domini veneziani tramite di informazioni sui turchi per gli spagnoli nel sec. XVI', in Hans-Georg Beck, ed., *Venezia centro di mediazione tra Oriente e Occidente (secoli XV–XVI)* (Florence, 1977), pp. 116–36.
10. Carnicer and Marcos, *Espías de Felipe II*, p. 146.
11. Philip to Guzmán, 14 September 1569; quoted in Carnicer and Marcos, *Espías de Felipe II*, p. 80.
12. Eric Dursteler, *Venetians in Constantinople: Nation, Identity, and Coexistence in the Early Modern Mediterranean* (Baltimore, 2006), pp. 4–6.
13. He was not the first Spanish resident ambassador in Venice to fail in this way. In the 1540s, Don Diego Hurtado de Mendoza suffered a similar fate; see Michael J. Levin, *Agents of Empire: Spanish Ambassadors in Sixteenth-Century Italy* (Ithaca, 2005), pp. 19–26.
14. Manuel Fernández Álvarez, *Tres embajadores de Felipe II en Inglaterra* (Madrid, 1951), pp. 132–90, and Mattingly, *Renaissance* Diplomacy, pp. 174–5.
15. Archivo General de Simancas, Sección Estado (henceforth, AGSE), 1398, #253: Philip to Guzmán, 26 November 1569.
16. Carnicer and Marcos, *Espías de Felipe II*, pp. 146–7, and Levin, *Agents of Empire*, pp. 26–9. For more on the precedence dispute, see Michael J. Levin, 'A New World Order: The Spanish Campaign for Precedence in Early Modern Europe', *JEMH*, 6 (2002), pp. 233–64.
17. Carnicer and Marcos, *Espías de Felipe II*, p. 88.
18. For a recent study of the war in the Mediterranean in these years, see Niccolò Capponi, *Victory of the West: The Great Christian-Muslim Clash at the Battle of Lepanto* (Cambridge MA, 2006).
19. Geoffrey Parker, 'Spain, her Enemies, and the Revolt of the Netherlands, 1559–1648', in Parker, *Spain and the Netherlands 1559–1569: ten studies* (reprint, London, 1990), pp. 17–42.
20. AGSE 1329, #23: Julián López to Philip, 16 March 1571.
21. AGSE 1329, #24: Guzmán to Philip, 16 March 1571.
22. AGSE, 1500, #3: Guzmán to Zúñiga, 17 March 1571.
23. AGSE 1501, #18: Zúñiga to Guzmán, 7 April 1571.
24. Fernand Braudel, *The Mediterranean and the Mediterranean World in the Age of Philip II*, trans. Siân Reynolds (2 vols, New York, 1972–3), ii. p. 1089.
25. See D. S. Chambers, *The Imperial Age of Venice 1380–1580* (London, 1970).

26. De Vivo, *Information and Communication in Venice*, pp. 37, 71–2.
27. AGSE 1329, #64: Guzmán to Philip, 14 June 1571.
28. AGSE 1329, #25: Guzmán to Philip, 29 March 1571. In years past, the Spanish embassy in Venice had an extensive intelligence network. For example, Don Diego Hurtado de Mendoza (ambassador from 1539 to 1546) had several informants inside the Collegio. Levin, *Agents of Empire*, pp. 170–1.
29. AGSE 1329, #31: Guzmán to Philip, 21 April 1571.
30. See Levin, *Agents of Empire*, pp. 93–9.
31. Luciano Serrano, ed., *Correspondencia diplomática entre España y la Santa Sede durante el pontificado de S. Pio V* (4 vols, Madrid, 1914), iv. pp. 272–3: Zúñiga to Philip, 7 May 1571.
32. Gaetano Cozzi, 'Venezia dal Rinascimento all'Età barocca', in Gaetano Cozzi and Paolo Prodi, eds, *Storia di Venezia, Vol. IV, 'Dal Rinascimento al Barocco'* (8 vols, Rome, 1992–1998), p. 52.
33. AGSE 1329, #25: Guzmán to Philip, 7 April 1571.
34. AGSE 1329, #44: Guzmán to Philip, 10 May 1571.
35. Capponi, *Victory of the West*, pp. 162–4.
36. AGSE 1329, #67: Guzmán to Philip, 3 July 1571.
37. See Edward Muir's classic work, *Civic Ritual in Renaissance Venice* (Princeton, 1981).
38. Iain Fenlon, 'Lepanto: Le arti della celebrazione nella Venezia del Rinascimento', in Vittore Branca and Carlo Ossola, eds, *Crisi e rinnovamenti nell'autumno del Rinascimento a Venezia* (Florence, 1991), p. 377.
39. Fenlon, 'Lepanto', pp. 373–406, and see also E. H. Gombrich, 'Celebrations in Venice of the Holy League and of the Victory of Lepanto', in Anthony Blunt, ed., *Studies in Renaissance and Baroque Art Presented to Anthony Blunt on His Sixtieth Birthday* (London, 1967), pp. 62–68.
40. AGSE 1329, #106: Guzmán to Philip, 22 October 1571.
41. For more on Philip's religious and imperial ideologies, see Geoffrey Parker, 'David or Goliath? Philip II and His World in the 1580s', in G. Parker, ed., *Success Is Never Final: Empire, War, and Faith in Early Modern Europe* (New York, 2002), pp. 16–38.
42. AGSE 1329, #112: Guzmán to Philip, 31 October 1571.
43. Joycelyne G. Russell, *Diplomats at Work: Three Renaissance Studies* (Wolfeboro Falls, 1992), p. 81.
44. AGSE 1329, #112: Guzmán to Philip, 31 October 1571.
45. AGSE 1329, #31: Guzmán to Philip, 22 October 1571.
46. The historian Kenneth M. Setton, for example, quotes Venetian municipal records of the celebrations, which mention Don John but not Philip. *The Papacy and the Levant (1204–1571)*, (4 vols, Philadelphia, 1976–1984), iv. 1060 n. 54.
47. Ludwig von Pastor, *The History of the Popes from the Close of the Middle Ages*, trans. Ralph Francis Kerr (40 vols, London, 1891–1953), xviii. 425.
48. Capponi, 1 *Victory of the West*, p. 310.
49. AGSE 1329, #111: Guzmán to Philip, 25 October 1571. The emphasis is mine.
50. *Correspondencia diplomática*, iv. 497–499: Juan de Zúñiga to Philip, 29 October 1571.
51. Martin Fernandez de Navarette, ed., *Colección de documentos inéditos para la historia de España* (113 vols, Madrid, 1842–1895), iii. pp. 292–303: Alba to Zúñiga. 17 November 1571.
52. *Correspondencia diplomática*, iv. 886–891: Philip to the delegates in Rome, 22 December 1571.
53. The historian N. M. Sutherland argues that France in fact would have invaded Italy in the early summer of 1572, had not the government been sidetracked by internal strife. See, 'The Massacre of St. Bartholomew and the Problem of Spain', in Sutherland, *Princes, Politics and Religion, 1547–1589* (London, 1984), pp. 173–82.
54. AGSE 1332, #2: Guzmán to Philip, 8 January 1572.

55. In 1573, Leonardo Donà, the Venetian ambassador to Spain, wrote a contemptuous report about Spaniards, who claimed to be more Catholic than anyone else, but in reality were all, 'so many baptized Jews and Moors'. James C. Davis, ed. and trans., *Pursuit of Power: Venetian Ambassadors' Reports on Spain, Turkey, and France in the Age of Philip II, 1560–1600* (New York, 1970), p. 97.
56. AGSE 1331, #19: Guzmán to Philip, February 1572.
57. AGSE 1331, #26: Guzmán to Philip, 19 March 1572.
58. AGSE 1331, #32: Guzmán to Philip, 8 April 1572.
59. In 1575, Guzmán wrote another letter complaining about being pestered by inventors of, 'clever secret machines of war', which were either impractical or ridiculous. ASGE 1334, #3: Guzmán to Philip, 8 January 1575.
60. *Correspondencia diplomática*, iv. 731–732: Zúñiga to Philip, 1 May 1572.
61. AGSE 1331, #40: Guzmán to Philip, 2 May 1572.
62. Braudel, *Mediterranean World in the Age of Philip II*, ii. pp. 1116–17.
63. See Parker, *Dutch Revolt*, pp. 126–30.
64. Luciano Serrano, *La Liga de Lepanto entre España, Venecia, y la Santa Sede (1570–1573)* (2 vols, Madrid, 1918–1919), i. p. 236.
65. Capponi, 1 *Victory of the West*, p. 310.
66. AGSE 1331, #69: Guzmán to Philip, 2 July 1572.
67. See Levin, *Agents of Empire*, pp. 203–8.
68. John Lynch, *Spain under the Habsburgs* (2 vols, New York, 1984), i. p. 246.
69. Braudel, *Mediterranean World in the Age of Philip II*, ii. p. 1118.
70. *Correspondencia diplomática*, i. 371–373: Philip to Zúñiga, 4 July 1572.
71. Braudel, *Mediterranean World in the Age of Philip II*, ii. p. 1118.
72. Setton, *Papacy and the Levant*, iv. pp. 1081–4.
73. AGSE 1331, #103: Guzmán to Philip, 10 September 1572.
74. *Correspondencia diplomática*, ii. chapter 9
75. AGSE 1332, #2: Guzmán to Philip, 2 January 1573.
76. AGSE 1332, #21: Guzmán to Philip, February [date unknown] 1573.
77. AGSE 1332, #19: Guzmán to Philip, 17 February 1573.
78. AGSE 1332, #23: Guzmán to Philip, 25 February 1573.
79. AGSE 1332, #26: Guzmán to Philip, 27 February 1573.
80. Guzmán was not the only one who was worried. On 19 March Pope Gregory XIII issued a papal bull threatening to excommunicate any League member who defected, and he clearly had the Venetians in mind. Setton, *Papacy and the Levant*, iv. pp. 1090–1.
81. Capponi, *Victory of the West*, pp. 310–12.
82. AGSE 1332, #30: Guzmán to Philip, 17 March 1573.
83. AGSE 1332, #36: Guzmán to Philip, 3 April 1573. As with many such encoded letters, the deciphered text appears in the margins.
84. AGSE 1332, #36: Guzmán to Philip, 3 April 1573.
85. AGSE 1332, #38: Guzmán to Philip, 4 April 1573.
86. AGSE 1332, #38: Guzmán to Philip, 4 April 1573.
87. Archivo de Zabálburu (Madrid), Caja 54, #34: Zúñiga to Philip, 12 April 1573.
88. Serrano, *La Liga de Lepanto*, ii. pp. 285–7.
89. See the letter from Cardinal Como, the papal secretary, to the papal nuncio in Madrid, 7 April 1573; published in Serrano, *La Liga de Lepanto*, ii. 413–14.
90. Davis, *Pursuit of Power*, p. 104.
91. Instituto de Valencia de Don Juan (Madrid), Caja 60, #96: Philip II to Antonio Pérez, no date. My thanks to Professor Geoffrey Parker for this reference.

92. AGSE 1332, #39: Guzmán to Philip, 8 April 1573.
93. AGSE 1332. #39: Guzmán to Philip, 8 April 1573.
94. Gaetano Cozzi notes that Leonardo Doná, among others, clearly felt ashamed of his government's actions. Cozzi, 'Venezia dal Rinascimento', pp. 53–4.
95. AGSE 1333, #10: Guzmán to Philip, 25 January 1574.
96. Requeséns was Governor-General of the Netherlands from 1573 until his death in 1576. He may have started out confident, but his tenure did not go very well; see Parker, *Dutch Revolt*, pp. 163–70.
97. AGSE 1333, #30: Guzmán to Philip, 17 March 1574.
98. Carnicer and Marcos, *Espías de Felipe II*, p. 159.
99. AGSE 1332, #72: Guzmán to Philip, July 1573 (date unknown).
100. See Daniel Goffman, *The Ottoman Empire and Early Modern Europe* (Cambridge, 2002), chapter 6.
101. Capponi, *Victory of the West*, pp. 127, 310–12.
102. AGSE 1333, #48: Guzmán to Philip, 11 June 1574.
103. Preto, *I servizi segreti de Venezia*, pp. 100–5.
104. AGSE 1332, #78: Guzmán to Philip, 13 August 1574.
105. AGSE 1334, #10: Guzmán to Philip, 22 January 1575.
106. AGSE 1333, #31: Guzmán to Philip, 26 March 1574.
107. AGSE 1333, #52: Guzmán to Philip, 15 June 1574.
108. See Levin, *Agents of Empire*, pp. 174–9.
109. See John Julius Norwich, *A History of Venice* (reprint, New York, 1989), p. 494, and Edward Muir, 'Images of Power: Art and Pageantry in Renaissance Venice', *AHR*, 84 (1979) pp. 16–52.
110. AGSE 1333, #57: Guzmán to Philip, 2 July 1574.
111. AGSE 1333, #65: Guzmán to Philip, 22 July 1574. On the ritual, see Muir, *Civic Ritual in Renaissance Venice*, p. 235.
112. AGSE 1333, #57: Guzmán to Philip, 2 July 1574.
113. See Parker, *Grand Strategy of Philip II*, pp. 80–5, and Manuel Rivero Rodríguez, *Felipe II y el gobierno de Italia* (Madrid, 1998), pp. 44–8.
114. Muir, 'Images of Power', pp. 43–5.
115. AGSE 1333, #68: Guzmán to Philip, no date.
116. See Robert C. Davis, 'The Spectacle Almost Fit for a King: Venice's *Guerre de'canne* of 26 July 1574', in Ellen E. Kittell and Thomas F. Madden, eds, *Medieval and Renaissance Venice* (Urbana, 1999), pp. 181–212, and Davis, *The War of the Fists: Popular Culture and Public Violence in Late Renaissance Venice* (New York, 1994).
117. AGSE 1333, #68: Guzmán to Philip, no date.
118. Davis, 'The Spectacle Almost Fit for a King', p. 204.
119. AGSE 1333, #66: Guzmán to Philip, no date. On the Book of Gold and the Venetian aristocracy, see D. S. Chambers, *The Imperial Age of Venice 1380–1580* (London, 1970), chapter 3.
120. Norwich, *A History of Venice*, p. 493.
121. AGSE 1334, #45: Guzmán to Philip, 10 June 1575.
122. See Levin, *Agents of Empire*, chapter 7.
123. Philip to Gregory XIII, 12 February 1577, in J. I. Tellechea Idígoras, *Felipe II y El Papado* (2 vols, Madrid, 2004–2006), ii. p. 87. My thanks to Geoffrey Parker for calling my attention to this reference.
124. Dursteler, *Venetians in Constantinople*, p. 5.
125. Braudel, *Mediterranean World in the Age of Philip II*, ii. chapter 5.

Chapter 2: Oxenstierna's Spies

1. L. Tandrup, ed., *Svensk agent ved Sundet; Toldkommissær og agent i Helsingør. Anders Svenssons depecher till Gustav II Adolf og Axel Oxenstierna 1621–1625* (Aarhus, 1971).
2. Heiko Droste, 'Johan Salvius i Hamburg: Ett nätverksbygge i 1600-talets Sverige', in Kerstin Abukhanfusa, ed., *Mare Nostrum: Om Westfaliska freden och Östersjön som ett svenskt maktcentrum* (Västervik, 1999), pp. 243–55.
3. Marika Keblusek, 'The Business of News: Michael le Blon and the Transmission of Political Information to Sweden in the 1630s', *ScJH*, 28 (2003), pp. 205–13; Badeloch Noldus, 'Dealing in Politics and Art: Agents between Amsterdam, Stockholm and Copenhagen', *ScJH*, 28 (2003), pp. 215–23.
4. Cools, Keblusek and Noldus, *Your Humble Servant*.
5. For the James Spens spy network in the context of other historical associations among the Scots in Northern Europe see Steve Murdoch, *Network North: Scottish Kin, Commercial and Covert Associations in Northern Europe, 1603–1750* (Leiden, 2006), pp. 251–79. For the Spens-Rutgers correspondence see Arne Jönsson, ed., *Letters of Sir James Spens and Jan Rutgers* (Stockholm, 2007).
6. James Dobreff, *Hermannus Samsonius to Axel Oxenstierna: Latin Correspondence from 1621–1630 with Linguistic and Historical Commentaries* (Lund, 2006).
7. Keblusek, 'The Business of News', pp. 205, 206, 213; Noldus, 'Dealing in Politics and Art', pp. 215, 224; Noldus, 'Loyalty and Betrayal: Artist Agents Michel le Blon and Pieter Issacsz, and Chancellor Axel Oxenstierna', in Cools, Keblusek and Noldus, *Your Humble Servant*, p. 58.
8. Noldus, 'Dealing in Politics and Art', pp. 223–4; Noldus, 'Loyalty and Betrayal', pp. 61–4.
9. Noldus, 'Loyalty and Betrayal', p. 63. It should be noted that occasionally the reports of the correspondents was considered of such significance that their reports were read out as the first order of business in the Swedish State Council (*Riksråd*), though this was very rare. See for example N.A. Kullberg, et al., eds, *Svenska Riksrådets Protokoll, 1621–1658*, (vols 1–18, Stockholm, 1878–1959) [hereafter *SRP*], i. 135: Riksråd minute, 29 May 1629.
10. Swedish Riksarkiv [SRA], Anglica, III, f. 66: James Spens to Gustav II Adolf, 20 September 1626; Murdoch, *Network North*, p. 270.
11. Karin Friedrich, *The Other Prussia: Royal Prussia, Poland and Liberty, 1569–1772* (Cambridge, 2000), p. 142.
12. Ragnhild Hatton, 'Count Nils Bielke's Prosecution for Treason', in Phyllis Mack and Margaret C. Jacob, eds, *Politics and Culture in Early Modern Europe: Essays in honour of H.G. Koenigsberger* (Cambridge, 1987), p. 104.
13. Dobreff, *Hermannus Samsonius*, pp. 98–9: Hermannus Samsonius to Axel Oxenstierna, 26 August 1626. Dobreff cites his reference as SRA, Oxenstierna samlingen, E709.
14. SRA, Oxenstierna samlingen (Axel Oxenstierna av Södermöre collection), and the Tidö Collection. The various Oxenstierna correspondence in these and other collections are discussed in Jönsson, *Letters of Sir James Spens and Jan Rutgers*, p. 7.
15. *Rikskansleren Axel Oxenstiernas Skrifter och Brefvexling* (series one, 16 vols and series two 13 vols, Stockholm, 1888–2010) [hereafter *AOSB*]. For the online edition of his letters see the Oxenstiernaprojectet [http://www.statensarkiv.se/default.aspx?id=9462&refid=4095, accessed 30 August 2009].
16. Keblusek, 'The Business of News', p. 209.
17. For more on this see Steve Murdoch, 'Diplomacy in Transition: Stuart-British Diplomacy in Northern Europe, 1603–1618', in A.I. Macinnes, T. Riis and F.G. Pedersen, eds, *Ships, Guns and Bibles in the North Sea and the Baltic States, c. 1350–1700* (East Linton, 2000), pp. 93–114.

18. Steve Murdoch, 'Anstruther, Robert (1578/9–1644/5?)', *Oxford Dictionary of National Biography* (Oxford University Press, September 2004); online edn, May 2009 [http://www.oxforddnb.com/view/article/63416, accessed 17 September 2009].
19. Alexia Grosjean, *An Unofficial Alliance: Scotland and Sweden 1568–1654* (Leiden, 2003), pp. 30–38 and passim. Richard Zygmunt Brzezinski, 'Spens, James, of Wormiston, Baron Spens in the Swedish nobility (d. 1632)', *Oxford Dictionary of National Biography* (Oxford University Press, September 2004); online edition, May 2008; online edn, May 2009 [http://www.oxforddnb.com/view/article/26142 accessed 9 September 2009].
20. SRA, Anglica, III: Copy of Instructions, James VI & I to James Spens, 20 April 1612.
21. SRA, Anglica, V: Scots language copy of a letter, Christian IV to Gustav II Adolf, 17 July 1612.
22. SRA, Anglica, V: Robert Anstruther to James Spens, 18 July 1612.
23. For more on Scottish kith and kin networks (and how these sometimes varied from other cultures) see Murdoch, *Network North*, chapter 1.
24. SRA, Oxenstierna samlingen, E724: James Spens's oath of loyalty to Gustav II Adolf, 28 October 1612.
25. SRA, Stegeborgssamlingen II, Karl Gustafs Arkiv, E161: Axel Oxenstierna to Karl Gustav, 24 March 1652. [Consulted online at: http://62.20.57.212/ra/ao/1516t_n.html, accessed 30 August 2009]. '*Ifrån Pålandh ähr här för någre dagar sedhan ankommen en envoyé benemdh Canasil, en francos, drotningens skattmästare, afferdatt under prætext att bedie Kongl. M:tt till fadder åth kongens i Pålandz nyfödde son, den där sedhan kortt efter sin födzle skall vara dödh bleffven. Hvad hans andre ährenden ähre, föruthan att espionera, ded veett jag intet*'. In translation this reads: 'There has been here for several days an envoy from Poland called Canasil, a Frenchman and the Queen's master of taxes, under the pretext of requesting Her Majesty to become Godparent to the king of Poland's newborn son, who died shortly after his birth. What his other duties are, apart from spying, I do not know'. Interestingly, this is the only direct reference to spying in the online edition of the Oxenstierna papers.
26. Keblusek, 'The Business of News', p. 208.
27. Droste, 'Johan Salvius', pp. 248, 252–3; Keblusek, 'The Business of News', p. 209. See also Keblusek, 'introduction' in Cools, Keblusek and Noldus, *Your Humble Servant*, p. 12.
28. Droste, 'Johan Salvius', p. 248; Heiko Droste, 'Sending a Letter between Amsterdam and Stockholm: A Matter of Trust and Precautions', in Cools, Keblusek and Noldus, *Your Humble Servant*, p. 141.
29. SRA, Oxenstierna samlingen, E724: Robert Anstruther to Sir James Spens, 18 July 1612.
30. SRA, Oxenstierna samlingen, E724: James Spens to Axel Oxenstierna, 3 August 1614. Ramsay is named as the courier in SRA, Oxenstierna samlingen, E724: James Spens to Axel Oxenstierna, 3 September 1614.
31. SRA, Oxenstierna samlingen, E724: Robert Anstruther to James Spens, 1 August 1624.
32. SRA, Oxenstierna samlingen, E556: Robert Anstruther to Axel Oxenstierna, 29 April 1613. In this letter he suggests the use of a secretary between himself and Oxenstierna should the Chancellor not be able to read his Danish – a rather curious statement perhaps used as a way of suggesting the employment of a go-between for other purposes.
33. SRA, Anglica, Engelska beskickningars memorial, 1591–1692: Robert Anstruther to Gustav II Adolf, 10 January 1614.
34. Anstruther had worked for Christian IV since 1606 and that should have made him suspect to the Swedish leadership. Oxenstierna played on this, saying Anstruther had been a 'good Dane' all his life in 1633. Yet Oxenstierna both praised his work and believed he was a man of integrity. For Oxenstierna's praise and trust of Anstruther see

several letters from *AOSB*, I:8, 570: Axel Oxenstierna to Charles I, 26 April 1633; and 669: Oxenstierna to Riksråd, 6 May 1633. For the 'Good Dane' comment see 688, 'Därtill medh att Amstrytter altijdh haver varit godh Dansk'. For Anstruther's distancing himself from Christian IV after 1629 see Murdoch, *Britain, Denmark-Norway and the House of Stuart*, pp. 71–2.

35. Keblusek, 'The Business of News', pp. 208–19; Noldus, 'Loyalty and Betrayal', p. 53.
36. O. Garstein, *Rome and the Counter-Reformation in Scandinavia* (2 vols, Leiden, 1922), i. xxxix; A. Biegańska, 'James Murray a Scot in the making of the Polish navy', in *Scottish Slavonic Review*, no.3 (Autumn 1984), p. 1; R. I. Frost, 'Scottish Soldiers, Poland-Lithuania and the Thirty Years' War', in Murdoch, *Scotland and the Thirty Years' War*, pp. 191–212; Dobreff, *Hermannus Samsonius*, p. 13.
37. Garstein, *Rome and the Counter-Reformation in Scandinavia*, i. xxx, xl, 403. For Posse see Garstein, *Rome and the Counter-Reformation in Scandinavia*, ii. 264, 287–8.
38. *SRP*, i. 2. Information contained in an extensive footnote.
39. A. Biegańska, 'The Learned Scots in Poland (From the Mid-Sixteenth to the Close of the Eighteenth Century)', in *Canadian Slavonic Papers*, vol. 43:1 (2001), p. 25. Biegańska cites AP, Gdansk: MS300, 53/1012: MNBC; MS 1772, ff. 474 *passim*. Biegańska is not explicit as to whether the men in Keith's circle were Scots or not, only that he controlled them.
40. Biegańska, 'The Learned Scots in Poland', p. 25.
41. *SRP*, i. 1628, 120–2. Riksråd interrogation of James Ross, 10 December 1628. This interrogation has been translated into English and reproduced in Murdoch, *Network North*, pp. 364–6.
42. SRA, Anglica, IV, f.14: Gustav II Adolf to Spens, 17 December 1614.
43. SRA, Oxenstierna samlingen, E724: James Spens to Axel Oxenstierna, 1 March 1615.
44. These letters from October 1614 are reprinted in A. F. Steuart, ed., *Papers relating to the Scots in Poland, 1576–1793* (Edinburgh, 1915), pp. 35–36. James VI's instructions on how Buik was to proceed with Sigismund can be found in SRA, Oxenstierna samlingen, E724: James Spens to Axel Oxenstierna, 1 March 1615; Frost, 'Scottish Soldiers, Poland-Lithuania and the Thirty Years' War', p. 198.
45. SRA, Oxenstierna samlingen, E724: James Spens to Axel Oxenstierna, 1 July 1615.
46. SRA, Oxenstierna samlingen, E724: James Spens to Axel Oxenstierna, 1 March 1615.
47. SRA, Oxenstierna samlingen, E724: James Spens to Axel Oxenstierna, 1 March 1615.
48. SRA, Oxenstierna samlingen, E604: Patrick Gordon to Axel Oxenstierna, 6 December 1615.
49. Forthelius served as a secretary in the Swedish chancellery and took part in negotiations with Britain in 1615/1616 and Brandenburg in 1616. Arne Jönsson notes only three extant letters exist in Oxenstierna samlingen from this man to Oxenstierna. Jönsson, *Letters from Sir James Spens and Jan Rutgers*, p. 600. Forthelius's return to Sweden with letters from Spens between missions is mentioned in *AOSB*, II:10, 179: Johan Skytte to Axel Oxenstierna, 20 February 1616.
50. SRA, Oxenstierna samlingen, E604: Patrick Gordon to Axel Oxenstierna, 6 December 1615.
51. SRA, Ämnessamlingar. Strödda historiska handlingar, vol. 24: Handlingar från Gust. II Adolfs tid 1612–1632: Patrick Gordon to Archibald Rankin, 18 August 1617; S. Tunberg, et al., *Den Svenska Utrikes Förvaltningens Historia* (Uppsala, 1935), pp. 74–5.
52. *AOSB*, II:10, 223–9: Johan Skytte to Axel Oxenstierna & Gustav II Adolf, 8 December 1617.
53. See Rankin's dispatches from London. SRA, Oxenstierna samlingen, E692: Dispatches from Archibald Rankin to Axel Oxenstierna, 20 December 1617, 2 January 1618, 20 March 1617/18 and 3 May 1618.
54. SRA, Oxenstierna samlingen, E724: James Spens to Axel Oxenstierna, 28 December 1618.

55. This man is variously called 'Johan Weijer' and 'Johannes Weiher'. Described as a colonel in Polish diplomatic service in 1617, he may actually have been the 'Joannes Weir' mentioned as a merchant of Edinburgh trading with Sweden in 1614. See SRA, Scotica I: Scottish Privy Council to Gustav II Adolf, 18 September 1614. For John Weir in the context of diplomatic agent see A. Norberg, *Polen i Svensk Politik 1617–1626* (Stockholm, 1974), pp. 59, 64; Jönsson, *Letters from Sir James Spens and Jan Rutgers*, p. 620.
56. SRA, Oxenstierna samlingen, E724: James Spens to Axel Oxenstierna, 17 March 1617; Norberg, *Polen i Svensk Politik*, p. 41.
57. Rankin names Spens as a faithful servant of the king of Sweden and tells Oxenstierna that he had written to Robertson to inform him about his pro-Swedish activities while in Denmark and that Skytte had arrived safely. SRA, Oxenstierna samlingen, E692: Archibald Rankin to Axel Oxenstierna, 20 December 1617. Skytte arrived in London from The Hague in the hope of bringing James VI & I into closer alliance with Sweden, but James wanted to see a treaty between Denmark and Sweden first. Norberg, *Polen i Svensk Politik*, p. 57.
58. SRA, Oxenstierna samlingen, E692: Archibald Rankin to Axel Oxenstierna, 20 March 1617/1618. As yet I have been unable to identify 'Herr Tinnagell'; Jönsson, *Letters from Sir James Spens and Jan Rutgers*, pp. 275–7: Jan Rutgers to Axel Oxenstierna, 14 February 1618.
59. SRA, Oxenstierna samlingen, E692: Archibald Rankin to Axel Oxenstierna, 3 May 1618.
60. SRA, Oxenstierna samlingen, E692: Archibald Rankin to Axel Oxenstierna, 3 May 1618.
61. SRA, Oxenstierna samlingen, E724: James Spens to Axel Oxenstierna, 7 March 1619.
62. Frost, 'Scottish Soldiers, Poland–Lithuania and the Thirty Years' War', p. 201.
63. M. Roberts, *Gustavus Adolphus: A History of Sweden 1611–1632*, (2 vols, London, 1953–1958), i. 203; R. Frost, *The Northern Wars, 1558–1721* (Harlow, 2000), p. 103.
64. This was perhaps due to a lingering grudge he held against Sweden. Having previously served in the Swedish army, Stewart found himself having to write to both the Swedish monarch and chancellor seeking satisfaction for himself and other associates in relation to the 30,000 *rdl* worth of copper he had been promised as payment agreed for his services during the Kalmar War (1611–1613). See SRA, Oxenstierna samlingen, E734: Robert Stewart to Axel Oxenstierna, 5 and 7 May and 19 June 1615. For discussion of the payment for his regiment see *AOSB*, I:2, 1606–1624, 51–2: Riksråd to Gustav II Adolf, 14 June 1612.
65. Tandrup, *Svensk agent ved Sundet*, pp. 291–2 and 341: Anders Svensson to Oxenstierna/Gustav II Adolf, 18 June and 30 September 1623; Norberg, *Polen i Svensk Politik*, pp. 175, 194–199; Grosjean, *An Unofficial Alliance*, p. 48; Dobreff, *Hermannus Samsonius*, p. 22. *If* this John Weir was the Scottish merchant, it shows an interesting relationship between failed commercial ventures leading to military action in revenge – particularly given Stewart's situation.
66. Tandrup, *Svensk agent ved Sundet*, p. 291: Anders Svensson to Oxenstierna/Gustav II Adolf, 18 June 1623 and *passim*.
67. Tandrup, *Svensk agent ved Sundet*, p. 295: James Spens to Oxenstierna/Gustav II Adolf, 24 June 1623 and fn.1 and 418, fn.10.
68. *AOSB*, I:2, 589–590: Axel Oxenstierna to the Representative for Peace Negotiations in Poland, 11 September 1623.
69. SRA, Anglica, IV, f. 22: Gustav II Adolf to James Spens, 23 September 1623.
70. SRA, Anglica, IV, f. 22: Gustav II Adolf to James Spens, 23 September 1623; Tandrup, *Svensk agent ved Sundet*, p. 363: Anders Svensson to Oxenstierna/Gustav II Adolf, 6 November 1623 and fn.10.
71. Tandrup, *Svensk agent ved Sundet*, 347–9: Anders Svensson to Oxenstierna/Gustav II Adolf, 10 October 1623.
72. Tandrup, *Svensk agent ved Sundet*, p. 361: Anders Svensson to Oxenstierna/Gustav II Adolf, 6 November 1623.

73. *RPCS*, XIII, 364–5: Gustav II Adolf to James VI and the Privy Council 23 September 1623.
74. SRA, Anglica III, f. 46a: James Spens to Gustav II Adolf, 16 February 1624.
75. *SRP*, I, 2; *AOSB*, II:2: Gabriel Gustafsson Oxenstierna to Axel Oxenstierna, 24 September 1625.
76. See also SRA, Anglica, 531: Copy of a letter sent by King James to Sigismund III, 10 October 1623.
77. SRA, Oxenstierna samlingen, E724: James Spens to Axel Oxenstierna, 10 March 1624.
78. SRA, Oxenstierna samlingen, E724: James Spens to Axel Oxenstierna, 10 March 1624.
79. SRA, Oxenstierna samlingen, E724: James Spens to Axel Oxenstierna, 10 March 1624.
80. SRA, Oxenstierna samlingen, E724: James Spens to Axel Oxenstierna, 10 March 1624. Thomas Reid, poet, philosopher and Latin secretary to King James VI & I from 1618–1624, as well as the founder of the first public reference library in Scotland (in Aberdeen). See *Die Matrikel der Universitat Rostock* (Rostock, 1889); G. P. V. Akrigg, ed., *Letters of King James VI & I* (London, 1984), 25; T. P. J. Edlin, 'Reid, Thomas (d. 1624)', *Oxford Dictionary of National Biography* (Oxford University Press, 2004) [http://www.oxforddnb.com/view/article/23341, accessed 21 September 2009].
81. SRA, Oxenstierna samlingen, E724: James Spens to Axel Oxenstierna, 3 November 1622.
82. SRA, Rigsregistraturet, vol. 147, 1624, Tysk och Latin, f. 67f: Gustav II Adolf to James Spens, 15 March 1624. John Fairbairne worked under a variety of different names including Johan Fairbairn, Johan Barinsfather/Bairnsfaither and Jean Fairbairne.
83. SRA, Anglica, 514, Korrespondenten Jean Fairbairne: John Fairbairne to Gustav II Adolf, 2 November 1623; Tandrup, *Svensk agent ved Sundet*, p. 376 fn. 1.
84. As early as 1612, Spens had reported that the Pope was supposed to be sponsoring the landing of 1,200 men in Finland backed by money from the Polish Catholic clergy. See National Archives, Kew, SP 95/1: James Spens to James VI, 11 October 1612.
85. SRA, Anglica, 514, Korrespondenten Jean Fairbairne: Two documents of contract between John Fairbairne and Hostier dated 10 October 1623; SRA, Anglica 514, Korrespondenten Jean Fairbairne 1623: Fairbairne to Gustav II Adolf, 2 November 1623; Tandrup, *Svensk agent ved Sundet*, pp. 375–376: Anders Svensson to Gustav II Adolf, 14 December 1623. Lehonard von Sorgen frequently handled the correspondence between Spens and his step-brother, Sir Robert Anstruther. If trusted by both men, this may indicate that Anstruther, the dual ambassador to and from Denmark and Britain, may also have had knowledge of Spens' anti-Polish network. See Tandrup, *Svensk agent ved Sundet*, pp. 491 and 511: Anders Svensson to Gustav II Adolf, 24 August 1624 and Svensson to Oxenstierna, 11 November 1624. For Sorgen, see letters of Jan Rutgers to Axel Oxenstierna 1620–1625 contained in SRA, Oxenstierna samlingen, E702.
86. SRA, Oxenstierna samlingen, E724: James Spens to Axel Oxenstierna, 26/16 Feb. 1624. See also SRA, Anglica, 514, Korrespondenten Jean Fairbairne: John Fairbairne to Gustav II Adolf, undated request for expenses and alternative employment. Rasche is mentioned over a dozen times in Oxenstierna's correspondence between 1623 and 1646, particularly in letters to him from Johan Adler Salvius and Ludwig Camerarius.
87. SRA, Oxenstierna samlingen, E724: James Spens to Oxenstierna, 26 April 1624; SRA, Anglica, 514, Korrespondenten Jean Fairbairne: John Fairbairne to Gustav II Adolf, undated request for expenses and alternative employment.
88. SRA, Oxenstierna samlingen, E724: James Spens to Axel Oxenstierna, 8 April 1624; SRA, Anglica, III, f. 48: James Spens to Gustav II Adolf, 26 April 1624; SRA, Anglica, III, f. 50: James Spens to Gustav II Adolf, 28 April 1624.
89. *AOSB*, I:3, 48, 768.
90. SP 95/2, f. 84. James Spens to James VI, 1623; SRA, Anglica, III, f. 43 and f. 46a: James Spens to Gustav II Adolf, 14/24 January and 16 February 1624; SRA, Oxenstierna

samlingen, E724: James Spens to Axel Oxenstierna, 10 March 1624; Tandrup, *Svensk agent ved Sundet*, p. 419 fn.12.
91. SP 95/2, ff. 86–8: James VI to James Spens, 6 July 1624.
92. SRA, Anglica, 514, Korrespondenten Jean Fairbairne 1623: John Fairbairne to Gustav II Adolf, 2 November 1623.
93. SP 95/2, ff. 86–88: James VI to James Spens, 6 July 1624.
94. *AOSB*, I:2, 767–9: Axel Oxenstierna to Ludwig Camerarius, 16 November 1624; Tandrup, *Svensk agent ved Sundet*, pp. 435–7, 441, 450, 508, 510.
95. Tandrup, *Svensk agent ved Sundet*, p. 419: Anders Svensson to Oxenstierna/Gustav II Adolf, 22 March 1624.
96. Tandrup, *Svensk agent ved Sundet*, p. 436 fn. 2.
97. *AOSB*, II:3, 86: Gabriel Gustafsson Oxenstierna to Axel Oxenstierna, 24 September 1625.
98. SRA, Oxenstierna samlingen, E724: James Spens to Axel Oxenstierna, 25 January 1626; J. K. Fedorowicz, *England's Baltic Trade in the Early Seventeenth century: A Study in Anglo-Polish Commercial Diplomacy* (Cambridge, 1980), p. 19; Biegańska, 'The Learned Scots in Poland', p. 21. For the distinction between merchant consuls and various levels of commercial factors in an early modern Scottish context see Murdoch, *Network North*, pp. 148–61.
99. Murdoch, *Britain, Denmark-Norway and the House of Stuart*, pp. 107–8.
100. SRA, Oxenstierna samlingen, E724: James Spens to Axel Oxenstierna, 25 January 1626.
101. SRA, Oxenstierna samlingen, E724: James Spens to Axel Oxenstierna, 25 January 1626.
102. Garstein, *Rome and the Counter-Reformation in Scandinavia*, i. 403; Biegańska, 'In Search of Tolerance', p. 48. Interestingly one of the names on Biegańska's list of Black Friars in Poland was that of a Francis Gordon, but I have not seen proof of any relationship to the Stuart agent.
103. Garstein, *Rome and the Counter-Reformation in Scandinavia*, i. 210.
104. *AOSB*, I:3, 313: Axel Oxenstierna to James Spens, 2 May 1626.
105. SRA, Oxenstierna samlingen, E724: James Spens to Axel Oxenstierna, 25 January 1626.
106. Murdoch, *Network North*, p. 131.
107. SRA, Oxenstierna samlingen, E724: James Spens to Axel Oxenstierna, 12 July 1626.
108. *AOSB*, I:3, 313: Axel Oxenstierna to James Spens, 2 May 1626; SRA, Oxenstierna samlingen, E724: James Spens to Axel Oxenstierna, 29 July and 28 August 1626; SRA, Anglica III: James Spens to Gustav II Adolf, 8 August 1626.
109. SRA, Oxenstierna samlingen, E724: James Spens to Axel Oxenstierna, 8 March 1626.
110. SRA, Anglica, IV, ff. 38–40: Gustav II Adolf to James Spens, 4 July 1626 and 28 August 1626.
111. SRA, Oxenstierna samlingen, E724: James Spens to Axel Oxenstierna, 12 July 1626.
112. SAR, Oxenstierna samlingen, E577: Ludwig Camerarius to Axel Oxenstierna, 8 June 1626 explicitly and 1 June 1626 implied.
113. SRA, Anglica, III, f. 66. James Spens to Gustav II Adolf, 20 September 1626.
114. SRA, Oxenstierna samlingen, E604: Francis Gordon to Axel Oxenstierna, various letters, 1627–1636.
115. *AOSB*, I:4, 1628–1629, 471: Axel Oxenstierna to Herman Wrangel, 14 April 1629.
116. *AOSB*, I:4, 1628–1629, 398–772: Numerous mentions of Gordon's correspondence. See Axel Oxenstierna to variously Gustav Horn, Francis Gordon, Herman Wrangel, Sir Thomas Roe, throughout 1629.
117. SRA, Oxenstierna samlingen, E604: Francis Gordon to Axel Oxenstierna, 14/24 May (Falconer) and 16/26 July 1630 (Keith); For their military service see KRA, Muster Roll, 1630/32,33; 1631/12–17 (Falconer); KRA, Muster Roll, 1630/28,30–33; 1631/12–15,17–19 (Keith). See also suspect information in letters of 19/29 May and 7 September 1629, that appear to reveal far more than they should about Poland's plans, etc.

118. SRA, Oxenstierna samlingen, E604: Francis Gordon to Axel Oxenstierna, 19/29 May 1629.
119. *C.S.P. Venetian*, 1636–1639, xxiv. 271: Anzolo Correr to Venice, 18 September 1637; For a broader description of Gordon's 'suspicious' activities between 1637–1640 see Murdoch, *Britain, Denmark-Norway and the House of Stuart*, pp. 107–8.
120. SRA, Anglica, IV, f. 40: Gustav II Adolf to James Spens, 28 August 1626; SRA, Oxenstierna samlingen, E724: James Spens to Axel Oxentierna, 26 November 1626.
121. SRA, Anglica, III, f. 70. James Spens to Gustav II Adolf, 18 October 1626; SRA, Anglica, III, ff. 85, 87 and 89: James Spens to Gustav II Adolf, 6, 24 and 27 April 1627.
122. SP 95/2, ff. 165–168: Charles I to James Spens, June 1627.
123. For Gordon's mission see Biegańska, 'The Learned Scots in Poland', p. 21.
124. SRA, Oxenstierna samlingen, E724: James Spens to Axel Oxenstierna, no date, c.1627.
125. SRA, Oxenstierna samlingen, E724: James Spens to Axel Oxenstierna, 14 August 1627.
126. SRA, Oxenstierna samlingen, E724: James Spens to Axel Oxenstierna, 3 September 1627.
127. *AOSB*, I:3, 678: Oxenstierna from Elbing, 2 November 1627; Grosjean, *An Unofficial Alliance*, p. 61.
128. The relationship is mentioned in SP95/2, f. 197: James Spens to Sir John Coke, Pillau, 30 October 1627. For more on Ramsay see A. N. L. Grosjean, 'Ramsay, James (1589?–1638/9)', *Oxford Dictionary of National Biography* (Oxford University Press, 2004) [http://www.oxforddnb.com/view/article/23084, accessed 7 January 2010].
129. SP 95/2, f. 173: James Spens to Sir John Coke, 13 August 1627 and SP 95/3, f. 6: James Spens to Secretary Coke, 17 May 1628.
130. SRA, Anglica, III, f. 9b: James Spens to Gustav II Adolf, 3 May 1629.
131. Murdoch, *Network North*, p. 284.
132. SP 88/7, II, f. 290: Instructions to Francis Gordon from Thomas Roe, 18 April 1630.
133. SRA, Oxenstierna samlingen, E692: Archibald Rankin to Axel Oxenstierna, Danzig, 23 Dec. 1629 and 13 January 1630.
134. SRA, Oxenstierna samlingen, E692: Archibald Rankin to Axel Oxenstierna, Danzig, 23 December 1629 and 13 January 1630.
135. For the importance of 'auld acquaintance' as a strong network linkage among early modern Scots see Murdoch, *Network North*, pp. 73–83.
136. Fedorowicz, *England's Baltic Trade*, p. 19.

Chapter 3: 'Woeful Knight'

1. Robert Walsh, *The True State, Case and Condition of Sir Robert Walsh* (London, 1687), p. 28. Walsh's father was mayor of Waterford and owned considerable property there. He lived in 'the Irish quarters' during the civil war, but he was it seems loyal to the Stuarts: *CSPI*, ii. 63. For both father and son see G. E. Cokayne, *Complete Baronetage* (5 vols, Exeter, 1900–1906), *1625–1649*, ii. 274.
2. Walsh, *True State, Case and Condition*, p. 11. He may well also have seen earlier service at the Île de Rhé under Buckingham in 1627. For the Bishops' Wars see Mark C. Fissel, *The Bishops' Wars: Charles I's Campaigns against Scotland 1638–1640* (Cambridge, 1994).
3. He said he was a 'Carvere to her Majesty'. He subsequently petitioned the House of Lords for release, citing his privilege as a royal servant. While he was eventually released, this order for debt would eventually come back to haunt him in 1661 and lead to further imprisonment. Walsh, *True State, Case and Condition*, p. 11.
4. Walsh, *True State, Case and Condition*, p. 12; *CSPI*, ii. 444–5, 619.
5. Walsh, *True State, Case and Condition*, p. 12.
6. According to Walsh he did this on his own; from other sources it is clear he was part of the royal cavalry under Prince Maurice and Edward Sackville, earl of Dorset, who

broke out together towards Oxford. Maurice's subsequent return enabled Sir Ralph Hopton to break out of the town with his infantry and the resulting battle of Roundway Down saw Sir William Waller's forces defeated on 13 July 1643 (*A True Relation of the Late Fight between Sir William Waller's Forces and those sent from Oxford* (1643)).

7. Initially Walsh had been sent to raise infantry, but this was 'not permitted', instead he raised some cavalry and then took them by ship to Pendennis castle. *CSPI*, ii. 444; also Sir Richard Bellings, *History of the Irish Confederation and the War in Ireland*, J. T. Gilbert, ed. (7 vols, Dublin, 1882–91), iii. 90–1.
8. *Severall votes and resolution of the Commons assembled in Parliament: for the drawing the Army under the command of the Lord Fairfax into garisons, in order to the late demands made by his Excellency. H. Elsynge, Cler. Parl. D. Com. Together with the proposition sent to the King, for security to those of Scotland, who assisted the Parliament of England. Also letters were read in both Houses, from the commissioners in the Isle of Wight. With His Majesties finall answer to both Houses, concerning the proposition for Ireland, and the Marquess of Ormond. And the princes sentence upon Sir Robert Welsh, concerning the Lord Culpepper* (London, 1648), p. 8; Thomas Carte, *The Life of James Duke of Ormond containing an account of the most remarkable affairs of his time* (6 vols, Oxford, 1851 edn), vi. 590–3; W. D. Macray, ed., *The History of the Rebellion and Civil Wars in England: Begun in the Year 1641 by Edward, Earl of Clarendon; Re-edited from a Fresh Collation of the Original MS in the Bodleian Library, with Marginal Dates and Occasional Notes* (6 vols, Oxford, 1958 fac. of 1888 edn), iv. 406–10; David L. Smith, 'Colepeper, John, first Baron Colepeper (bap. 1600, d. 1660)', *Oxford Dictionary of National Biography*, Oxford University Press, September 2004; online edn, October 2005 [http://www.oxforddnb.com/view/article/5876, accessed 31 December 2009].
9. Robert Walsh, *A True Narrative and Manifest set forth by Sir Robert Walsh* (London, 1679), p. 24. For Condé's army at this time see Eveline Charlotte Godley, *The Great Condé: A Life of Louis II de Bourbon, Prince of Condé* (1915), pp. 372–5, 380–90.
10. Indeed, Thurloe is almost coming to be seen as the '*eminence gris*' of the day, a return to the myths of the period. For which see, Patrick Little, 'John Thurloe and the Offer of the Crown to Oliver Cromwell', in Patrick Little, ed., *Oliver Cromwell: New Perspectives* (Basingstoke, 2009), p. 233.
11. In general the only full-dress biographies of Thurloe are poor. See Philip Aubrey, *Mr Secretary Thurloe: Cromwell's Secretary of State, 1652–1660* (London, 1990). The honourable exception to this is the biography in the *Oxford Dictionary of National Biography*: Timothy Venning, 'Thurloe, John (*bap.* 1616, *d.* 1668)', *Oxford Dictionary of National Biography*, Oxford University Press, September 2004; online edn, January 2008 [http://www.oxforddnb.com/view/article/27405, accessed 31 December 2009]. In addition, Gerald Aylmer's comments on Thurloe in, *The State's Servants: the Civil Service of the English Republic, 1649–1660* (London, 1973), pp. 165–7, 258–60, are still very pertinent.
12. Thurloe always underestimated and tended to besmirch Scot's good work, for which see Alan Marshall, *Killing Cromwell: The Death of the Leveller Party, 1649–1657* (forthcoming 2011).
13. Ruth Spalding, ed., *The Diary of Bulstrode Whitelocke, 1605–1675* (Oxford, 1990), p. 646.
14. Aylmer, *State's Servants*, pp. 165–7.
15. See Blair Worden, 'Oliver Cromwell and the Council', in Patrick Little, ed., *The Cromwellian Protectorate* (Chippenham, 2007), p. 97.
16. Michael Roberts, ed. and trans., *Swedish Diplomats at Cromwell's Court, 1655–1656. The Missions of Peter Julius Coyet and Christer Bonde* (Camden Society, 4th series, vol. 36, London, 1988), pp. 146, 114, 127, 162.
17. Robert Thomas Fallon, *Milton in Government* (Pennsylvania, 1993), p. 127.
18. Jason Peacey, 'Cromwellian England: a Propaganda state?', *History*, 91 (2006) pp. 176–99.

19. William Jessop was assistant secretary in foreign affairs, and had Henry Scobell to help. Walter Frost junior was given the title of 'treasurer for the council's contingencies'. Philip Medowes at first assisted and then virtually replaced the poet John Milton as Latin secretary until 1655 at least, when he in turn was sent on a diplomatic mission to Portugal. His post was then left vacant until 1657, when Andrew Marvell, another poet, was chosen to fill it. Samuel Morland acted as a clerk of the signet and Philip Nutley, the other clerk, acted in a general capacity. Morland, however, had some other special duties. Isaac Dorislaus worked in the Post Office and laboured over ciphers and public correspondence, while John Wallis at Oxford was employed to break any peculiar ciphers that came into the office.
20. See Peacey, 'Cromwellian England: a Propaganda state?', pp. 176–99; also Laura Lunger Knoppers, *Constructing Cromwell: Ceremony Portrait, and Print, 1645–1661* (Cambridge, 2009 edn), p. 137.
21. See Blair Worden, *Literature and Politics in Cromwellian England: John Milton, Andrew Marvell, Marchamont Nedham* (Oxford, 2009), p. 312; Aylmer, *State's Servants*, p. 72.
22. *Swedish Diplomats at Cromwell's Court*, p. 280.
23. Eucardio Momigliano, *Cromwell* (London, 1930), pp. 258–9.
24. Momigliano, *Cromwell*, pp. 258–9. For comparisons see Lucien Bély, *Espions et ambassadeurs au temps de Louis XIV* (Paris, 1990); Preto, *I Servizi Segreti di Venezia*; de Vivo, *Information and Communication in Venice*.
25. In Lambert's case see Worden, 'Oliver Cromwell and the Council', p. 87; *TSP*, iii. 329.
26. Bodleian Library, Rawlinson A, 24, f. 511.
27. William Harbutt Dawson, *Cromwell's Understudy: The Life and Times of General John Lambert* (London, 1938); for Swift see Rawlinson A, 22, ff. 517–29 and Rawlinson A, 59, f. 250.
28. Francis Dow, *Cromwellian Scotland* (Edinburgh, 1979), pp. 189–194; *TSP*, iv. 187, 221, 250, 271, 726; v. 500, 602–3. Also Patrick Little, 'An Irish Governor of Scotland: Lord Broghill, 1655–1656', in Andrew Mackillop and Steve Murdoch, *Military Governors and Imperial frontiers c.1600–1800. A Study of Scotland and Empire* (Brill, 2003), pp. 88–92; Patrick Little, *Lord Broghill and the Cromwellian Union with Ireland and Scotland* (Woodbridge, 2004).
29. *TSP*, iv. 105.
30. *TSP*, iv. 105.
31. *TSP*, iv. 324.
32. *TSP*, v. 18.
33. *TSP*, v. 18; see also Kathleen M. Lynch, *Roger Boyle, First Earl of Orrey* (Knoxville, 1963), p. 87.
34. See Marshall, *Killing Cromwell* (forthcoming 2011).
35. W. C. Abbott, *The Writings and Speeches of Oliver Cromwell* (4 vols, Oxford, 1947), iii. 656; for the Penruddock rising see A.H. Woolrych, *Penruddock's Rising 1655* (Historical Association Pamphlet, 1955, repr.1968).
36. Momigliano, *Cromwell*, pp. 264–5.
37. The classic case here being the penetration of the Royalist Sealed Knot. For which see David Underdown, *Royalist Conspiracy in England, 1649–1660* (New Haven, 1960); David Underdown 'Sir Richard Willys and Secretary Thurloe', *EHR*, 69 (1954) pp. 373–87; Geoffrey Smith, *The Cavaliers in Exile, 1640–1660* (Basingstoke, 2003); M. Hollings, 'Thomas Barret: A Study in the Secret History of the Interregnum', *EHR*, 43 (1928) pp. 33–56; Stephen K. Roberts, 'Sealed Knot (*act.* 1653–1659)', *Oxford Dictionary of National Biography*, online edn (Oxford University Press, October 2009) [http://www.oxforddnb.com/view/theme/98250, accessed 1 January 2010].
38. *C.S.P. Venetian* 1653–1654, xxix. 168.
39. *C.S.P. Venetian, 1653–1654*, xxix. 219, 222, 227, 230.
40. Rawlinson A, 55, ff. 313–14.

41. Rawlinson A, 55, ff. 251, 275, 279, 313–14, 318; Rawlinson A 57, f. 381.
42. *C.S.P. Venetian, 1653–1654*, xxix. 230.
43. *C.S.P. Venetian, 1653–1654*, xxix. 269, 283–4.
44. C. H. Firth, 'Thurloe and the Post Office', *EHR*, 13 (1898) p. 532.
45. Firth, 'Thurloe and the Post Office', p. 533.
46. Firth, 'Thurloe and the Post Office', p. 533.
47. Firth, 'Thurloe and the Post Office', p. 533.
48. Firth, 'Thurloe and the Post Office', p. 533.
49. *TSP*, i. 339; the fact that this letter is in Thurloe's papers proved that the ambassador's caution was more than justified. See also Bodleian Library, Rawlinson A, 9, f. 137.
50. *TSP*, i. 454.
51. Momigliano, *Cromwell*, pp. 264–5.
52. Marshall, *Intelligence and Espionage*, p. 55.
53. For examples see Marshall, *Intelligence and Espionage*, pp. 169–75.
54. *CSPDC*, xi. 293.
55. Bodleian Library, Clarendon MSS, 56, f. 82.
56. *TSP*, iv. 574.
57. Clarendon MSS, 56, ff. 83v.
58. Clarendon MSS, 56, ff. 84.
59. Clarendon MSS, 56, ff. 85.
60. British Library, Add. MSS, 4106, f. 254.
61. Clarendon MSS, 56, f. 86.
62. *CSPDC*, xi. 293.
63. Clarendon MSS, 56, f. 88; *CSPDC*, xi. 296.
64. Clarendon MSS, 56, f. 88v. There was an assassination plot, but Walsh was not involved in it, rather it was the ex-Leveller Edward Sexby's idea. See Marshall, *Killing Cromwell* (forthcoming 2011).
65. Clarendon MSS, 56, f. 89. *CSPDC*, xi. 294. Walsh notes a visit by a man called Owen whom he claimed was Broghill's 'intelligencer' in Bruges.
66. See J. Walker, *Pistols! Treason! Murder! The Rise and Fall of a Master Spy* (Melbourne, 2007), p. 41.
67. Walsh, *True Narrative and Manifest*, p.35; *CSPDC*, xi. 294.
68. *CSPDC*, xi.169. Broghill also seems to have had a hold over Walsh by threatening one of Walsh's brothers, who would be held until the information began to flow.
69. *TSP*, v. 683. There are hints that Walsh's time was spent productively in the Tower and the Fleet by supplying information on his fellow prisoners. Certainly his reputation amongst the Royalists remained dubious throughout this period, *CSPDC*, xi. 295, 296–7.
70. W. D. Macray et al, ed., *The Calendar of the Clarendon State papers* (5 vols, Oxford, 1869–1970), iii. 368.
71. British Library, Landsdowne MSS, 825, f. 106. Willys was later proved to be working for Thurloe. Richard Ollard, 'Willys, Sir Richard, first baronet (*bap.* 1614, *d.* 1690)', rev., *Oxford Dictionary of National Biography* (Oxford University Press, 2004) [http://www.oxforddnb.com/view/article/38135, accessed 1 January 2010].
72. Landsdowne MSS, 825, ff. 105v–6.
73. Landsdowne MSS, 825, f. 106.
74. Clarendon MSS, 56, ff. 98–106v.
75. For Bampfield see Alan Marshall, 'Bampfield, Joseph (1622–1685)', *Oxford Dictionary of National Biography*, Oxford University Press, September 2004; online edn, January 2008 [http://www.oxforddnb.com/view/article/1259, accessed 1 January 2010]; for Manning see Nicole Greenspan, 'News, Intelligence and Espionage at the Exiled Court at Cologne: the Case of Henry Manning', *MH*, 11 (2005) pp. 105–25.

76. Walsh, *True Narrative and Manifest*, p. 7. Further letters from Walsh, which detail his career post-1660, are in the Carte Papers in the Bodleian Library.
77. Walsh, *True Narrative and Manifest*, p. 4.
78. Aidan Clarke, *The Old English in Ireland, 1625–1642* (Dublin, 1966, repr. 2000), pp. 22, 25, 27. See also Kathleen M. Noonan, ' "The Cruel Pressure of an Enraged, Barbarous people": Irish and English Identity in Seventeenth-Century Policy and Propaganda', *HJ*, 41 (1998) pp. 151–77.
79. Alan Marshall, 'Irish Spies and Plotters in Seventeenth-Century Europe', *ISR*, 9 (1994–5) p. 12.
80. Clarendon MSS, 56, f. 102. Rather different from Walsh's dealings with Thurloe and his 'rigid humour', *CSPDC*, xi. 295.
81. Thomas V. Cohen and Elizabeth S. Cohen, *Words and Deeds in Renaissance Rome: Trials before the Papal Magistrates* (Toronto, 1993), p. 23; Elizabeth S. Cohen, 'Honour and Gender in the Streets of Early Modern Rome', *JIH*, 22 (1992) pp. 597–625; Stuart Carroll, *Blood and Violence in Early Modern France* (Oxford, 2006), pp. 49–54; Helen Langdon, *Caravaggio: A Life* (London, 1998), pp. 142–3.
82. Cohen and Cohen, *Words and Deeds in Renaissance Rome*, p. 25.
83. Walker, *Pistols! Treason! Murder!*, p. 49; Carroll, *Blood and Violence*, pp. 50–6.
84. Walsh, *True Narrative and Manifest*, p. 11.
85. Walsh, *True Narrative and Manifest*, p.[i]. See also David Booy, *Personal Disclosures: an Anthology of Self-Writings from the Seventeenth-Century* (Aldershot, 2002), pp. 4–5.
86. John Jeffries Martin, *Myths of Renaissance Individualism* (Basingstoke, 2004), p. 14. See also Jerome de Groot, *Royalist Identities* (Basingstoke, 2004), pp. 1–19 and Jerrold Seigel, *The Idea of the Self: Thought and Experience in Western Europe Since the Seventeenth Century* (Cambridge, 2005), pp. 5–6. Kevin Sharpe and Steven N. Zwicker, eds., *Writing Lives: Biography and Textuality, Identity and Representation in Early Modern England* (Oxford, 2008), pp.1–26.
87. Martin, *Myths of Renaissance Individualism*, p. 18.
88. Martin, *Myths of Renaissance Individualism*, p. 18.
89. Clarendon MSS, 56, f. 82.
90. Clarendon MSS, 56, f. 85v.
91. Walsh's part in Everard's career and the Popish Plot episode was obscure, but he was certainly later accused by Everard of dealings with Catholics in 1679. He denied it of course. See John P. Kenyon, *The Popish Plot* (London, 1972, 1974 pbk. edn), pp. 61, 224; John Pollock, *The Popish Plot: A Study in the History of the Reign of Charles II* (London, 1903), p. 174.
92. Walsh, *True Narrative and Manifest*, p. [iii].
93. Robert Walsh, *The Narratives of Sir Robert Walsh* (London?, 1680), p. 2.
94. Walsh, *True State, Case and Condition*, p. 17.
95. Walsh, *True State, Case and Condition*, pp. 17–18.
96. In this we can compare him with Joseph Bampfield. See Marshall, 'Bampfield'; also Marshall, *Intelligence and Espionage*, pp. 169–75.
97. Rawlinson A 175, ff. 274–8.
98. Rawlinson A, 175, f. 274.
99. Rawlinson A, 175, f. 274.
100. Rawlinson A, 175, f. 274. Walsh was still evidently wearing the medal of loyalty given to him long ago by Charles I, open proof to observers of his supposed loyalist credentials.
101. Rawlinson A, 175, ff. 274–5.
102. Rawlinson A, 175, f. 275.
103. Rawlinson A, 175, f. 275.

104. Rawlinson A, 175, f. 278. This entire affair finally came out in 1679 when Walsh found himself once again in trouble with the authorities in the course of the Popish Plot revelations.
105. T. Lucas, 'Memoirs of the Lives, Intrigues and Comical Adventures of the Most Famous Gamesters' (1714), in C. Cotton, *Games and Gamesters of the Restoration* ([London] 1930), p. 119.
106. Walsh, *True Narrative and Manifest*, p. [iv].

Chapter 4: Nathaniel Hooke and the Dynamics of Covert Operations in Eighteenth-century France

1. Gibson, *Jacobite Card*, p. 123.
2. National Archives of Scotland (henceforth NAS), GD 220/5/152/9: Adam Cockburn of Ormiston (Lord Justice Clerk) to James Graham, duke of Montrose, Edinburgh, 11 March 1708, 21.00 hrs; Daniel Szechi, ed., *'Scotland's Ruine'. Lockhart of Carnwath's Memoirs of the Union* (Aberdeen, 1995), pp. 227, 231.
3. Gibson, *Jacobite Card*, p. 127; Claude de Forbin, comte de Forbin, *Memoirs of the Count de Forbin, Commodore in the Navy of France: and Knight of the Order of St Louis* (2 vols, London, 1731), ii. 272.
4. Gibson, *Jacobite Card*, pp. 128; *Memoirs of the Count de Forbin*, ii. 275.
5. Gibson, *Jacobite Card*, pp. 128–9; *Memoirs of the Count de Forbin*, ii. 280.
6. http://eprints.nuim.ie/717/1/Thomas_Byrne_PhD_(2006)_-_From_Irish_Whig_rebel_to_Bourbon_d.pdf (accessed 31 December 2008): Thomas Byrne, 'From Irish Whig Rebel to Bourbon Diplomat: the Life and Career of Nathaniel Hooke (1664–1738)', unpublished NUI Maynooth Ph.D, 2006 (henceforth: Byrne, 'Hooke'), p. 326; *Memoirs of the Count de Forbin*, ii. 281–6.
7. Eveline Cruickshanks, *Political Untouchables. The Tories and the '45* (London, 1979), p. 52.
8. Gibson, *Jacobite Card*, pp. 93–7, 112–13; W. D. Macray, ed., *Correspondence of Colonel N. Hooke, Agent From the Court of France to the Scottish Jacobites, in the Years 1703–7* (2 vols, London, 1870), ii. 437–43: plan for 'l'Entreprise d'Ecosse', by Hooke, Charles-Honoré d'Albert de Luynes, duc de Chevreuse, and François de Callières, Paris, 23 July/2 August 1707; ii. 482–6: Hooke's plan, presented to Michel Chamillart, Minister of War, and Jean Baptiste Colbert de Croissy, marquis de Torcy, Secretary of State for Foreign Affairs, 16/27 September 1707.
9. Gibson, *Jacobite Card*, pp. 119–21; Bruce Lenman, *The Jacobite Risings in Britain 1689–1746* (London, 1980), p. 89; Frank McLynn, *The Jacobites* (London, 1985), p. 94.
10. Byrne, 'Hooke', *passim*. Dr Byrne's excellent thesis is without doubt the best survey of Hooke's career and its importance, and I am most grateful to him for permission to cite it here.
11. Byrne, 'Hooke', pp. 14–59.
12. Jonathan Scott, *England's Troubles. Seventeenth-Century English Political Instability in European Context* (Cambridge, 2000), pp. 182–204.
13. Byrne, 'Hooke', pp. 60–86.
14. Mark Goldie, 'John Locke's Circle and James II', *HJ*, 35 (1992) pp. 557–86; 'James II and the Dissenters' Revenge: the Commission of Enquiry of 1688', *HR*, 66 (1993) pp. 53–88.
15. Byrne, 'Hooke', pp. 87–99.
16. Byrne, 'Hooke', pp. 99–102.
17. Miller, *James II*, pp. 200–5; Speck, *Reluctant Revolutionaries*, pp. 118–21.
18. Byrne, 'Hooke', pp. 100–2.
19. Byrne, 'Hooke', pp. 102–4.

20. Childs, *Williamite Wars*, pp. 385–9.
21. Childs, *Williamite Wars*, p. 393.
22. Byrne, 'Hooke', pp. 105–6, 107–8.
23. Guy Rowlands, 'An Army in Exile: Louis XIV and the Irish Forces of James II in France, 1691–1698', *Royal Stuart Society*, Paper LX, p. 18; John A. Lynn, *Giant of the Grand Siècle. The French Army, 1610–1715* (Cambridge, 1997), pp. 21, 25, 336.
24. Edward Corp with Edward Gregg, Howard Erskine-Hill and Geoffrey Scott, *A Court in Exile. The Stuarts in France, 1689–1718* (Cambridge, 2004), pp. 119–21, 123.
25. Byrne, 'Hooke', pp. 111, 118.
26. This crisis centred on the question of who was to succeed to the Spanish empire when the ailing, childless Carlos (Charles) II died. There were two principal royal dynasties with a claim to this vast inheritance: the French Bourbons and the Austrian Habsburgs. The problem was that in the event that a Bourbon ruler succeeded Carlos the vagaries of inheritance might then have led to the unification of the French and Spanish empires under a single Bourbon monarch. The mere possibility of this appalled the governments of England and the Netherlands. Hence, when the Spanish grandees offered the crown to Philippe, duc d'Anjou (Louis XIV's grandson) after Carlos's death in 1700, and Philippe accepted, the two powers and the Austrian Habsburgs moved inexorably towards war with France and Spain.
27. Byrne, 'Hooke', pp. 220–72.
28. Byrne, 'Hooke', pp. 14–20.
29. *Correspondence of Colonel N. Hooke*, ii. p. vii. Hooke had theoretically been a 'Colonel réformé' since he arrived in France from Ireland in 1691, but he had been ranked only as a Major in the French military hierarchy. His promotion to full Colonel and commander of the regiment de Sparre in lieu of its proprietor (ii. 163–4: Hooke to Chamillart, Versailles, 28 February/11 March 1707) came on 28 December 1702/8 January 1703.
30. Byrne, 'Hooke', pp. 298–9.
31. *Correspondence of Colonel N. Hooke*, i. 53–4: 'Memoire Sommaire sur les Affaires d'Ecosse', 22 January/2 February 1704.
32. Edward M. Furgol, 'Fraser, Simon, eleventh Lord Lovat (1667/8–1747)', *Oxford Dictionary of National Biography*, Oxford University Press, September 2004; online edn, October 2006 [http://www.oxforddnb.com/view/article/10122, accessed 20 January 2009].
33. Byrne, 'Hooke', p. 273.
34. Lynn, *Giant of the Grand Siècle*, pp. 47–55, 210, 238, 261–2; Pierre Goubert, *Louis XIV and Twenty Million Frenchmen*, trans. Anne Carter (New York, 1970), pp. 242–7, and cf. François Bluche, *Louis XIV*, trans. Mark Greengrass (New York, 1990), pp. 522–3.
35. Hillel Schwarz, *The French Prophets. The History of a Millenarian Group in Eighteenth-Century England* (London, 1980), pp. 22–7.
36. David Chandler, *Marlborough as Military Commander* (2nd edn, London, 1979), pp. 123–50.
37. *Correspondence of Colonel N. Hooke*, i. 21–39: [memo on Scotland by Hooke] read to Louis XIV's royal council 29 November/10 December 1703.
38. James Macpherson, ed., *Original Papers; Containing the Secret History of Great Britain, from the Restoration to the Accession of the House of Hanover* (2 vols, London, 1775), i. 609–11: extracts, John Caryll, Jacobite Baron Caryll to Berry [James St Amand], 25 April/6 May and 10/21 August 1702; i. 623–5, 626–7: instructions for Captain James Murray, January 1703; i. 630: instructions for Captain John Murray, 24 April/5 May 1703.
39. Edward Gregg, 'France, Rome and the Exiled Stuarts, 1689–1713', in, Corp, *Court in Exile*, pp. 18–20, 30–6, 39–53.
40. Corp, *Court in Exile*, pp. 158–79.

41. J. R. Jones, *The Revolution of 1688 in England* (London, 1972), pp. 255–62; Childs, *The Army, James II, and the Glorious Revolution*, pp. 142–3.
42. Geoffrey Scott, 'The Piety of James II', in, Corp, *Court in Exile*, pp. 237–56; Miller, *James II*, pp. 234–6, 239.
43. Gibson, *Jacobite Card*, pp. 20, 25, 31, 38, 104; *Correspondence of Colonel N. Hooke*, i. 194–7: Hooke to Torcy, St Germain, 30 May/10 June 1705.
44. Byrne, 'Hooke', p. 252.
45. *Correspondence of Colonel N. Hooke*, i. 19: 'Memoire donné à Monsieur le Marquis de Torcy', 7/18 February 1703; i. 38, 39: [memo on Scotland by Hooke] read to Louis XIV's royal council 29 November/10 December 1703; Byrne, 'Hooke', p. 118.
46. Louis de Rouvroy, duc de St Simon, *The Memoirs of the Duke of Saint-Simon on the Reign of Louis XIV and the Regency*, trans. Bayle St John (3 vols, Philadelphia, 1890), ii. 5; *Correspondence of Colonel N. Hooke*, ii. 154: Hooke's instructions from Louis XIV, Marly, 27 February/9 March 1707.
47. *Correspondence of Colonel N. Hooke*, ii. 94: Hooke memo for Torcy regarding the Jacobite court, 28 December/8 January 1706/7.
48. *Correspondence of Colonel N. Hooke*, i. 122–6: Hooke to Marechal Victor Marie de Coeuvres, marquis de Coeuvres, 13/24 March 1704; i. 151–3: Hooke to Callières, Bruxelles, 16/27 May 1704; i. 157: extract, Hooke to Gualterio, Paris, 8/19 December 1704.
49. Bodleian Library, Oxford, Carte 180, f. 103r–107v: proposal for an invasion of England/Scotland submitted to Torcy, St Germain, 22 June 1704.
50. *Correspondence of Colonel N. Hooke*, i. 158–60: 'Memoire donné à Marechal [François de Neufville, duc de] Villeroy', 27 February/10 March 1705.
51. *Correspondence of Colonel N. Hooke*, i. 167–71: Hooke memo to Torcy, 6/17 April 1705; i. 203–8: official instructions for Hooke from Louis XIV, Versailles, 6/17 June 1705; i. 372, 373: Hooke's report for Torcy and Chamillart, Fontainebleau, 6/17 October 1705.
52. Daniel Szechi, *George Lockhart of Carnwath, 1689–1727. A Study in Jacobitism* (East Linton, 2002), pp. 50–60.
53. William Ferguson, *Scotland. 1689 to the Present* (Edinburgh, repr. 1994), pp. 102–10, 111–12, 129–30.
54. *Correspondence of Colonel N. Hooke*, i. 206–7: official instructions for Hooke from Louis XIV, Versailles, 6/17 June 1705.
55. *Correspondence of Colonel N. Hooke*, i. 383–98, 403–4, 406–8, 416–18: Hooke's report for Torcy and Chamillart, Fontainebleau, 6/17 October 1705.
56. *Correspondence of Colonel N. Hooke*, i. 38: [memo on Scotland by Hooke] read to Louis XIV's royal council 29 November/10 December 1703; i. 203–8: official instructions for Hooke from Louis XIV, Versailles, 6/17 June 1705.
57. *Correspondence of Colonel N. Hooke*, i. 385, 395, 397, 404, 406, 408, 409, 410: Hooke's report for Torcy and Chamillart, Fontainebleau, 6/17 October 1705
58. *Correspondence of Colonel N. Hooke*, i. 413, ii. 67–9, 156, 211–12, 269–70, 271–2, 335–6.
59. *Correspondence of Colonel N. Hooke*, i. 372–431: Hooke's report for Torcy and Chamillart, Fontainebleau, 6/17 October 1705, *passim*.
60. *Correspondence of Colonel N. Hooke*, i. 411, 413–17: Hooke's report for Torcy and Chamillart, Fontainebleau, 6/17 October 1705
61. *Correspondence of Colonel N. Hooke*, i. 418–19: Hooke's report for Torcy and Chamillart, Fontainebleau, 6/17 October 1705.
62. *Correspondence of Colonel N. Hooke*, i. 412–13: Hooke's report for Torcy and Chamillart, Fontainebleau, 6/17 October 1705.
63. *Correspondence of Colonel N. Hooke*, i. 342: Hooke to Torcy, Dunkirk, 14/25 September 1705.
64. *Correspondence of Colonel N. Hooke*, i. 372n.

65. Byrne, 'Hooke', pp. 8, 11.
66. *Correspondence of Colonel N. Hooke*, i. 342: Hooke to Torcy, Dunkirk, 14/25 September 1705.
67. *Correspondence of Colonel N. Hooke*, i. 299: 2 September 1705.
68. *Correspondence of Colonel N. Hooke*, ii. 1: Fleming to Hooke, Ostend, 22 December 1705/2 January 1706.
69. *Correspondence of Colonel N. Hooke*, ii. 23: French translation of Fleming's memo for the French government, 22 January/2 February 1706.
70. *Correspondence of Colonel N. Hooke*, ii. 22–31: French translation of Fleming's memo for the French government, 22 January/2 February 1706; ii. 31–7: Fleming to Queen Mary, February 1706; ii. 48: Hooke to Torcy, 25 March/5 April 1706.
71. Lynn, *Giant of the Grand Siècle*, pp. 53, 55; Chandler, *Marlborough*, pp. 151–83.
72. John Wells and Douglas Wills, 'Revolution, Restoration and Debt Repudiation: the Jacobite Threat to England's Institutions and Economic Growth', *JEcH*, 60 (2000) pp. 434, 436–7.
73. *Memoirs of the Duke of St Simon*, ii. 7; *Correspondence of Colonel N. Hooke*, ii. 155n, 183n and 165–6: Chamillart to Middleton, 5/16 February 1707.
74. N. A. M. Rodger, *The Command of the Ocean. A Naval History of Britain, 1649–1815* (London, 2004), pp. 166, 170–2, 175–7.
75. *Correspondence of Colonel N. Hooke*, ii. 155n.
76. *Memoirs of the Count de Forbin*, ii. 259.
77. *Memoirs of the Duke of St Simon*, ii. 7; *Memoirs of the Count de Forbin*, ii. 251–2.
78. *Correspondence of Colonel N. Hooke*, ii. 58: Hooke to Captain James Carron, 31 May/11 June 1706.
79. Chandler, *Marlborough*, pp. 166–83; Nicholas Henderson, *Prince Eugen of Savoy. A Biography* (London, 1966), pp. 125–33.
80. Allan I. Macinnes, *Union and Empire. The Making of the United Kingdom in 1707* (Cambridge, 2007), pp. 283–92.
81. *Correspondence of Colonel N. Hooke*, ii. 79: Hooke memo to Torcy, 18/29 September 1706.
82. *Correspondence of Colonel N. Hooke*, ii. 97: Hooke memo for Torcy and Chamillart, 22 December/3 January 1706/7; ii. 98–9: Hooke memo for Chamillart, 28 December/8 January 1706/7.
83. *Correspondence of Colonel N. Hooke*, ii. 118: Hooke to Perth, Versailles, 1/12 February 1707.
84. *Correspondence of Colonel N. Hooke*, ii. 165: Middleton to Hooke, St Germain, 28 February/11 March 1707; ii. 172–3: Queen Mary to Anne Erroll, 15/26 March 1707.
85. *Correspondence of Colonel N. Hooke*, ii. 178–9: Fleming to Marischal, 5/16 March 1707.
86. Macinnes, *Union and Empire*, pp. 292–306.
87. Sir Charles Petrie, *The Marshal Duke of Berwick. The Picture of an Age* (London, 1953), pp. 210–17.
88. Henderson, *Prince Eugen*, pp. 138–49.
89. *Original Papers*, ii. 80–2: Hooke's instructions from Chamillart, February 1707.
90. *Correspondence of Colonel N. Hooke*, ii. 347–409 *passim*: Hooke's account of his second journey to Scotland (given to Torcy and read in Council), 28 June/9 July 1707.
91. *Correspondence of Colonel N. Hooke*, ii. 349–52, 355, 358: Hooke's account of his second journey to Scotland (given to Torcy and read in Council), 28 June/9 July 1707.
92. *Correspondence of Colonel N. Hooke*, ii. 396–7: Hooke's account of his second journey to Scotland (given to Torcy and read in Council), 28 June/9 July 1707: 'Je traittay cet ecrit de ridicule'.
93. *Correspondence of Colonel N. Hooke*, ii. 388, 391: Hooke's account of his second journey to Scotland (given to Torcy and read in Council), 28 June/9 July 1707.

94. *Correspondence of Colonel N. Hooke*, ii. 368: Hooke's account of his second journey to Scotland (given to Torcy and read in Council), 28 June/9 July 1707.
95. *Correspondence of Colonel N. Hooke*, ii. 353, 355, 358, 360, 361, 365, 369–70, 372–4, 391: Hooke's account of his second journey to Scotland (given to Torcy and read in Council), 28 June/9 July 1707.
96. *Correspondence of Colonel N. Hooke*, ii. 375: Hooke's account of his second journey to Scotland (given to Torcy and read in Council), 28 June/9 July 1707.
97. *Correspondence of Colonel N. Hooke*, ii. 404: Hooke's account of his second mission to Scotland (given to Torcy and read in Council), 28 June/9 July 1707. He personally met 8 'seigneurs', saw pledges from 19 others and encountered up to twenty more whom he assessed as willing to rise (ii. 238–9: 'List of those the Lords that sign'd engage for', 7 May 1707; ii. 389, 404: Hooke's account of his second mission to Scotland (given to Torcy and read in Council), 28 June/9 July 1707).
98. *Correspondence of Colonel N. Hooke*, ii. 154–62: Hooke's instructions from Louis XIV, Marly, 27 February/9 March 1707; ii. 348: Hooke's account of his second journey to Scotland (given to Torcy and read in Council), 28 June/9 July 1707.
99. *Correspondence of Colonel N. Hooke*, ii. 375–89: Hooke's account of his second journey to Scotland (given to Torcy and read in Council), 28 June/9 July 1707.
100. *Correspondence of Colonel N. Hooke*, ii. 256–62: 'Memorial of the Scotch for the King of France', 7 May 1707.
101. *Original Papers*, i. 679: narrative of Captain John Murray, 19/30 May 1704.
102. *Correspondence of Colonel N. Hooke*, ii. 235: Hooke's list of clan chieftains Drummond represents, as dictated by Drummond, 2/13 May 1707; ii. 238–9: 'List of those the Lords that sign'd engage for', 7 May 1707.
103. *Correspondence of Colonel N. Hooke*, ii. 410, 411: Hooke to Chamillart and Pontchartrain, Dunkirk, 6/17 June 1707.
104. *Correspondence of Colonel N. Hooke*, ii. 427: Hooke to Torcy, Versailles, 28 June/8 July 1707.
105. *Correspondence of Colonel N. Hooke*, ii. 433: 13/24 July 1707.
106. *Correspondence of Colonel N. Hooke*, ii. 437–43: plan for 'l'Entreprise d'Ecosse', by Hooke, Chevreuse and de Callières, Paris, 23 July/2 August 1707.
107. *Correspondence of Colonel N. Hooke*, ii. 454: Ogilvie to Hooke, Dunkirk, 11/22 August 1707; ii. 455–6: Hooke to Ogilvy, 15/26 and 17/28 August 1707.
108. *Correspondence of Colonel N. Hooke*, ii. 473: Ogilvie's account of an interview with Chamillart, 31 August/11 September 1707; ii. 475–8: extracts of letters read in Council, 7/18 September 1707.
109. *Correspondence of Colonel N. Hooke*, ii. 482–6: Hooke's plan for setting out the expedition, presented to Chamillart and Torcy, 16/27 September 1707.
110. *Correspondence of Colonel N. Hooke*, ii. 487–8: Torcy's points for Ogilvie to write home about, 26 September/7 October 1707.
111. *Correspondence of Colonel N. Hooke*, ii. 495: 12/23 October 1707.
112. *Correspondence of Colonel N. Hooke*, ii. 513–15: Hooke to Middleton, Versailles, 7/18 November 1707.
113. *Correspondence of Colonel N. Hooke*, ii. 487–8: Torcy's points for Ogilvie to write home about, 26 September/7 October 1707; ii. 495–6: Hooke to Elizabeth Gordon, 12/23 October 1707.
114. *Correspondence of Colonel N. Hooke*, ii. 534–5: Hooke to Ogilvie, Versailles, 20/31 December 1707.
115. Daniel Szechi, *1715. The Great Jacobite Rising* (London, 2006).
116. Daniel Szechi, *Jacobitism and Tory Politics, 1710–14* (Edinburgh, 1984).
117. *Memoirs of the Count de Forbin*, ii. 288.

118. *Correspondence of Colonel N. Hooke*, i. 283–6: Fleming to Anne Erroll, Edinburgh, 27 August 1705; ii. 130: Perth to Mary Drummond, Countess Marischal, 31 January/10 February 1707; ii. 154: Hooke's instructions from Louis XIV, Marly, 27 February/9 March 1707.
119. Melville Massue de Ruvigny, marquis de Ruvigny and Raineval, *The Jacobite Peerage, Baronetage, Knightage and Grants of Honour. Extracted . . . from the Stuart Papers Now in Possession of His Majesty the King at Windsor Castle, and Supplemented by Biographical and Genealogical Notes* (Edinburgh, 1904), pp. 66–7; Byrne, 'Hooke', p. 347.

Chapter 5: The Fallen Politician's Way Back In

1. I should like to thank Nicola Cowmeadow and Dan Szechi for commenting on an earlier version of this chapter.
2. Christopher Storrs, 'Savoyard Diplomacy in the Eighteenth Century', in Daniela Frigo, ed., *Politics and Diplomacy in Early Modern Italy: the Structure of Diplomatic Practice, 1450–1800*, trans. Adrian Belton (Cambridge, 2000), pp. 210–53.
3. Archivio di Stato, Turin [hereafter AST]/Lettere Ministri [LM]/Spagna, mazzo [m]. 60: Marchese del Borgo to marquis d'Arvillars, Turin, 10 July 1732. This is undoubtedly the individual listed incorrectly in the archive catalogue as Marroni, exemplifying the problem in this underworld of names, identities and sources.
4. AST/LM/Spagna, m. 60: Marquis d'Arvillars to Victor Amadeus II [VAII], Madrid, 30 August, 4 October and 15 November 1728.
5. Cf. AST/LM/Inghilterra, m. 53: Charles Emmanuel III [CEIII] to cavaliere Ossorio, 20 August 1747. This dispatch throws invaluable light on the way intelligence was communicated, often in an indirect, roundabout way, and how one court sought to critically evaluate it.
6. AST/LM/Inghilterra, m. 53: Ossorio to CEIII, London, 18 August 1747, and CEIII to Ossorio, Turin, 20 August 1747.
7. AST/LM/Olanda, m. 44: Count Borré de la Chavanne to CEIII, Hague, 5 and 8 August and 6 September 1747, and AST/LM/Inghilterra, m. 53: CEIII to Chavanne, Turin, 20 August 1747; Ossorio to CEIII and to marchese di Gorzegno, London, 18 August 1747.
8. There is a substantial bibliography on espionage and Spanish policy before 1665. Cf. Charles Howard Carter, *Secret Diplomacy of the Habsburgs 1598–1625* (New York, 1964), Alain Hugon, *Au service du Roi Catholique. 'Honorables ambassadeurs' et 'Divins espions'. Representation diplomatique et service secret dans les relations hispano-françaises de 1598 a 1635* (Madrid, 2004), and Michael Levin's contribution to the present volume. A recent edition of a useful source/s is Diego Navarro Bonilla, *Cartas entre espías e intelligencias secretas en el siglo de los validos. Juan de Torres-Gaspar Bonifaz 1632–1638* (Madrid, 2007).
9. But cf. Christopher Storrs, 'Intelligence and the Formulation of Spanish Policy and Strategy (1665–1700)', *INS*, 21 (2006) pp. 493–519.
10. For espionage during the succession struggle cf. David González Cruz, *Propaganda e Información en Tiempos de Guerra. España y América (1700–1714)* (Madrid, 2009), pp. 200ff.
11. Given Macanaz's dramatic career, it is surprising how little has been done to redress the neglect noted by Henry Kamen as long ago as 1965, Kamen, 'Macanaz and the foundations of Bourbon power in Spain', *EHR*, 80 (1965) p. 699. Readers of Spanish can, fortunately, use Carmen Martín Gaite's biography, first published in 1969, Carmen Martín Gaite, *Macanaz. Otro paciente de la Inquisición* (Barcelona, 1982). Yet, Macanaz remains elusive; he is largely ignored, for example, by Concepción de Castro in her recent study of Philip V's secretary of state, José Grimaldo, and the administrative revolution of the

reign, despite the correspondence carried on by Grimaldo and Macanaz before and during the latter's exile, Concepción de Castro, *A la sombra de Felipe V. José de Grimaldo, ministro responsable (1703–1726)* (Madrid, 2004). The neglect is the more surprising in view of the source material provided by Macanaz himself: according to Kamen, by 1744 Macanaz had produced 201 manuscript volumes, Kamen, *The War of Succession in Spain 1700–1715* (London, 1969), p. 417; cf. Indice de los libros que durante su vida escribio Macanaz, in Fragmentos Históricos de la vida, Biblioteca Nacional, Madrid, MS 11029 f. 275ff. Despite the neglect, historians differ in their appreciations of Macanaz. Carmen Martín Gaite, whose biography is still arguably the best study of Macanaz, emphasises the extent to which Macanaz was above all a victim of the Inquisition. For his part, Kamen sees Macanaz as one of the founders of a new Bourbon Spanish state. More recently, José Cano Valero has argued that Macanaz was a proto-Enlightenment figure, Cano Valero, *Melchor Rafael de Macanaz (1670–1760): político y diplomático ilustrado* (Toledo, 2008). For François López, *Juan Pablo Forner y la Crisis de la Conciencia Española en el Siglo XVIII)* (Valladolid, 1999; original French edition, 1976), pp. 94–5, the marqués of Ensenada was Spain's most enlightened minister since Macanaz. Whereas these interpretations see Macanaz as a forward looking, 'modern' figure – emblematic in some respects of the way the new Bourbon dynasty revived a Spain brought low by the Habsburgs – and locate him in an emphatically domestic setting, M. Dolores Gómez Molleda has preferred to set Macanaz in an international context and to see him as backward looking – and unrealistic – by contrast with ministers such as Ferdinand VI's de facto prime minister, José Carvajal de Lencastre, who supposedly represented an alternative vision – more truly modern, more realistic, and more 'Atlantic' – of Spain and its international role from c. 1748. Gómez Molleda, 'Viejo y nuevo estilo político en la Corte de Fernando VI', *Eidos*, 6 (1957), pp. 43–76.

12. Cf. the comments of Martín Gaite, *Macanaz*, pp. 331ff. on Macanaz's account of an audience with Louis XIV in 1715 in the apologia he completed after his return to Spain, *Agravios que me hicieron mis enemigos*. There is a recent facsimile edition of this, edited by Francisco Mendoza Díaz-Maroto (Albacete, 2007).
13. Fragmentos Históricos de la vida de D.n Melchor Rafael de Macanaz, given as Valencia, 31 May 1788, see note 14 below.
14. The Inquisition trial papers are of relatively little value from this perspective.
15. What follows draws on Fragmentos Históricos de la Vida (BN), although this too must be used with caution, Martín Gaite, *Macanaz*, pp. 34–5; Fabrice Abbad and Didier Ozanam, *Les Intendants Espagnols du XVIIIe Siècle* (Madrid, 1992), pp. 122–4; and Ozanam, *Les diplomates espagnols du XVIIIe siècle*, (Madrid and Bordeaux, 1998), pp. 329–31.
16. The Audiencia was a high level court with important administrative functions, and was often a step to even higher office in Spain itself, cf. J. H. Parry, *The Spanish Seaborne Empire* (London, 1966), pp. 190ff.
17. On Portocarrero, cf. Antonio Ramón Peña Izquierdo, *La Casa de Palma. La familia Portocarrero en el gobierno de la Monarquía Hispánica (1665–1700)* (Cordoba, 2004).
18. For the count-duke of Olivares' largely abortive attempt to subvert these in the middle of the seventeenth century, cf. J. H. Elliott, *The Revolt of Catalonia* (Cambridge, 1961), *passim*.
19. Cf Janine Fayard, *Les Membres du Conseil de Castille 1621–1746* (Geneva, 1982), pp. 7, 57–8, 66, 81, 92, 112–13, 150; Fayard, 'La tentative de reforme du Conseil de Castille sous le règne de Philippe V (1713–15)', *Mélanges de la Casa de Velazquez*, II (1966) pp. 259–81.
20. There is a modern edition of this crucial text, Melchor de Macanaz, *Testamento Político Pedimento Fiscal*, Francisco Maldonado de Guevara, ed. (Madrid, 1972).
21. Among those he 'discovered' and promoted was the man who would become, as a reward for his role in negotiating a Concordat with Rome in 1717, marqués of la Compuesta, Fayard, *Les Membres*, p. 137.

22. For examples of satirical verses embracing Orry and Macanaz, the queen and the princess des Ursins, cf. Teófanes Egido López, *Opinión pública y oposición al poder* (2nd ed., Valladolid, 2002), pp. 103ff., and Egido López, *Sátiras políticas de la España moderna* (Madrid, 1973), p. 210.
23. Cf. Edward Armstrong, *Elisabeth Farnese: 'The Termagant of Spain'* (London, 1892).
24. Philip's exaggerated – and unusual – uxoriousness has attracted a great deal of comment, cf. Armstrong, *Elisabeth Farnese*, pp. 8ff., Kamen, *Philip V*, pp. 22ff., 133ff, and Charles C. Noel, ' "Barbara succeeds Elisabeth . . .". The feminisation and domestication of politics in the Spanish Monarchy, 1701–59', in Clarissa Campbell Orr, ed., *Queenship in Europe, 1660–1815: The Role of the Consort* (Cambridge, 2004), pp. 155–85.
25. For this dramatic episode, cf. William Coxe, *History of the Kings of Spain of the House of Bourbon* (5 vols, London, 1815), 2, pp. 177ff.; Armstrong, *Elisabeth Farnese*, pp. 25ff.; and Luciano de Taxonera, *Isabel de Farnesio. Retrato de una reina y perfil de una mujer (1692–1766)* (Barcelona, 1943), pp. 35ff.
26. Castro, *A la sombra*, p. 305. One of the architects of the marriage, and later chief minister, Cardinal Alberoni, claimed later (in exile) to have urged on the new queen the expulsion of Macanaz for his *Pedimento Fiscal*, Taxonera Vivanco, *El cardenal Julio Alberoni, forjador de una nueva Espana en el siglo XVIII* (Madrid, 1945), p. 251. The activity of the Spanish Inquisition in its last century or so has attracted far less attention than that in its first, but see Henry Kamen, *The Spanish Inquisition: An Historical Revision* (London, 1997) and Helen Rawlings, *The Spanish Inquisition* (London, 2005).
27. For the correspondence between Louis XIV and his grandson, an exchange which throws invaluable light on Louis's own understanding of kingship and 'absolute' monarchy, cf. Henri Marie Alfred Baudrillart, *Philippe V et la Cour de France* (5 vols, Paris, 1890–1900), 1, *passim*; and Francisco Javier Guillamón Álvarez and J. D. Muñoz Rodríguez, eds., *Educando al Principe. Correspondencia privada de Luis XIV a Felip V durante la Guerra de Sucesión* (Rosario, 2008).
28. Macanaz undoubtedly made a major error in referring to his services to Philip's first wife.
29. Robinet was dismissed a month later, Martín Gaite, *Macanaz*, pp. 326–7. According to one Madrid informant of the French foreign secretary, Torcy, Macanaz's dismissal threatened plans for an expedition to recover the island of Majorca, which was still held by supporters of 'Charles III', but Isabel Farnese pressed for his dismissal. For one foreign diplomat's reporting of the dismissal of Macanaz, cf. AST/LM/Spagna, m. 57: Morozzo to VAII, Madrid, 11 February 1715. In June 1715 Philip reversed Macanaz's reform of the council of Castile.
30. Martín Gaite, *Macanaz*, pp. 331ff., denies Macanaz's claim that the king had allowed him to go to France to take the waters for his health.
31. Carlos II's widow, Mariana of Neuburg, had met Isabel Farnese at Pau in 1714, Martín Gaite, *Macanaz*, p. 311. His proximity may explain why, later that year, the Savoyard minister in Madrid reported that Macanaz, had been recalled, but with orders not to be in Madrid, AST/LM/Spagna, m. 57: Morozzo to VAII, 27 May 1715.
32. On confiscation by the Inquisition, cf. Henry Kamen, 'Confiscations in the Economy of the Spanish Inquisition', *EcHR*, NS 18 (1965) pp. 511ff.
33. This community has been extensively studied by Virginia León Sanz, cf. her 'Represión Borbónica y Exilio Austracista al Finalizar la Guerra de Sucesión Española', in Antonio Álvarez-Ossorio, Bernardo J. García García and V. León, eds, *La Pérdida de Europa. La guerra de Sucesión por la Monarquiá de España* (Madrid, 2007), pp. 567ff., and references there.
34. Castro, *A la sombra, passim*.
35. Archivo General de Simancas [AGS]/Estado [E]/4690: Macanaz to Grimaldo, Pau, 25 May 1717.

36. AGS/E/4690: Macanaz to Grimaldo, Pau, 8 June 1717. A large part of Philip V's army was stationed in the Aragonese territories - and above all Catalonia - after their recovery.
37. AGS/E/4690: Macanaz to Grimaldo, Pau, 28 September 1720.
38. AGS/E/4690: Macanaz to Grimaldo, Pau, 25 May 1717.
39. Henri Marie Alfred Baudrillart, 'Les Prétentions de Philippe V à la Couronne de France d'après des documents inédits', *Revue des Questions Historiques*, 41 (1887), pp. 96–149.
40. J. H. Shennan, *Philippe Duke of Orléans* (London, 1979) pp. 53, 57, 136–8.
41. AGS/E/4690: Grimaldo to father Daubenton, Buen Retiro, 13 March 1723.
42. For the debate, cf. Kamen, *Philip V*, pp. 173ff.
43. AGS/E/4690: Macanaz to Grimaldo, Pau, 29 January 1724.
44. AGS/E/4690: Macanaz to Grimaldo, Pau, 25 March 1724.
45. Derek McKay and H. M. Scott, *The Rise of the Great Powers 1648–1815* (Harlow, 1983), pp. 121ff.
46. In his congress diary, in the National Archives of Scotland, GD 158/2124, one of the British plenipotentiaries at Cambrai, Patrick Hume, earl of Marchmont, recorded the receipt of an anonymous offer of intelligence about the French court in return for 50 *louis d'or*. The British representatives replied that if the intelligence was of consequence they would pay. Bély, *Espions*, focuses on the congress of Utrecht.
47. AGS/E/4346: Lawless to Orendayn, Paris, 11 April 1724. For Lawless, one of many Jacobite exiles who had a successful career in Spain after 1713, cf. Ozanam, *Les diplomates*, pp. 313–14.
48. AGS/E/4690: Macanaz to [?], 29 May 1724. Cf. AGS/E/4690: Macanaz's Reflexiones a las demandas echas por los Ministerios Imperiales en su escrib. de 28 de abril de 1724.
49. AGS/E/4690: Bermúdez to Grimaldo, San Ildefonso, 18 July 1724. On Bermúdez, a Spanish Jesuit, cf. Baudrillart, *Philippe V*, 2, pp. 549–50. In the spring of 1722, Philip V granted Macanaz 50 *doblones* a month, AGS/E/4690: Macanaz to Grimaldo, Pau, 31 March 1722. Macanaz may well have received the same amount from Luis I: in May 1724 Macanaz acknowledged receipt of a letter for 50 *doblones* received from the then Secretary of State, Orendayn, AGS/E/4690: Macanaz to Orendayn, 23 May 1724.
50. AGS/E/4690: Berat de Cortiada to Grimaldo, Zaragoza, 19 September 1724.
51. AGS/E/4690: Macanaz to Grimaldo, Paris, 19 September 1724.
52. AGS/E/4690: Macanaz to Grimaldo, Paris, 30 October 1724.
53. On this episode, cf. Baudrillart, *Philippe V*, pp. 143ff., Colin Jones, *The Great Nation* (London, 2002), pp. 79–80, and Jeremy Black, *From Louis XIV to Napoleon: The Fate of a Great Power* (London, 1999), pp. 74–5.
54. That Macanaz himself felt there were some in Paris who did not wish him well, cf. AHN/E/2490: Macanaz to Grimaldo, Bayona, 13 May 1725.
55. AHN/E/2490/4: Lawless to Grimaldo, Paris, 27 March and 5 April 1725.
56. National Archives, SP 78/, f. 63: [Thomas Robinson?] to Charles Delafaye, Paris, 3 April 1725.
57. SP 78/, f. 63: Robinson to Delafaye, Paris, 2 June 1725. However, the Genealogia in the Fragmentos Históricos, f. 293, claimed that Macanaz was of Irish origin.
58. AHN/E/2490/8: Monteleon to Grimaldo, San Lorenzo de las Aguas, 10 April 1725. The same point was made by Macanaz himself, AHN/E/2490: to Grimaldo, San Lorenzo de las Aguas, 10 April 1725. By this time, del Giudice had long fallen out of favour, but the Inquisition case remained open.
59. AHN/E/2490/4: Lawless to Grimaldo, Paris, 5 April 1725.
60. AHN/E/2490/4: Lawless to Grimaldo, Paris, 27 March 1725.
61. AGS/E/4690: Macanaz to Grimaldo, Poitiers, 19 April 1725.

62. AGS/E/4690: Macanaz to Grimaldo, Bordeaux, 2 May 1725.
63. Cf. Puntos q piden resolucion . . ., in AHN/2490/6: Lawless's letters from Paris of 5 and 10 April 1725.
64. AHN/2490/6: Lawless to [Grimaldo], Paris, 5 and 10 April 1725.
65. AGS/E/4690: Macanaz to Grimaldo, Bayona, 13 May 1725.
66. AGS/E/4691: Macanaz to Grimaldo, Brussels, 13 July 1725.
67. For one Flemish noble, the marquis de Conflans (b. 1712) who went to Spain, married a member of Isabel Farnese's household and received the command of a company in the Walloon Guards, cf. Didier Ozanam, *La Diplomacia de Fernando VI. Correspondencia entre Carvajal y Huescar, 1746–1749* (Madrid, 1975), p. 215.
68. AGS/E/4691: Macanaz to Grimaldo, Brussels, 27 July 1725. For the Ostend Company, cf. Derek McKay, *Prince Eugene of Savoy* (London, 1976), pp. 184–5, 209–12, 218–23.
69. AGS/E/4691: Macanaz to Grimaldo, Brussels, 13 July 1725, and petition of D. Joseph Carlos Brambilla, [May 1725?]. On Spain's consular service, cf. Ozanam, *Les diplomates*, pp. 107ff.
70. AGS/E/4691: [Grimaldo?] to [Macanaz?], 2 September 1725.
71. Martín Gaite, *Macanaz*, p. 397.
72. AGS/E/4691: Macanaz to Grimaldo, Brussels, 6 December 1725.
73. Martín Gaite, *Macanaz*, pp. 397ff. Macanaz's wife is a rather shadowy figure: there are no letters until her return to Spain in 1747: cf. AGS/E/4695: Macanaz to Maria Maximiliana, Huy, 1, 22 and 29 March 1748.
74. AGS/E/4692: Macanaz to marqués of la Paz, [Paris, November] 1728.
75. AGS/E/4961: Macanaz to marqués of la Paz, Liège, 20 December 1725.
76. Savoyard industrial development in this period rested in part on luring English artisans to Piedmont, often illegally, cf. Geoffrey Symcox, *Victor Amadeus II* (London, 1983), p. 210. In October 1746, Macanaz encouraged the Parisian watchmaker, Jean-Léonard Bourgeois, who had fled to Liège because of his debts, to go to Spain, AHN/E/4027: Macanaz to Huescar, 16 October 1746, cited by Ozanam, *Diplomacia*, p. 307.
77. AGS/E/4961: [Minute of a reply to a letter from Macanaz] 21 January 1726.
78. AGS/E/4961: Macanaz to marqués of la Paz, Liège, 30 May 1726. For the fall of Ripperda, who took refuge in the British embassy, offering to reveal Spanish state secrets, before eventually entering the service of Spain's enemies in north Africa, cf. Coxe, *Memoirs of the Kings of Spain*, iii. 128ff.
79. AGS/E/4961: Macanaz to marqués of la Paz, Liège, 3 July 1726.
80. On the collapse of the Dutch Republic as a Great Power after 1713, cf. Jonathan I. Israel, *The Dutch Republic. Its Rise, Greatness, and Fall 1477–1806* (Oxford, 1995), pp. 959ff.
81. AGS/E/4961: Macanaz to marqués of la Paz, Liège, 17 July 1726.
82. AGS/E/4961: Macanaz to marqués of la Paz, Liège 14 January 1727.
83. AGS/E/4961: Minute of reply to Macanaz to marqués of la Paz, Liège, of 14 January 1727.
84. AGS/E/4692: Macanaz to [?], Liège, 22 Apr. 1727, encl. paper, and minute of a reply to Macanaz, 9 June 1727.
85. AGS/E/4962: Macanaz to marqués of la Paz, Liège, 29 April 1727.
86. AGS/E/4692: Macanaz to marqués of la Paz, Liège, 11 October 1727, enclosing copy of Eugene to Macanaz, 13 September 1727; AGS/E/4695: same to same, Liège, 9 November 1727, enclosing copy of latest letter from Eugene; AGS/E/4692: same to same, 22 November 1727, encl. copy of Eugene's last letter, and of Macanaz's reply of 6 December 1727; AGS/E/4692: same to same, enclosing letter from Eugene of 7 April 1728. The correspondence is only cursorily dealt with by Max Braubach, *Die Geheimediplomatie des Prinzen Eugen von Savoyen*, (Cologne, 1962) and is omitted by McKay, *Prince Eugene*.
87. Martín Gaite, *Macanaz*, p. 401; McKay and Scott, *Rise of the Great Powers*, pp. 134ff.
88. AGS/E/4695: Macanaz to [?], Liège, 9 November 1727.
89. AGS/E/4695: Macanaz to [?], Liège, 9 November 1727.

90. AGS/E/4695: Macanaz to [?], Liège, 9 November 1727.
91. AGS/E/4695: Macanaz to [?], Liège, 17 November 1727.
92. AGS/E/4962: Macanaz to marqués of la Paz, Paris, 15 December 1727.
93. AGS/E/4692: Minute of a reply for Macanaz, end December 1727.
94. AGS/E/4695: Marqués of la Paz to Count Königsegg, El Pardo, 23 February 1728.
95. AGS/E/4690: Macanaz to Grimaldo, Pau, 25 May 1717; AGS/E/4691: same to same, Brussels, 10 August 1726.
96. AGS/E/4692: [Doc], [January 1728].
97. AGS/E/4692: [Summary of letter from Macanaz, 1728].
98. AGS/E/4692: Macanaz to marqués of la Paz, Paris, 22 December 1727, and summary/minute of reply.
99. Macanaz gave his thoughts, for example, on the admission of more states to the congress, AGS/E/4692: Macanaz to marqués of la Paz, Paris, 16 February 1728.
100. Martín Gaite, *Macanaz*, pp. 410–11. For the use of that cipher, cf. AGS/E/4692: Macanaz to marqués of la Paz, Paris, 5 July 1728.
101. AGS/E/4692: Marqués of la Paz to Macanaz, El Pardo, 22 March 1728.
102. Martín Gaite, *Macanaz*, p. 419.
103. AGS/E/4692: Macanaz to marqués of la Paz, Soissons, 20 June 1728.
104. AGS/E/4692: Macanaz to marqués of la Paz, Paris, 5 July 1728.
105. AGS/E/4692: Macanaz to marqués of la Paz [end 1728].
106. For the congress of Soissons, cf. Arthur McCandless Wilson, *French Foreign Policy during the Administration of Cardinal Fleury* (Cambridge, Mass., 1936), pp. 192ff.; McKay and Scott, *Rise of the Great Powers*, pp. 134ff.
107. AGS/E/4693: Macanaz to marqués of la Paz, Paris, 10 March 1729.
108. Cf. SP 78/190, f. 374: copy of Keene to Poyntz, Cadiz, 24 March 1729.
109. One Spaniard who miscalculated was the marqués of Tabuérniga. Believing that Philip V was not rightful king, he nevertheless failed to convince the Prince of Asturias to act; indeed, Ferdinand betrayed the marqués to Philip and Isabel. Imprisoned, Tabuérniga eventually escaped abroad, to London where he became an intimate of the Prince (and above all of the Princess) of Wales, and an informer on them to Thomas Pelham-Holles, duke of Newcastle. During the War of the Austrian Succession, the British government hoped to exploit Tabuérniga's contacts to open negotiations with the Spanish court via Lisbon. For Tabuérniga, whose career as both exile and agent offers interesting comparisons and contrasts with that of Macanaz, cf. Richard Lodge, ed., *The Private Correspondence of Benjamin Keene*, (Cambridge, 1933), pp. 100ff.
110. SP 78/190, f. 133: Poyntz to Keene, Paris, 5 February 1729 [in close cypher].
111. Cf. AHN/E/3381/2: Macanaz to marqués of la Paz, Paris, 26 September 1729.
112. Martín Gaite, *Macanaz*, p. 420.
113. Martín Gaite, *Macanaz*, p. 422.
114. Martín Gaite, *Macanaz*, pp. 428–9.
115. AGS/E/4693: Macanaz to marqués of la Paz, Paris, 13 November 1730.
116. AGS/E/4693: Marqués of Castelar to [?], October/November 1730. Although Macanaz was allowed 50 *doblones* a month by the Spanish court, it was paid irregularly. In [June] 1726 Macanaz complained of the failure to pay his monthly allowance, and the want of any financial help for 14 months, AGS/E/4961: Orendayn to Grimaldo, Palacio, 29 June 1726. Orendayn replied that a letter had been sent to Macanaz for 410 *doblones* to end June 1726. For Macanaz's account of what was owed him to end December 1729, totalling more than 26,000 *libras*, cf. AGS/E/4695: Macanaz to marqués of la Paz, Paris, 2 January 1730. For his account to end September 1730, cf. AGS/E/4695: Macanaz to marqués of la Paz, [Paris] 30 November 1730, and the enclosed account.
117. AGS/E/4693: Marqués of la Paz to Macanaz, Seville, September 1731.
118. AGS/E/4693: Marqués of Castelar to marques of la Paz, Paris, 3 December 1731.

119. Martín Gaite, *Macanaz*, p. 438.
120. José Luis Gómez Urdáñez, *Fernando VI* (Madrid, 2001), pp. 39–40.
121. Martín Gaite, *Macanaz*, pp. 426–7. In 1747 the British minister, John Montagu, earl of Sandwich, thought Macanaz' wild ideas were in part explained by the fact that he had spent thirty years with his head in books, Richard Lodge, *Studies in Eighteenth Century Diplomacy* (London, 1930; 1970), p. 241.
122. The self-styled noble from Lucca in Italy, Colonel Gamberini, was exemplary. In October 1731, he contacted the British ambassador in Paris, James, Earl Waldegrave, claiming to have important intelligence to communicate. His elaborate precautions for a first meeting were the stuff of the modern thriller: he would be found, between 2 and 3 pm, on the terrace of the Tuileries, sitting on the third bench as one entered by the little gate off the rue Saint Honoré, he would be wearing a white English-style frock coat, black waistcoat and stockings, and have a black sword; he would be holding a red handkerchief; his contact would have to address him thus: 'Sir, your very humble servant', which would be the signal for him to reveal the intelligence which could not be entrusted to the posts, SP/78/199 f. 290: 'le Zelé Inconnu' to Mylord, Paris, 24 October 1731. Waldegrave accordingly sent one of his servants to the Tuileries, and his report on the meeting is in SP/78/199 f. 292: Burnaby to [Waldegrave], Paris, October 1731. Paris's public spaces may have facilitated such encounters and the transmission of intelligence in this way.
123. For the role of clerics in espionage and related activities in the recently concluded War of Spanish Succession, cf. AST/LM/Spagna, m. 57: Morozzo to VAII, 20 May 1715, and Bély, *Espions, passim*. One Abbé Granata, from Messina, was suspected of being a double agent in that conflict, AST/LM/Spagna, m. 57: same to same, 1 April and 8 May 1715.
124. None of the rival versions explains how the Sicilian abbés came to be in Madrid; they may well have been part of that migration prompted by the collapse of Spanish Italy noted earlier. According to the anonymous source cited by Ozanam, *Diplomacia*, p. 128, Caracciolo was the nephew of the duke of Granada and sent him intelligence from Paris.
125. William Coxe, *Memoirs of Horace Walpole* (2 vols, London, 1820), i. 250ff.
126. Cf. James Frederick Chance, *The Alliance of Hanover* (London, 1923), pp. 317, 743–4, Wilson, *French Foreign Policy*, pp. 134, 163n. In the summer of 1728, for example, the abbés supplied Horace Walpole with a list of Spanish ships then fitting out, SP 78/190, f. 242: Walpole to [?], Paris, 31 July 1728.
127. In 1731, Waldegrave reported that the abbés frequently asked him for money, complaining that they had received nothing for 5 months, and that Walpole used to give them 100 *louis d'or* every 5 months. Waldegrave had given them 50 *louis d'or* on account, but wished to know what to do, believing that since they had established contact with the new Spanish minister in Paris, Castelar, they would be useful. He calculated that their allowance would total 240 *louis d'or* a year, or about £270, SP 78/199 f. 120: Waldegrave to Walpole, Paris, 22 March 1731.
128. For a positive assessment, cf. David Bayne Horn, *The British Diplomatic Service 1689–1789* (Oxford, 1961), p. 266. But Armstrong, *Elisabeth Farnese*, pp. 205–6, dismisses the intelligence supplied by the abbés regarding the content of the secret treaty of Vienna of 1725 (and its supposed commitment to the restoration in Britain of the Old Pretender), noting that not all British ministers were as trusting as Horace Walpole. Cf. SP 78/194: Waldegrave to Newcastle, Paris, 10 November 1730.
129. SP 78/188, f. 332: Stanhope and Walpole to Newcastle, Fontainebleau, 27 October 1728 [most secret].
130. SP 78/188, f. 416: Stanhope and Walpole to Newcastle, Paris, 22 December 1728 [most secret].

131. SP 78/190, f. 95: Poyntz to Newcastle, Paris, 1 February 1729.
132. SP 78/190, f. 133: Poyntz to Keene, Paris, 5 February 1729 [in close cypher].
133. SP 78/190, f. 174: Poyntz to Newcastle, Paris, 22 February 1729.
134. SP 78/192: Walpole to Delafaye, Pateau, 3 Aug. 1729, encl. Popple to Walpole, Paris, 1 August 1729.
135. British Library, Add. 32,772, f. 82: Intelligence received from the Sicilians, enclosed with Waldegrave to [?], Paris, 26 March 1731.
136. Cf. Bély, *Espions*, pp. 61ff.; Alan Williams, *The Police of Paris, 1718–1789* (London, 1979).
137. Peter R. Campbell, *Power and Politics in Old Regime France 1720–1745* (London, 1996), pp. 150–51. Cf. also Arlette Farge, *Subversive Words. Public Opinion in Eighteenth Century France* (Oxford, 1994), pp. 18ff.
138. Bennett, *Tory Crisis*, pp. 297–8.
139. Bennett, *Tory Crisis*, p. 305. Cf. Baudrillart, 'Prétentions de Philippe V', p. 98, for the seizure of the papers of the Abbé Montgon, another agent of Philip V in Paris at this time.
140. SP 78/190, f. 261ff: Poyntz to Newcastle, Paris, 8 March 1729 [extract].
141. SP 78/190, f. 310ff: Poyntz to Newcastle, Paris, 12–23 March 1729.
142. Cf. SP78/203, f. 280: Thomas Pelham to Delafaye, 9 September 1733, for the expulsion of Sempill and others.
143. Martín Gaite, *Macanaz*, pp. 439ff.
144. AGS/E/4694: Marqués of Villarias to marqués of Salas, San Lorenzo, 30 November 1745. Cf. Martín Gaite, *Macanaz*, pp. 440ff.
145. AGS/E/4694: Marqués of Villarias to Macanaz, El Pardo, 13 January 1746.
146. AGS/E/ 4695: [?] to marqués of la Ensenada, El Pardo, 3 March 1746, on the dispatch to Macanaz of 700 *doblones* to pay his debts in Paris and cover the costs of his journey.
147. Ensenada to Huescar, 22 September 1746, cited in Ozanam, *Diplomacia*, p. 128. Cf. also pp. 132–3 for Macanaz's efforts to secure a Spanish pension for Caracciolo, February 1747.
148. Cf. Ozanam, *Diplomacia*, p. 17.
149. Martín Gaite, *Macanaz*, pp. 448, 454; Ozanam, *Diplomacia*, pp. 29–30 and references there.
150. Cf. M. S. Anderson, *The War of the Austrian Succession, 1740–1748* (Harlow, 1995), pp. 196–8, and Lodge, *Studies*, pp. 215ff; and Ozanam, *Diplomacia, passim.*
151. M. Dolores Gómez Molleda, 'El "Caso Macanaz" en el Congreso de Breda', *Hispania*, 18 (1958), pp. 62–128, at pp. 82–3, citing the contemporary memoires of the marqués of Valdeolmos. A new Inquisitor General had been appointed following the accession of Ferdinand VI, in July 1746, Ozanam, *Diplomacia*, p. 111.
152. AHN/E/3457/36. For the following account of Macanaz at Breda, unless otherwise indicated, cf. Gómez Molleda, 'El "Caso Macanaz" ', Lodge, *Studies*, and Ozanam, *Diplomacia*.
153. Macanaz was not accompanied by his wife and daughter; they abandoned Paris on 1 February 1747 and arrived in Madrid on 29 March 1747.
154. AST/LM/Olanda, m. 44: Chavanne to CEIII, Hague, 8 and 11 February 1747.
155. AST/LM/Olanda, m. 44: Chavanne to CEIII, and same to Gorzegno, Breda, 6 March 1747. Chavanne met Macanaz for the first time on 5 March. According to Macanaz, in expectation of a prompt settlement with the allies, he had urged Ferdinand VI to withdraw the Spanish troops then in Languedoc closer to the Spanish border.
156. AST/LM/Inghilterra, m. 53: Ossorio to CEIII, London, 24 and 38 March 1747. It is worth noting, in connection with the Don Quixote comparison, that the British minister, Carteret (later Lord Granville) was a great devotee of this work, such that the image may have more readily come to mind, in the case of some English politicians at least at this time.

157. AST/LM/Olanda, m. 44: Chavanne to CEIII, Breda, 18 April 1747.
158. AST/LM/Olanda, m. 44: Chavanne to CEIII, Hague, 22 March 1747.
159. AST/LM/Olanda, m. 44: Chavanne to CEIII, Hague, 12 March 1747. English ministers acknowledged the role of Chavanne in getting Macanaz to drop his insistence on the return of Gibraltar, AST/LM/Inghilterra, m. 53: Ossorio to Gorzegno, 18 April 1747.
160. AST/LM/Olanda, m. 44: Chavanne to CEIII, Hague, 12 March 1747. Chavanne also had instructions from CEIII on how to deal with Macanaz, AST/LM/Olanda, m. 44: CEIII to Chavanne, Turin, 11 March 1747.
161. AHN/E/193/71: Macanaz to Huescar, Hague, 19 February 1747. Cf. also, AHN/E/193/71: Reflexiones [of Huescar] on the peace terms agreed by Macanaz and Sandwich, 3 May 1747.
162. AST/LM/Olanda, m. 44: Chavanne to CEIII, Hague, 24 May 1747.
163. AST/LM/Olanda, m. 44: Chavanne to CEIII, Hague, 3 and 18 June 1747. For negotiations in Liège in the summer of 1747, cf. AST/LM/Inghilterra, m. 53: Ossorio to CEIII, London, 26 September 1747.
164. AST/LM/Olanda, m. 44: Chavanne to CEIII, Hague, 7 June 1747.
165. Apparently, Macanaz showed Sandwich a letter he claimed to have received from the brother of Ferdinand VI's chief minister, Carvajal which purported to say that the Spanish king was annoyed with Huescar for suppressing letters from Macanaz during the Breda conferences, AST/LM/Olanda, m. 44: Chavanne to CEIII, Hague, 21 April 1747.
166. AGS/E/4695: Macanaz to Carvajal y Lancaster, Liége, 11 July 1747.
167. AGS/E/4694: Macanaz to Carvajal y Lancaster, Liége, 12 July 1747.
168. Cf. AHN/E/4074: Wall to Huescar, 1 December 1747 (and AHN/E/4166: Carvajal's order to Wall, 30 December 1747), in Ozanam, *Diplomacia*, p. 266.
169. AHN/E/193/71: Macanaz to Huescar, Breda, 5 May 1747. This was no doubt the same Darieau, Macanaz's secretary for thirty years, who also recruited skilled Flemish and French workers for Spain, Ozanam, *Diplomacia*, p. 103. In May 1747, Darieau offered to reveal things [about Macanaz] to Huescar, Ozanam, *Diplomacia*, pp. 193, 207.
170. Ozanam, *Diplomacia*, p. 295.
171. Ozanam, *Diplomacia*, p. 295.
172. Cf. Carvajal to Huescar, 15 December 1746 and 13 May 1747, in Ozanam, *Diplomacia*, pp. 110–11, 190–1.
173. Martín Gaite, *Macanaz*, pp. 449, 461–2. In May 1748, Ensenada ordered the securing of those of Macanaz's papers still in Huy; the young Spanish secretary of embassy, Felix Álvarez de Abreu, was sent to recover them, taking formal possession of eight chests of documents. Ensenada wanted to know who Macanaz's correspondents were and whether he had copied his instructions.
174. Ozanam, *Diplomacia*, p. 317.
175. AHN/E/2850/21: Representación de Macanaz al Rey [1749].
176. Macanaz's heirs continued to press for payment of what was owed him long after his death. Cf. AGS/E/4695: petitions of D. Pedro and Da. Gregoria de Macanaz, Madrid, 24 February 1790, and of D. Pedro de Macanaz, San Lorenzo, 16 November 1790, and the certification by D. Francisco Hurtado de Mendoza, official and archivist of the Secretariat of Estado y del Despacho, Madrid, 27 October 1798.
177. H. M. Scott, 'Diplomatic culture in old regime Europe', in H. M. Scott and Brendan Simms, eds, *Cultures of Power in Europe During the Long Eighteenth Century* (Cambridge, 2007), pp. 58–85.
178. It may simply be that we are not aware of (all of) those women who operated in this murky world. They certainly existed. It is highly likely that the Neapolitan noblewoman, Anna Pinelli, wife of Giuseppe Antonio Pignatelli, prince of Belmonte (commander of the Austrian forces in Naples during the War of the Polish Succession), and who was twice banished from Naples for her opposition to the Bourbon regime

there, passed on to the opponents of the latter useful intelligence, Eurigio Tonetti, ed., *Correspondenze Diplomatiche Veneziane da Napoli: Dispacci*, XVII, (Rome, 1994), pp. 290–1, 748, 759: Bartolini to Venetian Senate, 17 October 1741, and Bernardo Tanucci, *Epistolario*, II, R. P. Coppini and R. Nieri, eds (Rome, 1980), p. 210: Piatti to Senate, 8 August and 28 November 1747 and Tanucci to Corsini, 14 March 1747.

Chapter 6: Giacomo Casanova and the Venetian Inquisitors

Sources

Giovanni Comisso, ed., *Agenti segreti di Venezia 1705–1797* (Milan, 1984), pp. 113, 173, 176–80, 185, 188, 191, 200, 202, 206, 209–10, 233, 234, 236, 238, 240, 251, 253, 255–7, 260, 265.

Nicola Mangini, 'Casanova, Giacomo', in *Dizionario biografico degli italiani* (Rome, 1978), vol. 21, pp. 154–67.

Preto, *I Servizi Segreti di Venezia*, pp. 46, 62, 279, 341, 384, 440–1, 461, 502, 512–13, 524–9, 546, 548, 552, 556, 582.

1. This was published posthumously early in the nineteenth century in French, and later in German, Italian and other languages, but the original complete version only reappeared in Jacques Casanova, *Histoire de ma vie* (12 vols, Wiesbaden, 1960–2).
2. Preto, *I Servizi segreti di Venezia*, pp. 533–4.
3. Preto, *I Servizi segreti di Venezia*, pp. 11–12.
4. Preto, *I Servizi segreti di Venezia*, pp. 455–6.
5. Preto, *I Servizi segreti di Venezia*, pp. 457–8.

Index

9781845860608